SIR ROBERT CLAYTON
AND THE ORIGINS OF
ENGLISH DEPOSIT BANKING,
1658–1685

Sir Robert Clayton: portrait by Lorenzo da Castro. By permission of the Governor
and Company of the Bank of England

SIR ROBERT CLAYTON
AND THE ORIGINS OF
ENGLISH DEPOSIT BANKING,
1658–1685

•

FRANK T. MELTON

Associate Professor of History
University of North Carolina at Greensboro

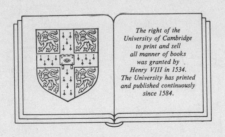

The right of the
University of Cambridge
to print and sell
all manner of books
was granted by
Henry VIII in 1534.
The University has printed
and published continuously
since 1584.

CAMBRIDGE UNIVERSITY PRESS

Cambridge

London   New York   New Rochelle

Melbourne   Sydney

Published by the Press Syndicate of the University of Cambridge
The Pitt Building, Trumpington Street, Cambridge CB2 1RP
32 East 57th Street, New York, NY 10022, USA
10 Stamford Road, Oakleigh, Melbourne 3166, Australia

First published 1986

Printed in Great Britain at the University Press, Cambridge

British Library cataloguing in publication data
Melton, Frank T.
Sir Robert Clayton and the origins of English
deposit banking, 1658–1685.
1. Clayton, *Sir* Robert, *1629–1707* 2. Banks and
banking – England – History – 17th century
I. Title
332.1′0942   HG1552.C6

Library of Congress cataloguing in publication data
Melton, Frank T.
Sir Robert Clayton and the origins of English deposit
banking, 1658–1685.
1. Deposit banking – England – History. 2. Clayton,
Robert, Sir, 1629–1707. I. Title.
HG2999.E54M45 1986   332.1′752′0942   85–22373

ISBN 0 521 32039 9

To my parents

CONTENTS

———— • ————

ILLUSTRATIONS

———— • ————

ACKNOWLEDGEMENTS

———————— • ————————

The sources of this book are widely scattered, and I am indebted to many people who made the Clayton papers available to me. I regret that limitation of space prevents my mentioning the names of all the archivists and librarians who gave me their patient assistance. I thank the staffs of the British Library, the Guildhall Library, the Bodleian Library, the Memorial Library of the University of Illinois at Urbana-Champaign, the Butler Library at Columbia University, the British Library of Political and Economic Science in the London School of Economics (especially Miss Angela Raspin), Mr H. A. Hanley of the Buckinghamshire Record Office and Mr Stephen Parks, curator of the Osborn Collection in the Beinecke Library at Yale. Deserving special praise is A. E. J. Hollaender, formerly archivist of the Guildhall Library, and his successor Mr Christopher Cooper. Albert Hollaender first put me on the trail of the Clayton papers, and since 1971 Chris Cooper has directed my attention to catalogues of Clayton items which have come to auction. Miss G. M. A. Beck, formerly archivist of the Guildford Muniment Room, gave me her help in Guildford, and then delivered the Abbott and Clayton ledgers under her care to London to be microfilmed.

Lady Fairfax of Cameron allowed me to inspect the Clayton papers in her library, offered me her gracious hospitality while I was there and permitted me to reproduce material in this book. In the course of their own research Dr John Broad, Dr Stephen M. Macfarlane and Mr Andrew Federer came across valuable references to Clayton and banking which they shared with me. For their advice, friendship and generosity I am grateful to Dr Ann P. Saab, Dr Nancy Ellenberger, Mr Colin Corness, Mr Brian

Jenkins, Mr J. C. Judy and Mr J. R. Stow, as well as the University of North Carolina at Greensboro and the National Science Foundation, which supported the completion of this book through grant no. SES–7913413.

My greatest obligation is to Professor Donald C. Coleman. Over a long period he answered my many questions, in other instances assured me that certain problems held answers which were not intractable, and in other ways encouraged my research. Most important, he read an earlier draft of this work, making many valuable suggestions and saving me from errors, though whatever faults remain are entirely my own.

ABBREVIATIONS

————————— • —————————

A.	Robert Abbott
B.L.	British Library
Bod. Lib.	Bodleian Library
Buc. R.O.	Buckinghamshire Record Office
C.	Robert Clayton; after 1671, Sir Robert Clayton
C.L.R.O.	Corporation of London Record Office
C.S.P. Dom.	*Calendar of State Papers Domestic*
C.T.B.	*Calendar of Treasury Books*
C.U.	Butler Library, Columbia University, New York
D.N.B.	*Dictionary of National Biography*
Ex. R.O.	Essex Record Office
Fairfax Collection	Papers of Lord Fairfax, Gay's House, Berkshire
G.L.	Guildhall Library, London
G.M.R.	Guildford Muniment Room
H.M.C.	Historical Manuscripts Commission
I.U.	Memorial Library, University of Illinois at Urbana-Champaign
J.R.L.	John Rylands University Library of Manchester
K.A.O.	Kent Archives Office
L.J.	*Journals of the House of Lords*
L.R.O.	Leicestershire Record Office
L.S.E.	British Library of Political and Economic Science, London School of Economics
M.	John Morris
N.R.O.	Norfolk Record Office

Northants. R.O.   Northamptonshire Record Office
Osborn, Yale   James Osborn Collection, Beinecke Library, Yale
                   University
P.R.O.   Public Record Office, London
S.R.O.   Surrey Record Office
U.L.   University of London Library

INTRODUCTION

———— • ————

The title of this book represents a compromise of several topics, longer in time and greater in subject than the description suggests. More precisely, this study is a business history of two generations of a money-scrivening firm established by Robert Abbott in 1636 and taken over upon his death in 1658 by his nephew Robert Clayton and another apprentice in the shop, John Morris. The time-span of the book does not conform to the biographical contours of the three partners, as it begins with the Jacobean money-scriveners and ends with a description of private banking in London after the Bubble crisis in the 1720s. Clayton becomes in the title a banker, an attribution his contemporaries never bestowed. The title concentrates upon a category best explaining the role of the man and his work. Banking problems define all the chapters of the book, reiterating the greater framework absorbing the complex evidence from the Clayton papers. In ascribing a role to the money-scriveners in banking history – and to this one scrivener's operation in particular – Robert Abbott and John Morris are deprived in the title of a recognition in banking history. Precise credit is difficult to assess. Morris and Clayton were so closely ravelled in their affairs that the individual efforts of each man to the firm are rarely apparent. It was not the intention of this book to assign each man his proper contribution, even if that were possible. Clayton was the most visible of all three partners, both then and now. Since the main sources of this book are known as the Clayton papers, his name became a likely subject for a title, concentrated at the same time upon the history of banking.

Memory of Sir Robert Clayton has not faded entirely. Today his fame rests upon his leadership of the City Whigs during the time of the Popish

1

Plot. By supporting the exclusion of the Duke of York to the throne, Clayton helped initiate the chain of events culminating in the Revolution of 1688–9. The most remarkable feature of Clayton's story was his rise to great wealth from a humble, rural origin, but details of his financial success were distorted by his critics, and then largely forgotten by later generations. Clayton's role in the history of banking is commemorated by his service as governor of the Bank of England from 1702 until 1707; upon his death the history of his own bank and the innovations he brought to mortgage finance were all but forgotten. No one who actually knew Clayton ever composed the facts of his long life into a whole, or left a reliable account of his character. He died in his seventy-sixth year, outliving the people who knew him best. No children survived him: his fortune descended through his nephew William Clayton. The family preserved Sir Robert Clayton's business papers, and were it not for this archive, little justification could be given for trying to rescue this man from his obscurity and for claiming that his greatest achievements were in banking finance.

Clayton himself encouraged posterity to remember his public life. He wrote his own epitaph for his tomb in the church of St Mary in Bletchingley, Surrey, where visitors encounter a family monument overwhelming the east end of the south chapel. Under a classical canopy supported with Corinthian columns stand two life-size figures of a man and a woman, with a baby between them, in striking contrast to the common recumbent funeral effigies of the past. Sir Robert Clayton and his lady, with their infant son Robin, were carved with meticulous attention to their persons and dress by Richard Crutcher in the early eighteenth century, but Clayton posed for the artist in his mayoral robes of 1679–80, and Lady Clayton's dress is from the same period. The Claytons chose to be remembered in marble splendor for their place some two and a half decades before their deaths, when events brought this rich money-scrivener into the political arena. *Non vultus instantis tyranni*: whatever else the observer might hear, Clayton wished to be remembered for the part he played in averting the rule of the Catholic Stuarts and the restoration of popery in England. Clayton dismissed the controversy surrounding the fortune he amassed with the comment that 'by the justest methods and skill in business he acquired an ample fortune.'

With rightful pride Clayton could point to a record of public service and benefactions few of his contemporaries could rival. He rarely chose to do things by halves. His political career began in 1670, with his election to the Court of Aldermen, where he sat until the City's charter was withdrawn in

Fig. 1. Tomb of Sir Robert and Lady Clayton, Church of St Mary, Bletchingley, Surrey. By permission of the National Monuments Record

1683. After the revolution he was elected alderman again and continued to be re-elected until his death. In parliament Clayton was returned to the House of Commons in the three successive assemblies of 1679, 1680 and 1681, and after the revolution he sat in the legislatures elected in 1690, 1695, 1698, 1701 (February) and 1701 (December), 1702 and 1705. Upon his election as one of London's sheriffs in 1671, he was knighted, and in 1679–80 Clayton served the City as Lord Mayor. He was colonel of the Orange Regiment of the militia in 1680–1, 1689–90 and 1694–1702, and President of the Honourable Artillery Company from 1690 to 1703. Supplementing these civic positions Clayton was Commissioner of the Customs, 1689–97, and an Assistant to the Royal African Company, 1672–81.

When the Tory pamphleteers attacked Clayton in the years before the Revolution, they ignored his philanthropic commitments. The Whig politician and plutocrat had softer, charitable instincts encouraged by his friend Thomas Firmin, who appealed to his self-help sympathies. From 1676, when he first supported Firmin's workhouse school in Little Britain Street, Clayton became vice-president of the workhouse. Firmin was probably responsible for Clayton's connection with Christ's Hospital, where in 1672 he became involved with the foundation of the Royal Mathematical School. According to John Strype, Clayton told him he had first come to believe in the idea of a mathematical school by reading an account of how Louis XIV had established schools in maritime towns in France to teach children the principles of navigation. Clayton became a governor of Christ's Hospital in 1675. He and Morris donated money to build a new Girls' Ward in the hospital, and the two men may also have contributed anonymously to the rebuilding of some of the hospital's wards in 1676–7.[1]

In 1689 Clayton became a governor of Brideswell Hospital, but his interest in that institution as well as Christ's Hospital waned after the revolution, as the opportunity arose for him to run St Thomas's Hospital. In 1692 he was elected president and held that position until his death. The historian of St Thomas's gives Clayton credit for rebuilding the hospital during his presidency, but until his death, when he bequeathed £2,500 to the hospital, his support was probably not so much in the form of cash as in starting a subscription fund for that purpose.

The personality behind this largesse and power is difficult to capture. His critics held a somewhat ironical view of the man's politics, when they

[1] B. D. Henning, *The House of Commons 1660–1690* [History of Parliament] (London, 1983), 84–7; S. M. Macfarlane, 'Studies in Poverty and Poor Relief in London at the End of the Seventeenth Century,' Oxford D.Phil. thesis, 1982, 283, 287, 362 and ch. 7, *passim*.

saw, darkly, his business dealings to be in contrast with his public life. Swindler and at the same time purifier was Nahum Tate's verdict in the second part of *Absalom and Achitophel*:

> 'Mongst these extorting Ishban first appears,
> Pursued by a meagre troop of bankrupt heirs.
> Blest times – when Ishban, he whose occupation
> So long has been to cheat, reforms a nation!
> Ishban, of conscience suited to his trade,
> As good a saint as usurer ever made.

Once he acquired a critical audience this ambiguity pursued Clayton to his end. From 1659 to 1672, when he built his fortune, he lived modestly, unnoticed by those writers who described the social scene. His reputation invites comparison with a fellow self-made Midas, Sir Stephen Fox (1627–1716). Their long lives both spanned the political turmoils of the century of revolution. Whereas Fox could describe himself as 'a wonderful child of providence,'[2] for whom the doors of success opened so easily from his childhood to his mature age, Clayton's future was never quite so self-assured until 1666, when he and Morris appropriated Abbott's bank from his heirs. Clayton was unable to discard the rudeness of his background. His wealth never brought him much into court circles. Fox was an amiable man, able to absorb the intricacies of court life, and this ability brought him to the coffers of state, where he made his fortune. Only after 1671 did Clayton begin to display his wealth in his new mansion in the Old Jewry and his country seat at Marden Park.

In the City Clayton lived on a grand scale, as he climbed the political ladder. John Evelyn attended one of his lavish feasts in the Old Jewry in 1672, where he was duly impressed with the wealth expended to build and equip the scriveners' quarters. He returned there in 1679 with Lady Sunderland for a celebration of Clayton's election to the mayoralty, that 'she might see the pomp & ceremonie of this Prince of Citizens, there never having been any, who for the stateliness of his Palace, prodigious feasting & magnificence exceeded . . . ' Two years earlier Evelyn had visited the Claytons at Marden Park, where the new house, built at great cost, was surrounded by gardens and plantations of a lushness and design which impressed even his discriminating taste in such matters.[3]

[2] C. Clay, *Public Finance and Private Wealth: The Career of Sir Stephen Fox, 1627–1716* (Oxford, 1978).
[3] John Evelyn, *Diary*, ed. E. S. deBeer (6 vols., Oxford, 1955), Vol. III, 625–6; Vol. IV, 110–11, 121–2, 170, 173, 185–7, 191, 195.

This great display of wealth reflected an immense fortune. At the time Evelyn was the guest of the Claytons, in the City and country, the scrivener's annual rents amounted to £3,869, and his yearly interest on loans was £3,515.[4] His disposable income was greater than those figures indicate, for after his election to the mayoralty, he gave several lavish feasts costing £6,955.[5] No accounts of his income and expenses survive after 1685. At his death Luttrell reported that he had left about £7,000 in legacies and an annual income of £5,000 to his heir,[6] which seems a low estimate. By the standards of his own time Clayton was seriously rich, comparable today to a millionaire.

For Daniel Defoe, observing Clayton's ostentation at a greater distance than Evelyn, qualms arose as to how this great wealth arose.

> And yet he Covets without Rule or End
> Will sell his wife, his Master, or his Friend –
> To boundless Avarice a constant Slave,
> Unsatisfy'd as Death, and Greedy as the Grave.[7]

Death and the grave – the metaphor could translate to another reference of Defoe, in *A Journal of the Plague Year*. According to the novelist, Clayton bought the land used for a burial pit during the Plague in 1665. So anxious was he to get on with his building schemes that he excavated the site before some of the corpses were fully rotted.[8]

This rich scrivener's political career and his benefactions never succeeded in erasing suspicions that his wealth came through exploitation of a particularly unscrupulous kind. His greatest victim was thought to be the Duke of Buckingham, though Clayton was also accused of ruining Lord Peterborough's fortune.[9] Sir Stephen Fox loaned money on a grand scale also, without suffering the criticism directed toward Clayton. Clayton became vulnerable to charges that his wealth was ill-gotten because of the novelty of his particular sort of banking, coupled with his ostentation.

Part of the complexities of any system involving credit is that it is not

---

[4] J. R. Woodhead, *The Rulers of London 1660–1689* (London & Middlesex Archaeological Society, London, 1965), 48.

[5] Henning, *House of Commons*, 85.

[6] N. Luttrell, *A Brief Historical Relation of State Affairs from September 1678 to April 1714* (Oxford, 1857), Vol. VI, 193.

[7] Quoted in M. E. Novak, *Economics and the Fiction of Daniel Defoe* (Berkeley and Los Angeles, 1962), 131.

[8] *A Journal of the Plague Year*, ed. A. W. Secord (New York, 1935), 233.

[9] Henning, *House of Commons*, 84; and see below, pp. 198–205.

understood completely by individuals outside the operation. Deposit banking was a relatively new form of finance in Abbott and Clayton's time. Known commonly as scribes and conveyancers, these men stood somewhat outside the ordinary perception of banking. Their contemporaries were more likely to regard bankers as offering specific services, such as moneylending and cash-keeping, than they were to view their operations as integrated within a complete cycle of credit, where bankers made their fortunes on the use of their deposits. With this fragmented view their clients did not always accept the necessary part of the process of true banking, even at its most basic levels. To cite one example, from the moment bankers accepted money on deposit they also offered to store valuables, including coins, for their clients, to keep the distinction clear that in one instance they returned different coins of equal value to the original deposit, and, in another, they returned a parcel, such as a bag of gold, preserving the same coins intact in their chests. As late as 1672 Morris had to state this same-or-similar principle to one of his clients, who demanded the original coins he had placed in his ordinary deposit.[10]

This interpretation of Clayton's role in the history of banking is based largely upon his business papers, which happened to survive his death. The later Claytons preserved this archive until 1929, when the collection was carelessly dispersed. The Clayton papers in their scattered state comprise the earliest and largest of all the archives of private banking in England. In their range, depth and diversity the mountain of Clayton documents make the surviving archives of the goldsmith-bankers seem like molehills. The Clayton papers score several archival achievements, for the earliest examples of checks are among this evidence, as are the first bankers' notes, the first statements of account, the earliest banking cashier's book and the first banking ledgers, supplemented by the most extensive surviving banking correspondence and a welter of documents relating to mortgage finance. In their chronological range of banking material the Clayton papers begin with the cashier's book which Robert Abbott kept from 1634 to 1636 during his apprenticeship. The last major source of the bank is the ledger of the firm, kept to 1686, though there are fragments of family papers of the Claytons and Abbotts before 1636 and after 1685. Within this large assortment of papers there are disappointing gaps, most serious in the sequence of ledgers. After 1685 the papers of the bank end abruptly, with only a few family records of the Claytons in the following period. The

---

[10] See below, p. 97.

last twenty-two years of Clayton's life and the fate of the bank cannot be drawn so clearly as the period when his fortune was established.

The embarrassment of riches which are the Clayton papers confound as much as they clarify, leaving a trail of imprecise answers to questions vital to the banking process. Partly this is due to the passage of time, to the accidental loss of evidence and to obscurities buried in the language and practice of the seventeenth century. At the same time, these records were at times deliberately destroyed and falsified in their own day by men aiming to disguise parts of their business from their clients and the government. There were no rules about what records were kept in good faith, and the modern researcher must be especially cautious about the evidence in account books and contracts. The gaps and omissions in this material present difficulties of their own, apart from the problem of the dispersed archives, where parts of what were originally single letters now lie separated by the Atlantic.

This modern analysis restores Clayton to his rightful place in banking history, which would surprise neither Evelyn nor Defoe. Both men understood that the man known as a scrivener performed the functions of a banker. In his novel *Roxana* Defoe presented Clayton as the only real figure amid fictional characters, to explain what he understood about private banking. No evidence ties Defoe directly to Clayton, but even if he observed the scrivener from a distance and based his impression upon hearsay, his characterization in a work of fiction comes closer than any other contemporary description to an accurate perception of the scrivener's business. Certain references in *Roxana* conform to the workings of the bank as reflected in the Clayton papers. For instance, when Roxana makes a deposit, Clayton presents her with a receipt, making an oral promise to repay her with interest. This accords with the scrivener's peculiar note-issue, which was unlike the corresponding forms surviving from the goldsmith-bankers. In another example, Clayton calculates the possibilities of Roxana's investment with his interest tables. Later, Defoe refers to Clayton's specialty as investing in mortgage loans.[11] The two references to moneylending with real security at the base come closer than any other contemporary analysis of the actual nature of Clayton's business.

The courtesan Roxana described Clayton as faultless, 'thoroughly versed in the arts of improving money, but thoroughly honest . . . ' Twice she refers to him as her 'faithful counsellor' for his advice on how to

---

[11] *Roxana, The Fortunate Mistress*, ed. D. Blewett (New York, 1982), 207–8, 210.

increase her capital. She confesses to 'acknowledge myself much a debtor, not only to the justice of his dealings with me, but to the prudence and conduct which he guided me to, by his advice, for the management of my estates.' In her first encounter with the scrivener, Roxana deposits £14,000 with Clayton who then invests the capital at five per cent in an estate worth £1,800 a year, bound to the lady. Clayton then advises her to add to her investment £1,000 every year, to accrue with compound interest. Roxana lacks the scrivener's prudence, wishing to spend her capital at once rather than wait until her old age to reap its reward. Later, she appears with £1,400 which Clayton takes in on deposit, promising to pay six per cent on the money until the following year, when the deposit can be put out on good mortgage. Then, at another juncture, Clayton advises the woman to marry a wealthy merchant he had found.[12] (The scrivener's role of marriage broker in rich spouses is documented in the Clayton papers.)[13]

Defoe described the two roles which Clayton's clients and the general public observed of the banker: that of a cashier who received money and accounted for it, and that of a loan-broker who found borrowers for his clients' capital. What they did not witness, however, were the complex series of events between the time his clients' deposits reached Clayton's hands and the time their capital was placed out on loan in their names. During the interval Clayton loaned his deposits for his own purposes. In this intervening stage Clayton's role transcended that of cash-keeper and simple broker to assume the functions of a banker, giving him the means to lend money which was not his own capital.

Distinctions between simple brokerage and banking are rarely apparent from public view. Sir Stephen Fox was a broker, receiving money from his clients which he placed in both royal and private loans. In this instance brokerage is entirely profit-based, the broker's capital deriving exclusively from interest and fees, regulated in the Usury Acts.[14] A broker who has only his profits to reinvest is no more a banker than a merchant who invests his profits in loans. Such a broker is like a banker, for both intermediaries take money on deposit, while most merchants do not accept deposits from their clients. If the intermediary is unable to extend his brokerage functions to tap his deposits in other ways, for other reasons, to

[12] *Ibid.*, 204, 207–12, 223–4, 240, 246, 303–4.
[13] See below, p. 48.
[14] 'The interest rate was reduced from ten per cent to eight per cent in the Usury Act of 1625 and from eight per cent to six per cent in 1652. The brokerage rates remained constant, however. Brokers were allowed 5s. per £100, 'or forbearing of £100 for a year, and so ratably . . .' The conveyancing charges were set at 12d. for the original contract as well as its renewal, 'or forbearance thereof . . .'

create a system of moneylending greater than his ordinary source of capital, he has not fulfilled the role of banker.

In a modern context bankers borrow from some in order to lend to others, and this process is regular and ordinary. A broker like Sir Stephen Fox might receive sums of money from friends and others to invest in loans, but only occasionally. The money-scriveners Abbott, Clayton and Morris were bankers in the true sense. In one capacity they acted as brokers and realized large profits from interest and fees, but the bulk of their wealth derived primarily from their role as depositaries, where they manipulated the capital of their clients to create their own source of lending capital.

Clayton and Morris acted as cash-keepers and accountants when they received and paid their clients' capital and kept records of this activity. These demands led them to issue notes and checks, receive and collect inland bills of exchange, issue statements of account and receive valuables for safe-keeping. In merely handling their depositors' capital they executed other services, making themselves their clients' London agents. They could act in a steward-like capacity when they ran the household affairs of clients absent from the capital. And they often paid bills their depositors incurred with tradesmen. This range of services derived from the depositing nexus of banking, which was by no means limited to the passive receipt of capital.

Like their services as cashiers, which implied several functions beyond the ordinary use of that term, loan-brokerage initiated a sequence of actions following the placement of lenders and borrowers in conjunction with each other. Usually the scriveners and their clerks wrote the indenture forms of contracts and thus became conveyancers. For legal actions arising from lending contracts, the scriveners drew upon their own expertise and either acted themselves (before 1660) as attorneys or hired lawyers to do this work. In this connection as money-brokers Clayton and Morris specialized their role and achieved their greatest innovation in banking history by introducing the mortgage in fee to banking practice. This depended upon an accurate form of land assessment which they perfected. To their basic function as money-brokers, scribes, conveyancers and lawyers, the scriveners added further stages and, as a result, they and their agents acted also as land-valuers, rent-collectors and estate-managers.

The conventional account of early banking does not make a clear distinction between functions commonly associated with banking and the various groups of money-men who practiced as bankers during the seventeenth century. The term 'banker' at that time was not a precise word, but the laws forbidding the taking of usury made a distinction between the roles of broker, conveyancer and moneylender. The usury laws were framed to control simple, direct moneylending as practiced by Shylock, and brokers who did no more than pass money between lending parties. Fees charged by brokers were regulated apart from the maximum legal interest rate, though both actions were controlled in the same pieces of legislation.

Banking arose after the first usury laws were enacted. During the careers of Clayton and Morris, however, these bankers performed a range of functions – as conveyancers, scribes, rent-collectors and estate-managers – that could be explained away as fee-paid services but which in fact were so close to interest and the usury laws that distinctions became muddled. The complex entrepreneurial activities which deposit banking gradually presented, especially after 1660, created a gulf between the intent and limitations of the law and the realities of the brokerage aspect of banking absent from simple and direct moneylending. Evasion was not merely a question of blatant disregard for control of a cultural and ethical position: banking created problems and changes unaccounted for in the 'just profit' principle of the usury laws. The categories of moneylender and broker as conceived in legislation were too narrow to accommodate the functions deposit banking could adopt. Once brokers assumed direction of a series of credit operations culminating in loans, they often performed a variety of services more extensive than merely transferring capital between their clients.

Legal regulation of the interest rate clearly did not retard the growth of banking. Private banking emerged over a long period when the usury rate was falling. When the maximum level fell from eight per cent to six per cent in 1652, the profits from moneylending would decrease likewise, or so it would seem. Lenders to the Protector and later to the Crown received a subsidy in addition to the maximum rate, but during the same time other banks appeared bearing little or no relation to governmental finance. It seems unlikely that bankers as a general practice disregarded the usury laws by charging excessive rates; if the government pursued the matter, as it did in 1672, each usurious contact made the lender and his broker liable to prosecution through the courts. Evasions might have been widespread yet carefully concealed, but after 1672 the goldsmith-bankers suffered few criticisms that their loans exceeded the legal rate – whereas in the early part of the century, money-scriveners were suspected of being masters of usurious deceit. On the other hand, the profit rate may have fallen alongside the interest rate; while many private banks were founded after 1660, few of them managed to survive to 1700.

The context of Clayton's bank lay outside the royal castles, the mint and the ports. Throughout the seventeenth century deposits of private bankers came from country gentlemen, giving banking a connection with the rural economy it never lost. Country capital was the thread binding the scriveners to the goldsmiths. At the same time, banking in its earliest stages followed a course of expansion at variance with the general state of agriculture. Scrivener-banking grew during a rural depression. The price of wool leveled off during the early years of the Stuart age, and England's retail markets in the Baltic suffered, but during the peaceful years of Charles I's reign the scriveners enjoyed their greatest prosperity. Regardless of how dislocated agriculture became during this period, fortunate landowners still required London agents to receive their capital in town and to provide a series of services in their absence from London. Social life in the capital and the growth of consumer trades in luxury articles continued to attract landowners to the court and City. Both civil wars were followed by severe depressions which hit a cumulative bottom in 1651. Robert Abbott's bank flourished during those hard times. If disorder did not support banking, neither did it interrupt its progress.

The rural economy was resilient to temporary upsets. Sheep-farming and the woolen industry did not decline in the early seventeenth century to the degree once thought. As long as the population rate remained stable, demand for woolen textiles was built into the domestic consumption market. The export trades, especially in the Baltic markets, were hit harder than the home trades. Where distress was most common, long-term leaseholders paying rents set at the high woolen prices of the early part of the century found it difficult to meet their rents. Unless there was a surfeit of tenants nearby to take up the deserted tenancies, few landlords wished to depopulate their lands and thereby reduce their rent rolls. If deserted copyholds were common during this period, there is no reason to believe that this was a permanent movement, directly connected with resolute landlords determined to force tenants to meet rents they could not pay. Pillaging and looting of the armies dislocated agriculture, and the prospect of a military career encouraged farmers to leave their holdings for another life. But in the same period of rural dislocation, tenants took their plows to the meadows to revive arable farming. From the same bleak picture of the Interregnum economy, where deposit banking grew, changes in the countryside were slowly to bring the means to offset the long-term effects of too much sheep-farming.

The change from less pasture to more tillage became increasingly common after 1650. Revival of arable farming encouraged changes that went beyond leasing transformation. Waste land came under the plow as swamps were drained and primitive forms of irrigation were laid out near river and stream beds to water fields during floods. Before the new agriculture evolved, permanent pasture and permanent tillage were common. As new lands were plowed, the arable culture implemented tended to be temporary. Grain was raised for one year, then the lands were untilled while flocks were herded to the fallow lands to manure them. This was up-and-down husbandry. By taking fewer of the natural nutrients from the soil and by adding manure, farmers increased grain production dramatically. Up-and-down husbandry was centered in the Midland counties where farmers were more likely to have leys for raising grain and fodder, thus keeping in tandem a relationship between stock-farming and arable farming. In another part of the agricultural sector, a brisk business was done leasing pasture lands to shepherds fattening Irish and Welsh cattle on a long journey to London. Market gardening was well advanced in the Home Counties and directed toward a captive clientele in London.[15]

Under the direction of Clayton and Morris the bank's operations became actively integrated into the rural economy, rather than merely receiving country rents which landowners delegated to the bank's money-chests. The main problem Clayton faced after 1660 was how the long-term mortgages which he negotiated could be repaid with expectations that rents would fall during the lives of the loans. This concern forced the scriveners to pay the closest attention to agricultural affairs. Throughout the 1660s the scriveners and their agents witnessed approvingly the changes of the new agriculture. Short-term arable rent-charges, set at current market prices, were more attractive credit than antiquated pastoral rents fixed at high woolen prices. Other problems arose during the 1670s when the consequences of the new agriculture meant that recent solutions could only be temporary. So much grain was grown that corn prices fell. During the 'hungry seventies' farmers again revived stock-farming, for meat, hides and dairy products. Success lay in maintaining both stock and crops, directed toward annual market expectations. From London Clayton commanded a communications network greater than the king's postal system. He knew, for instance, that letters could be sent to

---

[15] A. H. John, 'The Course of Agricultural Change, 1660–1760,' in *Studies in the Industrial Revolution Presented to T. S. Ashton*, ed. L. S. Pressnell, (London, 1960), 125–55; E. Kerridge, *The Agricultural Revolution* (New York, 1968); J. Thirsk, 'Seventeenth-Century Agriculture and Social Change,' in *Seventeenth-Century England*, ed. P. S. Seaver (New York and London, 1976), 72–110; D. C. Coleman, 'Labour in the English Economy of the Seventeenth Century', in *ibid.*, 112–38; D. J. Bowden, *The Wool Trade in Tudor and Stuart England* (London, 1962); *The Agrarian History of England and Wales*, ed. J. Thirsk, Vol. IV: *1540–1640* (Cambridge, 1967).

Kent by the water carriers at the Queen's Head, Billingsgate, and that the Egham coach at the White Hart in the Strand carried letters to Windsor and Staines, where other couriers could deliver correspondence to other points.[16] Through his correspondence from the country during the growing season and his knowledge of market gossip in London, Clayton commanded a position to advise farmers how best to choose their options at the harvest.

The various service roles which Clayton and Morris assumed, such as those of rent-collector and conveyancer, have precise terms, more so than the portmanteau word of the profession. Abbott, Morris and Clayton were rarely referred to in their own lifetimes as 'bankers.' All three men were apprenticed as Scriveners and made free of the company, which claimed Abbott and Clayton as Wardens. In their own day they were all known by the honorifics as 'Scriveners' or 'scriveners' when their financial work was referred to. Robert Abbott was closer to the early tradition of money-scriveners than Clayton and Morris, and to refer to him as a scrivener is to allude to an activity somewhat different from that of the goldsmith-bankers. Clayton and Morris were transitional figures in banking history when the money-scriveners and the Scriveners' Company were in decline, yet they were the greatest of its practitioners and the last prominent members of the Stuart company. By the 1690s the work of a few goldsmith-bankers came close to their own operations as money-scriveners. Clayton's business lacked continuity beyond his own lifetime to acquire the more important and accurate term of 'bank.' To a modern mind the term 'banker' has a specific, relevant meaning which 'scrivener' lacks. In attempting to trace the scrivening traditions from which banking emerged, I have often used the word 'scrivener' to describe these men who in many ways executed the notarial and legal functions associated historically with the money-scriveners. 'Banker' I have used more in the modern sense to describe the practice of private banking once it was recognized as a business apart from the craft of goldsmiths and scriveners. For the sake of convenience, I have used the two words interchangeably.

These variants in terminology support the disjointed view of early banking which this study aims to unify. According to this book deposit banking in Stuart England grew as a linear development in the private sector; scrivener-banking of the early period and the goldsmith-banking of the

---

[16] Sir Thomas Culpeper to M. & C., August 9, 1671, Clayton MS A.1/2, Buc. R.O.; John Thynne to M., August 14, 1672, *ibid.*

later period are part of a continuous development. Clayton's bank was a transitional institution, an enterprise between banks themselves and the early and late episodes of seventeenth-century banking. This one firm – the bank of Abbott, Clayton and Morris – became a bridge between the two phases of Stuart banking. Over a century of private banking associations is represented by this one business which observed the two distinct periods of private banking in the Stuart period. Robert Abbott's master Francis Webb and Webb's master Nicholas Reeve bear a link with the earliest stages of deposit banking, in which skills were passed through four generations of scriveners until the bank of Clayton and Morris ceased its operations. At the opposite end of the historical spectrum, Clayton and Morris witnessed the birth of goldsmith-banking which before Clayton's death had become, in several cases, the family banking firms of the eighteenth century.

CHAPTER 1

ENGLISH BANKING IN HISTORICAL PERSPECTIVE

———————— • ————————

From the point of view of economic history, there is a certain difficulty inherent in the history of banking, as usually understood. It separates facts which should be kept together, and combines different objects. On the one hand, banking means giving of credit as a whole. In this case the besetting sin of the study of economic history, that of taking the cloud for Juno, or believing *quod non est in actis non est in mundo*, is particularly serious; for there can be little doubt that the well-authenticated part played by public banks, up to the middle of the nineteenth century, has been small in its bearing upon the credit system when compared with what was done by private bankers, goldsmiths, scriveners, money-lenders, and usurers, though their activities were often kept in darkness and sometimes held in ignominy.

Eli Heckscher, 'The Bank of Sweden and Its Connection with the Bank of Amsterdam,' in *The History of the Principal Public Banks*, ed. J. G. van Dillen (The Hague, 1934), 161

Before the reign of Elizabeth I banking in England was closely associated with royal credit. As early as the twelfth century the Crown exploited the wealth of its citizens, Jews and Italian bankers to raise loans supplementing the ordinary royal income. After the Jews were expelled in 1290 and the Crown thereafter gradually discontinued its policy of relying upon Italian bankers to finance its debts, Englishmen began to form syndicates raising money to lend to the kings. Often these men were merchants whose ventures into royal moneylending were temporary enterprises. They lacked the institutional structures which can with certainty be called banks, and most of their fortunes did not last beyond their own lifetimes. Nevertheless, these men have a historical visibility memorialized in the history of banking. Figures like William de la Pole in the fourteenth century, Richard Whittington in the fifteenth, and Thomas Gresham in the sixteenth are all associated with high finance in their own time.[1]

In medieval Europe a distinction existed between moneychangers, deposit bankers and merchant bankers.[2] In seventeenth-century Amsterdam exchange banking and foreign credit performed by financiers were recognized as different activities altogether from domestic credit banking performed by merchants.[3] But in England, from the time English deposit banking began until well into the late seventeenth century, the two traditions of banking to the Crown and private banking had not matured to the same levels of specialization as in medieval Europe. In the years after the Restoration the position of the royal moneylenders declined as the Crown improved its own finances, thus reducing its reliance upon private funds. The royal finances were reorganized under the Treasury after 1660. As the foreign and colonial trades expanded, the Crown's income from customs likewise increased. When England and France formed an alliance against the Dutch in 1670, Louis XIV agreed to pay Charles II a handsome pension, and this bounty was renewed when James II ascended the throne in 1685. Charles II defaulted on his loans to his moneylenders in 1672, and

---

[1] C. M. Baron, 'Richard Whittington: The Man Behind the Myth,' in *Studies in London History Presented to Philip Edmund Jones*, ed. A. E. J. Hollaender and W. Kellaway (London, 1969), 197–248; H. Buckley, 'Sir Thomas Gresham and the Foreign Exchange,' *Economic Journal*, XXXIV (1924), 589–601; J. W. Burgon, *The Life and Times of Sir Thomas Gresham*, 2 vols. (London, 1839); D. K. Clark, 'Edward Backwell as a Royal Agent,' *Economic History Review*, IX (1938), 45–55; R. de Roover, *Gresham on Foreign Exchange* (Cambridge, Mass., 1949); E. B. Fryde and M. M. Fryde, 'Public Credit with Special Reference to North-Western Europe . . . ,' in *The Cambridge Economic History of Europe*, Vol. III (Cambridge, 1963), 430–63; A. V. Judges, 'The Origins of English Banking,' *History*, XVI (1931), 138–45; M. D. O'Sullivan, *Italian Merchant Bankers in Ireland in the Thirteenth Century* (Dublin, 1962), 22–3; R. B. Outhwaite, 'Royal Borrowing in the Reign of Elizabeth I: The Aftermath of Antwerp,' *English Historical Review*, LXXXVI (April 1971), 251–63; Thomas Wilson, *A Discourse upon Usury . . .* [1572], ed. R. W. Tawney (London, 1925).

[2] R. de Roover, 'La Structure des banques au moyen age,' in *Congrès et Colloques: Troisième Conférence Internationale d'Histoire Economique. Munich, 1965* (5 vols., Paris, 1968–74), Vol. V, 165.

[3] J. G. van Dillen, 'La Banque de change et les banquiers privés à Amsterdam aux XVIIe et XVIIIe siècles,' in *ibid.*, 178, 181–2. See also R. de Roover, 'Un contraste: La Structure de la banque continentale au XVIIIe siècle,' in *ibid.*, 225.

even though they were eventually compensated, the Stop of the Exchequer in 1672 marked the end of the old tradition of a small clique of bankers who throve on the Crown's inability to meet its own financial needs completely. The Crown still continued to raise subscription loans from the City of London after 1672, secured upon anticipated parliamentary revenues.[4] When the Bank of England was created in 1694, to fund the war debt, public banking reached its climax. State banking had assumed several forms during the seventeenth century, with antecedents in royal moneylenders like Edward Backwell and an even older linkage to the king's bankers of the Middle Ages. So prominent was this transition in public moneylending that the terms 'bank' and 'banking' ordinarily referred to the various schemes supporting royal finance, and less frequently to businesses lending money to private persons. When private banks were referred to, the term usually was hybridized to conform to the particular class of financiers such as the 'goldsmith-bankers,' though their places of operation were called 'shops.' The several applications of the term during the seventeenth century contributed to the confusion between public banking and private banking, to the degree that the more prominent form of finance – public banking – sired the private banks of the day.

Does English private banking trace its genealogy back to the royal moneylending traditions of the king's bankers, or did it develop from other sources altogether, as Heckscher suggested? According to the oldest theory of the origins of English deposit banking the true progenitors of private banking were not the royal moneylenders but the lesser goldsmith-bankers who survived the crisis of 1672. This description was published anonymously in 1676 in the pamphlet *The Mystery of the New Fashioned Goldsmiths*, and it remained the only explanation of the origins of English banking for almost two hundred years. According to this description, goldsmiths ventured into the new finance when they first began to offer facilities such as cashiers, which brought them exchange dealings. At a somewhat later date these cash-keepers then began to accept deposits for which they paid interest. In turn, they then loaned these reserves at a greater rate of interest paid to their depositors. In the time before their clients recalled their deposits, these financiers were free to speculate with their capital.

Over the years this explanation – what A. V. Judges called the

---

[4]P. G. M. Dickson, *The Financial Revolution in England* (London and New York, 1967), 341–92; C. A. F. Meekings, 'The City Loans on the Hearth Tax, 1664–1668,' in *Studies in London History*, ed. Hollaender and Kellaway, 335–70.

'catastrophic' explanation of the origins of English banking[5] – has been challenged. That suddenly complex financial institutions like banks should arise at a date when other economic institutions were well developed seemed suspicious. By 1877 F. G. Hilton Price had found evidence that certain goldsmiths during the 1650s had begun lending their deposits at high rates of interest and allowing their clients to draw drafts on demand.[6] The standard work on the subject of the origins of banking is R. D. Richards's *Early History of Banking in England*. Richards was reluctant to discredit the contributions of the bankers to the government in the development of private banking. He gave much attention to the Vyners and Backwell and their techniques with high finance. With considerable capital at their command and with their influence in international finance, especially foreign exchange, the state bankers set a pattern, he believed, which their successors imitated. This transmission of experience from the last generation of Crown bankers to the goldsmith-bankers who survived them is credible in part by the uneven weight of evidence.[7] More material survives recording the activities of the Vyners and Backwell than for the lesser goldsmith-bankers whose records today are sparse.

Backwell was like no other banker before or after him. The 'father of English banking' executed several of the functions absorbed by the Treasury and later the Bank of England. He took in deposits from London goldsmiths and then loaned the money to the government.[8] After the Restoration he received the money on behalf of the king for the sale of Dunkirk. Sir John Finch witnessed the event in 1662, when Backwell provided forty-six carts to carry the £350,000 – all in silver – to the mint.[9] The Houblon brothers deposited into Backwell's hands Portuguese coins, silver bars and occasionally blocks of tin, which were balanced with the exchange of commodities in other ports. They did not leave for long periods sums of money on deposit with him, and there is no evidence that Backwell speculated with their specie on deposit.[10] Backwell's fortune did not begin with interest-bearing deposits, nor did those of the Vyners and four or five other goldsmiths of the 1650s. They offered facilities not

[5] Judges, 'The Origins of English Banking,' *History*, 138–45.

[6] F. G. Hilton Price, 'Some Notes on the Early Goldsmiths and Bankers to the Close of the 17th Century,' *Transactions of the London and Middlesex Archaeological Society*, V, Part II (August 1877), 271.

[7] R. D. Richards, *The Early History of Banking in England* (London, 1929).

[8] F. G. Hilton Price, 'Some Account of . . . Edward Backwell,' *Transactions of the London and Middlesex Archaeological Society*, VI (1890), 204.

[9] Historical Manuscripts Commission, *7th Report*, Appendix (London, 1879), 514.

[10] Lady A. A. Houblon, *The Houblon Family: Its Story and Times* (London, 1907), Vol. I, 170, 172–3.

unlike the Italian *cambio* bankers of the Middle Ages, discounting notes and issuing bills of exchange. Only after the Restoration did they traffic in loans to the public, and this was toward the end of their careers. At an earlier period they received no money on deposit from private clients.[11]

Before Richards, R. H. Tawney removed from the goldsmiths their historical attribution as the first private bankers, and in doing so, he pushed back to an earlier period the origins of banking. Within the complex world of the Elizabethan money market he isolated an obscure class of financiers, the scriveners, who had begun to take in deposits from an unexpected source. Before their flocks had been driven to London and sold for slaughter at Smithfield market in late summer, certain graziers from the Midland counties instructed their drovers to leave a part of these profits on deposit with scriveners. From these deposits domestic credit banking began. Tawney's discovery separated private banking from state finance altogether. At the roots of English banking was agriculture, whereas much of the banking business of the Middle Ages had been constructed around foreign trade and moneychanging. Deposits which came the scriveners' way from domestic, agrarian roots did not exclude the possibility that at a somewhat later date control over the same source of capital could fall to the first goldsmith-bankers. Banking skills, according to Tawney, were not the monopoly of a few great moneylenders to the Crown who then passed their secrets down to their lesser brethren.[12] Scrivener-banking was a simpler process than the state banking of the greater goldsmith-bankers. According to the author of *The Mystery of the New Fashioned Goldsmiths*, by 1676 the rents and other income of country gentlemen formed the deposits of the goldsmith-bankers surviving the Stop of the Exchequer. Tawney's essay suggested that there was a continuous tradition in banking history through its agrarian sources, and bankers to the Crown seemed incidental to this connection.

Banking was destined to develop in London, though it would seem to bear a close affinity to provincial towns, where stock and commodities could be sold at the local markets and deposited there with less trouble than if the same were sent to London. Two banks are traced to provincial origins in the Stuart period. Before 1650 the Gurneys in Norwich were receiving the money of merchants in the town and the gentry nearby and performing other banking functions as well, such as granting loans and

---

[11]D. K. Clark, 'A Restoration Goldsmith-Banking House: The Vine on Lombard Street,' in *Essays in Modern British History in Honor of Wilbur Cortez Abbott* (Cambridge, Mass., 1941), 4–5.

[12]Wilson, *A Discourse upon Usury*, ed. Tawney, 1–172.

making drafts in London. In another instance the firm of Abel Smith in Nottingham by 1658 was acting as a bank to local tradesmen; by the eighteenth century Smiths had established their headquarters in London.[13] The way deposits were invested in loans placed London at the center of banking history, as much as where depositaries received their reserves. There was a logical connection between landowners and scriveners. The one group turned to the other to receive their deposits and pay their debts in London because they had already used their services in conveyancing land. As the sessions of parliament became longer and more frequent, the squires and lords who sat at Westminster spent more time and money in London than before. The fashionable clothes, furniture and other commodities bought on credit from London artisans and tradesmen were often paid for by their agents.[14] From one type of middlemen – conveyancers and agents – the scriveners moved into another intermediary position, that of loan-brokers. Because they knew who was buying and who was selling land, the scriveners were in a situation to put lenders – their depositors – in touch with the new purchasers. The landowners who had put money on deposit with them had left more capital than was necessary to pay their debts.[15] Deposits in the capital reached a wider potential loan market than the neighborhood, and the implication is that those who deposited money in London did so anticipating that a large part of their capital would be loaned.

Virtually nothing is known about banking credit in this early period. How was credit-worthiness determined? Did the broker ascertain the lender's ability to repay the loan or was that the responsibility of the lender? Did the borrower submit his accounts for inspection? A check was certainly made in the public registers to see what loans were outstanding. One of the earliest glimpses we have of Clayton as a young man is his searching through the small-loans registers of the Mayor's Court in London.[16] The records of registration were so disorganized that the process of inspection was haphazard. There were four Exchequer record repositories at Westminster by 1610, but before then these records had been housed in other buildings in the kingdom. Chancery records were kept in the king's wardrobe in the Tower until 1657, when the Close Rolls

---

[13] W. H. Bidwell, *Annals of an East Anglian Bank* (Norwich, 1900), 11–12; J. A. S. L. L. Boyce, *Smiths the Bankers* (London, 1958), 1–15.

[14] M. G. Davies, 'Country Gentry and Payments to London, 1650–1714,' *Economic History Review*, second series, XXIV (1971), 15–36.

[15] Wilson, *A Discourse upon Usury*, ed. Tawney, 97–8.

[16] Henry Montague to C., May 4, 1676, Box 9, L.S.E.

were all assembled in the Rolls Chapel.[17] Even after the transfer the methods of arranging these records were unreliable. In 1661 Clayton's clerks found in the Office of the Petty Bag a recognizance signed four years earlier but never written on the Rolls, and these omissions were not unusual.[18] Even so, land registration and the records of loans were much better kept in England than in any country on the continent.[19]

Lending money through brokers was so bound up with the registration of the lending contracts that it was impossible to separate this aspect from transfer of capital between parties. The public enrollment of the documents comprising the loan protected its validity, and for all large-scale commitments outside the Duchy of Lancaster, this took place in the capital. Registration was thus another force working toward the centralization of banking in London. With the Hales Commission in 1652 a fruitless proposal was made to establish registers in each county, where a record of title transfer, as well as the encumbrances upon the property, would be available for local inspection.[20] Periodically this suggestion arose again, though it was not until the early eighteenth century that the first county register was established, in Yorkshire. Had the movement succeeded during the first century of banking, local credit would have been strengthened. As long as the only public registers remained in London, this became a force working toward the concentration of the process in London. The great Lord Chancellor Lord Nottingham observed that after the Restoration it was the practice for most securities for money to be transferred in London. As equity law had become so complex, it was likely that legal questions arising out of lending contracts would arise in the courts in London. If the indentures were sealed in London, and witnessed by persons living in the metropolis, it would be more convenient to summon them to the courts, should any question arise, than it would be to ask witnesses in the country to travel to London to give testimony.[21]

[17] *Guide to the Contents of the Public Record Office* (London, 1963–8), Vol. I, i.

[18] John Thompson's letter, July 12, 1660, Clayton papers, 1661 Jul.–Dec., Osborn, Yale.

[19] S. Rowton Simpson, *Land Law and Registration*, Cambridge, 1976, 91–2.

[20] H. Robinson, *Certain Proposals* . . . (London, 1652). See Anon., *A Treatise Showing How Usefull, Safe, Reasonable and Beneficial, the Inrolling & Registering of all Conveyances of Land, may be to the Inhabitants of this Kingdom* (London, 1694), 1, 5, 23; W. Leach, *Propositions for Recording and Registering of Deeds and Conveyances* (London, 1651), 7; W. Pierrepoint, *A Treatise Concerning Registers* (London, *c.* 1670), in *Harleian Miscellany* (London, 1744–6), Vol. III, 321; F. Philipp, *The Pretended Perspective-Glass* . . . (London, 1669); *idem., The Reforming Registry* . . . (London, 1671). See also Simpson, *Registration*, 93–4.

[21] *Lord Nottingham's 'Manual of Chancery Practice,'* ed. D. E. C. Yale (Cambridge, 1965), 159.

According to one observer, the failure to establish county registers produced among rural moneylenders a desire for 'scrupulous lenders' rather than for greater risks to extend credit, and caused a situation in which loans in the country went at eight per cent, whereas loans in the City cost five per cent, solely because of the familiarity with the Rolls which the scriveners and goldsmith-bankers had acquired.[22]

As it was, even in the City, the system was so lax that the opportunities for fraud were rife. In 1585 an Elizabethan statute required that all recognizances known as Statutes Staple were to be enrolled within a year and a day after their signing.[23] Much could be done to a conveyance before that time. The document itself could be altered, and where the witnesses had died or disappeared, these changes were difficult to prove. Honest errors often appeared in the several copies made of the deed. The copy of the transaction left with the Master of the Rolls was the supreme copy of the deed, the one to which all other copies were referred. Over the years this recognizance, as well as the Statute Merchant, had declined in use, partly because after the signing and before registration, other claims might be secretly assigned on the security. In 1674 an order of Lord Chancellor Nottingham changed the process of registration by decreeing that no recognizance, of whatever type, written on the Rolls more than six months after it was made was to be valid.[24]

Like recognizances, all titles conveyed by freehold, inheritance or years' purchase were registered on the Close Rolls, a tradition of enrollment going back to the reign of Henry VI. Through these conveyances land was secured by mortgage, which meant that copies of most long-term, large-scale lending contracts were supposedly deposited in these records. The money-scriveners searched the public registers in deplorable conditions to see if titles were free of encumbrances and what commitments the prospective lender had made through bonds. But under the same circumstances these men who negotiated the money for the loan and also cleared the security acquired an expertise amid the maze of fraud and confusion. It was as much as conveyancers who registered documents and knew the loopholes in the process as it was as scribes who actually wrote out the documents of the loan that the role of the scriveners becomes clearer in early banking history.

The scriveners lacked the continuity in their history that the goldsmiths

---

[22]N. Philpot, *Reasons and Proposals for a Registry* . . . (London, 1671), in *Harleian Miscellany*, Vol. III, 317.
[23]27 Eliz. I c. 4, sections 7, 8 and 9; made perpetual 39 Eliz. I c. 18.
[24]*Ordines Cancellariae* . . . (London, 1698), 183–6.

had. There were two successive companies of Scriveners, though a lapse of years separated the medieval gild from the new craft founded in James I's reign. In the Middle Ages the Company of Court Letter Scriveners included scribes and limners among its membership, while at the same time outside the gild there flourished notaries who performed some of the same functions as the gild members.[25] With the advance of printing, the need for handwritten work contracted sharply, and the company declined. By 1565 the scriveners left in the medieval company were absorbed into the Ironmongers' Company.[26] What demands remained in the market for inscribed forms lay in conveyancing, through title deeds, money bonds and all other financial and legal transactions which were not yet executed on printed forms. From the reign of Henry VIII until well into the seventeenth century a group of scribes who were called, variously, brokers, notaries and scriveners executed these writings.[27] Most of the writings prepared for James I's signature until 1621 were prepared by scriveners, who lost this source of income when the Crown's clerks took over these duties.[28]

Contemporaries charged the scriveners with incompetence at making conveyances, which were said to be filled with so many errors and contrivances that all men must beware these charlatans.[29] But in the Tudor and Stuart periods great experimentation was made in conveyancing, to accommodate the complexities of land ownership following the dissolution of the monasteries, as well as the financial arrangements settled upon overseas expansion. Many deeds and other financial contracts were drawn up by scribes, who worked out various conveyancing precedents, occasionally published as clerks' manuals.[30] In the course of the seventeenth century lawyers gradually took over these functions, but before then, scriveners and notaries played a role in legal history which went

[25] B. G. C. Brooke, 'London Notaries and Their History' [typescript in the Guildhall Library of a lecture delivered at the Society of Genealogists on March 22, 1967], 2–3; *Records of the Society of Gentlemen Practisers* (London, 1897). See also C. R. Cheney, *Notaries Public in England in the Thirteenth and Fourteenth Centuries* (Oxford, 1972).

[26] *Notes & Queries*, seventh series, X (1890), 464.

[27] *Records of the Society of Gentlemen Practisers* (London, 1897), xiii.

[28] *Bibliotheca Lindesiana: A Bibliography of Royal Proclamations of the Tudor and Stuart Sovereigns and Others Published under Authority 1485–1714*, ed. R. R. Steele (Oxford, 1910), Vol. I, 156.

[29] Anon., *Poems upon Divers Occasions with a Character of a London Scrivener* (London, 1667), 131–2.

[30] G. Bird, *Practising Scrivener and Modern Conveyancer* ... (London, 1729); N. Covert, *The Scrivener's Guide* (London, 1695, 1700); R[obert] G[ardiner], *Ars Clericalis* ... (2 vols., London, 1690, 1692, 1698); [Robert Gardiner], *Enchiridion Clericale* ... (London, 1701, 1712); *Compleat Clark* ... (var. edns, London, 1664–83), *Young Clerk's Tutor Enlarged* ... (var. edns, London, 1664–1735); (J[ohn]) H[ernel], *Modern Assurancer* ... (London, 1658),

beyond the mere copying out of documents.[31] Imperfect as their legal training might have been, practical experience remained with scriveners and notaries who must have known what conveyances the courts would accept. A scriveners' guide published in 1655 drew upon the learning and experience of a century of legal cases and title registrations.[32] At the same time the scriveners created new conveyances, a margin of error and loss could be predicted as newly formed indentures reached the bench. Innovative, and possessed of a certain wisdom which few others had, the scriveners produced work probably of a consistently reliable standard; otherwise they could not have gained the confidence of landowners to accept money on deposit.

Best known of these early scriveners was John Milton, senior, the father of the poet. Son of a farmer, he came to London and took up the work of a scrivener long before the second Company of Scriveners was formed. It was the sort of occupation a man could enter who could not afford to be apprenticed. Interestingly, when this Milton took on two apprentices himself in 1628, he remitted two-fifths of the normal apprenticing fee, which by that time had become rather high. Milton grew wealthy in the business before he retired. In his shop all manner of conveyances were drawn up, but according to one of his servants, the mainstay of his income came from putting out other men's money at interest.[33] In other words, he was a money-broker, commonly known as a money-scrivener during the seventeenth century.

A contemporary of Milton was Hugh Audley, also trained as a scrivener before the Stuart company was founded in 1617. His master was a clerk in the court of Poultry Compter in the City. This man flourished by finding bail for men imprisoned for bad debts. When Audley established his own shop, his financial investments broadened. He discounted notes and dabbled in land, but his great success came after he obtained a place in the Court of Wards:

he gained money ... in hindering some great persons to make a prey of young Heirs ... he was father to the fatherless ... he watched the incumbrances that lay upon

General Tutor . . . (London, 1659); Sir R. Hutton, Young Clerks Guide . . . (var. edns, London, 1649–91), Clerk's Vade mecum . . . (London, 1655), The Compleat Clark and Scriveners Guide . . . (London, 1655), Exact Clerk and Scrivener . . . (London, 1656, 1659, 1672); H. J.,Young Clerk's Tutor . . . (London, 1660, 1662), The Third Part of the Young Clerkes Guide . . . (London, 1659).

[31] Records of the Society of Gentlemen Practisers, xiii.
[32] The Compleat Clerk and Scriveners Guide . . . , [i].
[33] J. M. French, Life Records of Milton (New Brunswick, N.J., 1949–58), Vol. I, 54; idem, Milton in Chancery, M.L.A. Monograph Series, X (New York, 1939), 36–7.

the Estates that came thither and he undertook them, complying with the necessities of the owners, insomuch that he had at one time an hundred & fourteen mortgages, statutes and judgements.[34]

From the group of clerks there arose a clique of men, like Milton and Audley, who called themselves 'scriveners.' There is no reason to believe that their work was different from other men who performed writing skills.[35]

In 1617 the Scriveners received a charter of incorporation.[36] Through incorporation they acquired the privilege of investing in the Londonderry Company, in which they soon became one of the largest investors of the smaller London companies.[37] All in all, this advantage became the main benefit of the company, for no provision in the charter gave the Scriveners a monopoly over conveyancing, which would have extinguished those activities of their rivals, the attorneys.

During the Jacobean period Lord Chief Justice Hobart attacked the attorneys when he said that 'it did no more belong to an attorney to make writings than it did to an apothecary to make physic,'[38] but this was an opinion rather than an order of restraint, and it is doubtful whether the Scriveners ever had a legal monopoly over the drawing up of minor contracts, or whether they stuck to their oaths not to draw up the deeds of major contracts such as inheritance.[39] In the company's by-laws, composed in 1635, it was ordered that no member of the gild was to keep in his service any person other than an apprentice who was not free of the society.[40] This underlined the inherent weakness of the company: that the writing skills of the Scriveners were so simple to learn that those who had not undergone the same training could perform the same skills. After 1666 the Scriveners allowed attorneys who paid quarterage to the company to practice conveyancing along the same lines as the former, although there

---

[34] *The Way to be Rich, According to the Practice of the Great Audley* ... (London, 1662), 4, 6, 8,15; *The Oppressions and Wrongs to the value of above ten thousand pounds done by Hugh Audley to Sir Philip Knivett, Bt.* . . . . [London, 1661].

[35] The first generation of new scriveners learnt their skills from the last generation of the old company, and this transmission of experience was perpetuated by the Stuart Scriveners, Abbott, Clayton and Morris were trained in an apostolic succession of eight generations of master–apprentice relationships beginning in 1425: *Scriveners' Company Common Paper 1357–1628*, ed. F. W. Steer, London Record Society, Vol. IV (London, 1968), 22, 26, 29, 46, 61, 116, 122.

[36] *Ibid.*

[37] T. W. Moody, *The Londonderry Plantation 1609–41* (Belfast, 1939), 442–3.

[38] *Records of the Society of Gentlemen Practisers*, xii–xiv.

[39] F. W. Steer, *A History of the Worshipful Company of Scriveners of London* (London and Chichester, 1973), 22–5.

[40] B.L., Harleian MS 2295, fol. 21.

is no record that a single attorney availed himself of this privilege.[41] It seems likely that this concession of the Scriveners was an attempt to raise money to rebuild their hall – which the homeless attorneys might use – rather than a bona fide dispensation of privileges which the attorneys had not enjoyed before.

The early years of the new Company of Scriveners were its most prosperous. In 1628 the Scriveners bought a hall, Bacon House, near the church of St Mary Staynings.[42] When this building was destroyed by the Great Fire of 1666, the members constructed another hall, but by 1682 the fortunes of the company had declined to the point that their meeting-place was leased to the Hudson's Bay Company and later sold to the Coachmakers and Coach Harnessmakers.[43] The dwindling number of Scriveners could no longer support their own hall. In 1672 the company asked the Court of Common Council of London to amend its charter to include a monopoly over conveyancing, claiming that their group was the same as the medieval company having that privilege. It was an unsuccessful plea, a misrepresentation of the true history of the company.[44]

The turnover of land influenced the growth and contraction of the second Scriveners' Company. The company was founded at approximately the same time the number of land transactions from 1560 to 1699 reached its peak. But soon thereafter this number declined sharply until about 1625, when the numbers of transactions remained constant until 1640. Similarly, during the period 1627–37 the company registered more apprentices than it did in any other decade for which registration records survive. After 1660 the numbers of apprentices enrolled by the company declined drastically, just as the numbers of land transactions sharply contracted.[45] On the other hand, apprenticeships did not increase significantly during the land sales of the Puritan Revolution, which, admittedly, was a period when the normal training of apprentices was interrupted. During a period when the gilds generally were losing their power to control their charters, this right of the Scriveners' Company was always uncertain and never existed as a privilege to be lost.

[41] Brooks, 'London Notaries,' 2–3.
[42] J. Stow, *Annales* . . . (London, 1631), 1043–4.
[43] *Scriveners' Company Common Paper*, xiii.
[44] Bod. Lib., Rawlinson MS D.734, fols. 85–6.
[45] From 1617 through 1626 the company registered sixty-seven apprentices. During the next decade, 1627 through 1636. eighty-one men became apprentices. During the next decades the enrollments were, respectively, 1637 through 1646, thirty-seven; 1647 through 1656, thirty-five; and 1657 through 1666, fifty-three: *Scriveners' Company Common Paper*, 57–62, 114–27.

What this suggests is that the Scriveners' Company had little effect in improving its members' status. In 1640 twelve aldermen compiled a list of the wealthiest men of their wards, listing such persons as were capable of contributing towards a large loan to the kind. Of the 1,090 men who were polled only five were scriveners.[46] Over a broader period covered by the company's records, only a few men can be traced beyond the company's register. Even though they were vilified as usurers, it seems likely that, all in all, those scriveners who were moneylenders – the money-scriveners – were such small-scale financiers that their relative transgressions were likewise menial. Conveyancing was the mainline of business of most of the scriveners, not moneylending. Their most serious rivals were the attorneys.

Before the late seventeenth century any person could represent another person's or group's interest in the lower courts; if he was not a lawyer proper, he was referred to as an attorney. Attorneys, like the scriveners, acquired much practical experience in their work searching through court records and writing conveyances for clients. During the course of the seventeenth century the attorneys were forbidden to attend the Inns of Court, and a sharper distinction was made between those who had formal legal training and those whose expertise was self-acquired, like the attorneys.[47] As the legal profession became better trained and as the problem of land transfer and settlements became more complicated, lawyers and even attorneys, until after the Restoration, acquired a reputation for accuracy and knowledge which redounded to the discredit of other groups trained as writers who had formerly performed these skills. The attacks upon the scriveners, that they 'crack'd titles,' either through deceit or ignorance, rested upon the assumption that some other group could do this better. As the scriveners began to lose land title transfer to attorneys and lawyers, they were left with the residue of petty contracts. By the eighteenth century the scriveners had become notaries, while the attorneys, especially in the country, managed estates, negotiated loans and put out their own money, much as did the money-scriveners of the past.[48]

During the years of the brief prosperity of the scriveners their place as early bankers changed from the receivers of deposits to financiers who

---

[46]T. C. Dale, 'List of the Principal Inhabitants of London in 1640,' in *Miscellanea Genealogica et Heraldica*, second series, Vol. II (1888), *passim*.

[47]Sir W. Dugdale, *Origines juridicales* (London, 1671), 311; B. A. Holderness, 'The English Land Market in the Eighteenth Century: The Case of Lincolnshire,' *Economic History Review*, second series, XXVII (1974), 560.

[48]M. Birks, *Gentlemen of the Law* (London, 1960), 182; R. Robson, *The Attorney in Eighteenth-Century England*, Cambridge Studies in English Legal History (Cambridge, 1959), 26–7; Holderness, 'The English Land Market,' 560.

handled more complex financial operations. By about 1628 scriveners were managing the estates of clients, and within the next two decades Hugh Audley, Humphrey Shalcrosse and Robert Abbott had all become actual trustees for some of their clients' affairs.[49] As a result of their entry into the land market, scriveners were led to policy decisions regarding reinvestment and credit and acquired in the process a degree of limited liability. Soon after the company was founded, the writer of a broadside complained that the late Thomas Frith, Scrivener, 'being a putter forth of much money for other men at interest,' was arrested when he went broke, but his own estate and the property he left to his widow and heirs had never been attached for his debts.[50] In 1668 and again in 1680 Chancery defined the limited liability of scriveners who acted as money-brokers. If the security to a loan failed, the lender had no recourse to the broker, but rather to the one who put up credit. If the scrivener forfeited the security, it was no different than losing the same by theft or fire:

Where one places money in a scrivener's hands with this general trust for him to put it out where he pleases there by that general trust or authority the payment back to the scrivener is good payment [except] if the lender keep the security himself...[51]

As the scriveners became involved in trusteeships and estate management, two other banking precedents developed. The first involved credit. In 1668 Chancery recognized the rights of a scrivener to investigate his clients' affairs, beyond merely the estates which he held in trust for him.[52] In fact, Hugh Audley, Humphrey Shalcrosse, Robert Abbott, Robert Clayton, and John Morris had done exactly that long before the court decision, which recognized a role scriveners had played in determining credit some time before. Long-term credit, based upon landed income, led the scriveners to policies involving the valuation of estates. In 1667 a writer complained:

---

[49] J. M. Holden, *History of Negotiable Instruments in English Law* (Cambridge, 1955), 205, n. 4.

[50] *The Contents of a Bill, preferred by the Creditors of Thomas Frith, late of London, Scrivenor, deceased* . . . [London, 1621?].

[51] Ld. Nottingham's clarification of Southcote's case, in which he expressed doubts on the legitimacy of detinue of goods. The case was not finally disallowed until 1703. *Lord Nottingham's Chancery Cases*, ed. D. E. C. Yale, Vol. I, Publications of the Selden Society, LXXIII (1957), civ–cv, n. 5; *Clerk v. Perryer* (January 1680), in *ibid.*, I, civ–cv; *Sir Henry Henn v. Sir Henry Conisby* (1668), in A. Keck, *Cases Argued and Decreed in the High Court of Chancery from the 12th year of King Charles II to the 31st* (London, 1697).

[52] L.R. Ch. (1668–93), 608 [21 Car. II, 1669–70].

When he is examining an estate, you would imagine him casting its water to find what disease it labours of, and to be sure (like a knavish surgeon) he will either find a cure of it, or make one.[53]

Ethically or not, this is testimony to the role that the scriveners had made in the development of land assessment, which is unlike anything attributed during the same period to the goldsmith-bankers. When Samuel Purchase published his own method of valuing land in 1680, he chastened his rivals, warning purchasers to beware of 'scriveners' law, and their books of precedents' in this matter, which at the same time is a back-handed recognition of their accomplishments.[54]

The first five or six decades of English banking were years of growth and change. From the scanty evidence available to draw a comparison it appears that scriveners of the Commonwealth had not expanded their receipt of deposits much beyond the days of Shakespeare, when their deposits were attuned to the cycles of the harvest. The price of wool leveled off as English merchants lost their traditional markets in the Baltic. As the normal flow of trading to Flanders was cut off during the Thirty Years War, more capital for speculation was available at home.[55] The banking operations which R. D. Richards described for the 1650s were dependent upon this capital accretion in London and its subsequent reinvestment in the mercantile and colonial enterprises which the Protector encouraged. Only one scrivener whose career is documented became a part of this transition. Sir Martin Noel was so successful in trading to both the East and West Indies that even Oliver Cromwell sought his advice on commercial matters.[56]

It was a group of goldsmiths, however, who were to rise to prominence from this change. The goldsmiths were an old and honorable company whose membership was tightly regulated. By the end of the fifteenth century the goldsmiths of London produced wares of such high quality and beauty as to strike the admiration of foreigners.[57] During the following

---

[53] *Poems upon Divers Occasions with a Character of a London Scrivener*, 131. See also Bacon, 'Of Riches,' *Essays*, XXIV ('The scriveners and broaker doe valew unsound men').

[54] S[amuel] P[urchase], *The City and Country Purchaser and Builder*, 2nd edn (London, 1680), 12.

[55] B. E. Supple, *Commercial Crisis and Change in England, 1600–1642* (Cambridge, 1959); J. A. Chartres, *Internal Trade in England 1500–1700*, Studies in Economic and Social History (London, 1970); A. Friis, *Alderman Cockayne's Project and the Cloth Trade . . . 1603–1625* (Copenhagen and London, 1927).

[56] D. K. Clark, 'The Vine . . . ,' in *Essays*, 5; E. B. Sainsbury, ed., *A Calendar of the Court Minutes of the East India Company 1655–1659* (Oxford, 1916), xiii.

[57] T. F. Reddaway and L. Walker, *The Early History of the Goldsmiths' Company 1327–1509* (London, 1975).

century the fortunes of the goldsmiths expanded further. Through the spoliation of the monasteries much mineral wealth fell into their hands, to be fashioned into wares. Later, Queen Elizabeth bought gold from these men, who probably by that time had added Spanish bullion to their stock. A few of these highly skilled artisans had acquired positions in the royal mint in the Middle Ages, and in Tudor England this connection grew even stronger. The Crown depended upon the goldsmiths of London more than any other gild as deputies to the officials in the mint. From 1572 to 1579 Richard Martin, goldsmith, farmed the mint as his own operation.[58]

By the seventeenth century the goldsmiths had acquired another connection with the state which arose out of the Crown's need for public borrowing. Between 1603 and 1640 the goldsmiths enjoyed preferential powers as moneylenders to the Stuart kings.[59] As the finances of the state fell into chaos in 1640, the goldsmiths continued this practice. When Edward Backwell received deposits from other goldsmiths of London during the Interregnum and then loaned this money to the government, he merely concentrated a long-established practice.

When troubles between king and parliament erupted in 1640, the gentry and nobility began to melt down their plate, much of which they left with the goldsmiths. To safeguard these reserves goldsmiths then placed their deposits in the royal mint. Rude coins were made from this metal. When they came into circulation many goldsmiths profited from clipping the grosser coins of their excess weight. At the same time they took merchants' capital into their hands, paying fourpence a day for the use. Other merchants who needed credit to replenish their stocks found they could borrow through the goldsmiths. To increase the cycle of deposits and loans some of the goldsmiths then undertook to receive gentlemen's rents as they were paid into London, and since the gentry were more likely to leave the bulk of their capital on deposit longer than merchants, the ebb and flow of capital from the shops of goldsmiths worked in harmony.[60]

During the twelve years from 1640 to 1652 the goldsmiths had entered the private banking market for reasons independent of their role as royal moneylenders and minters. But after Cromwell became Lord Protector, they began to channel their investments back into governmental loans, through agents like Backwell. It is probably not incorrect to assume that before the Restoration their clients were not principally in the country. In 1652 the goldsmiths were described as 'cashiers of the merchants of

---

[58] C. E. Challis, *The Tudor Coinage* (Manchester and New York, 1978), 34, 40, 41, 43.
[59] R. Ashton, *The Crown and the Money Market* (Oxford, 1960).
[60] Such is the explanation in *The Mystery of New Fashioned Goldsmiths*.

London,'[61] and if these deposits formed the bulk of their reserves, they were not in competition with the money-scriveners. The origins of goldsmith-banking and scrivener-banking sprang from different sources at different times. If eventually the goldsmiths were to supersede the scriveners in the banking market, the time of that eclipse lay some time in the future.

The relative positions of the goldsmith-bankers before and after 1660 is unclear, but it seems safe to conclude that the stable years following the Restoration of Charles II were not ones of unparalleled growth, as Dorothy Clark suggested.[62] Historical accounts of these financiers during the period 1640–87 describe bankers performing different functions, and they cannot be truly compared. Goldsmiths receiving money on deposit are not necessarily the same financiers specializing in foreign exchange and loans to the government. Before the Exchequer crisis of 1672 laid the foundations of ruin for the banking tycoons – the king's bankers – the Plague of 1665 caused a run on the reserves of the banking community in London, probably accounting for the bankruptcy and disappearance of some of the establishments founded during the Interregnum.[63] The size of the goldsmith-banking community becomes clearer in 1670, and at selected intervals thereafter, from the lists which F. G. Hilton Price compiled during the nineteenth century. While these are sometimes unreliable, the general pattern of his work seems correct: that the many banking foundations of the late seventeenth century had only brief lives. In 1670 there were at least thirty-one separate goldsmith-banks; in 1687 forty-three houses are accounted for in Hilton Price's lists. Only eleven of these banks founded by 1670 survived to 1687.[64]

In spite of the brief lives of most of their banks, the goldsmiths have seemed especially compelling as pioneers in early banking for the reason that by working in gold and silver they became directly involved with capital, yet according to the author of *The Mystery of the New Fashioned Goldsmiths*, most of the goldsmith-bankers soon lost this direct connection with fashioning specie. By 1676 the bulk of the goldsmith-

[61] Richards, *Early History of Banking*, 24.
[62] D. K. Clark, 'The Vine . . . ,' in *Essays*, 5; Richards, *Early History of Banking*, chs. 2 and 3.
[63] *Memoirs of the Verney Family*, ed. M. M. Verney (reprint edn, New York, 1970), Vol. IV, 116; see also Clark, 'The Vine . . . ,' in *Essays*, 22–3.
[64] See Appendix 3.

bankers' reserves came from their deposits.[65] Not until the eighteenth century did the bankers who were also goldsmiths finally relinquish their role as artisans in gold and silver.[66] Nevertheless, there is a consistent theme among historians of English banking that the origins of banking are necessarily related to the artisanship of particular drafts. The scriveners lacked the same orientation to specie as the goldsmiths, and, at any rate, the scriveners faded from a scene the goldsmiths captivated. With so little documentary evidence to the contrary, confidence seems to rest in the belief that the goldsmiths' affinity with gold and silver complemented their role as progenitors of early banking.

Behind the forms which these early bankers assumed – distorted by their relationships to their gilds – the banking functions of the scriveners and goldsmiths were strikingly similar. Their contemporaries were apt to describe private bankers as 'cashiers,' financiers who processed money from its receipt on account until the time it was disbursed. According to J. Houghton, banking meant 'to receive and pay other men's money, whereby the owners were freed from much trouble, and loss of bad money; and instead of going over the town, they might, many of them, meet with all their cash in one man's shop, and thus came in the banking.'[67] This definition is craft-free, applicable to both the money-scriveners and goldsmith-bankers. Dudley North concurred in this definition of banking as cash-keeping,[68] as did the author of The Mystery of the New Fashioned Goldsmiths, though the latter was concerned with only one of the groups which performed these functions. According to his explanation it was the cash-keeping skills of the goldsmiths which first attracted banking deposits into their hands. Among the merchants of London it was the practice for their apprentices to keep their books and handle their cash. When these young men went off to the civil wars, merchants delegated these duties to goldsmiths who then received their first deposits. This statement that the absence of clerks could disorientate capital from one business to another is a powerful testimony to the importance of cash-keeping services.[69]

'Cashier' referred to a greater range of operations in seventeenth-

---

[65] The Mystery of the New Fashioned Goldsmiths (London, 1676), 5. This fluctuation should not be taken to be the same as a bankruptcy rate. The inability of bankers to find suitable replacements in the succeeding generation could account for some failures; it is possible that some banks merged.
[66] The Mystery of the New Fashioned Goldsmiths, 4–6.
[67] [J. Houghton,] An Account of the Bank of Credit in the City of London [1683], 5.
[68] Roger North, The Life of the Honourable Sir Dudley North, Knt (London, 1744), 148.
[69] The Mystery of the New Fashioned Goldsmiths, 1.

century banking than it does in modern use, in which the word implies receiving and paying functions integrated within a single organization. A cashier in the seventeenth century acted outside the framework of businesses and households of private clients, rendering services absent from the simple bureaucracies of those groups. Cashiers might handle the finances of a corporation or act as deputies in handling certain stages of governmental commissions, such as tax-farming. In modern usage these commissions would be termed 'receiverships.' The bankers to Cromwell and Charles II, such as the Vyners and Edward Backwell, were prominent in this aspect of cash-keeping; after 1672, other bankers handled similar commissions on a smaller scale. The goldsmith-bankers Coggs, Hornby, Fowle, Price and Smith all acted during the 1690s as receivers of naval affairs and other governmental commissions arising from the salt tax and excise.[70]

The visible character of banking – the one their clients saw – was the work of cashiers. In large banks, like Clayton's, hundreds of men entered the shop each month to transact a variety of business. There they met scribes working at what must have seemed a bewildering display of notation, all reconciled in ledgers. Often receipts and bankers' notes were issued for each deposit, which might also be registered in a cashiers' book or the bank's ledgers, open for each client to inspect his account. Each withdrawal was written for the appropriate sum. Somewhere nearby were other scribes copying indentures for loans, and records of these trans- actions were recorded in the ledgers also. Other chits were written for valuables stored for safe-keeping, as tapestries, jewels, pictures, plate and legal writings were duly received and stored. Often accounts were pre- sented with each deposit (as in the instance of Clayton's rent-collectors), audited and checked against the ledgers. For the casual observer, who never advanced much beyond the threshold, this was the work of banking he was most likely to see. There was a powerful logic and control presented in the work of the clerks, likely to inspire confidence in the banker's clients and others impressed with the public image of banks as a series of well- coordinated cash-keeping functions.

When cashiers took in and paid out the monies of their clients, they per- formed extensive bookkeeping services, often more advanced than their clients and their stewards were capable of themselves. In 1727 Jonathan Swift wrote Alexander Pope he was willing to pay two or three hundred

---

[70]F. G. Hilton Price, *Handbook of London Bankers* (London, 1890–1), 40, 61, 84, 110, 134.

pounds a year to an accountant or cashier to handle his affairs.[71] Cashiers' records were important in an age in which the records of credit were imprecise or otherwise non-existent. Seventeenth-century banking ledgers were semi-public documents. When the cashier-banker made his own accounts testifying to the credit of his clients, he was able to present, often, the only reliable records of credit in London for certain financial transactions. It goes without saying that bankers would try to keep good accounts, but bearing in mind the importance their clients placed upon cashiering, a good bookkeeping image was an outward and visible sign of an inward cash-keeping grace.

A cash-keeper's skills could put him in a position of offering to lend money to his clients. Working with their capital and records gave him an exact knowledge of where lay his clients' credit. If cashiers took the steps to lend money, they performed another service that raised their skills to something recognizable as banking. This was problematical. Not all their commissions led to lending money to their clients, and contemporaries who described banking did not assume that cashiers were necessarily moneylenders. Cash-keeping facilities, apart from any considerations of lending, were acknowledged by their clients as valuable services in themselves. The cashier provided a London base for his clients, and for his establishment he must pay his clerks and meet all the other expenses of his work. He might charge his clients fees for his services. When the cashier acted overtly as a banker, he might sometimes give interest on his deposits, but this practice was uncommon. The line was not clearly drawn between what were banker's deposits and what were cashier's accounts, because the two functions of banker and cashier were often one and the same and similarly indistinct.

When cashiers received money on account, they inspected English coins for clipping, and they converted English bills and tallies to gold. These exchange negotiations were an integral feature of cash-keeping rather than a separate, distinctive feature of banking. Deposit banking did not emerge from the merchant class. The most prominent goldsmiths, with royal commissions, were more likely to deal directly in foreign exchange than the smaller fry of goldsmith-bankers and money-scriveners, who ordinarily would have no means of knowing exchange rates until they made inquiries among merchants or brokers on the Royal Exchange. Generally bankers

---

[71]H. Erskine-Hill, ' "Dexterous Attorney": Peter Walter, Esq. of Stalbridge (1664?–1746),' in H. Erskine-Hill, ed., *The Social Milieu of Alexander Pope: Lives, Examples and the Poetic Response* (New Haven, 1975), 119.

were not in a position to offer credit over a wide area. There may be isolated examples of goldsmiths who made arrangements for their notes to be cashed outside London,[72] but ordinarily bankers before the 1690s had no such facilities.

In their role as cashiers bankers were ordinarily passive agents who received money in the City but did not collect money in the country. In this respect the goldsmith-bankers and the money-scriveners labored under the same limitations of a lack of any institutional means of transporting capital throughout the kingdom. Private individuals provided their own means of returning capital to London and other places. Bankers had no means of transporting their clients' capital to London, except in a few exceptional instances, such as the bank of Clayton and Morris. Perhaps none of the preconditions which worked toward the origins of banking was as striking as this negative barrier seeming to obviate deposit banking: the inability of banks to return their clients' deposits in the country to London. Some idea of the seriousness of this problem comes from an example in the Verney papers. In 1683 Sir Ralph Verney transported by armed bodyguard a large sum of money from Claydon to Thame, though the risks of robbery were still so great on a journey scarcely more than fifteen miles that he was determined never to make such a trip again.[73] The Verneys and other gentry families found a more consistent method of returning money to London: they lived in the capital for several months a year and needed to support their stays there, however modest their living arrangements may have been. They and their families carried cash to the capital, but they also relied heavily on their stewards, tenants, merchants, drovers and other travelers who could be trusted to take their capital to their London residences, accountants, cashiers, scriveners or goldsmiths. The system of returning money from the country to London had more linking possibilities than between points within the country.[74] Edmund Verney in 1681 paid a debt in Oxford of £1,000 by sending the money to London to John Verney who found a man to transport the money to Oxford.[75] Banking depended upon an elaborate network of travelers to and from the metropolis who were not the servants of bankers themselves.

The banker's practice of expropriating capital depended upon the

---

[72]See below, p. 216.

[73]I am indebted for this information from the Verney papers at Claydon House to Dr John Broad, who kindly allowed me to read and refer to his unpublished paper 'Country Gentry and Payments to London 1650–1714: A Comment.'

[74]Davies, 'Country Gentry and Payments to London,' 15–36.

[75]See n. 73.

awkward, difficult return of capital from the country to the City and the rhythms of the agricultural economy controlling the ebb and flow of capital to London. On February 16, 1676, Sir Richard Newdegate wrote his scriveners that he had instructed his servant to add £2,000 to his deposit of £1,500 with them. Only a portion was earmarked for investment. Not until Easter term would he draw upon his account, and then only for £400 or £500.[76] Newdegate's plans let the scriveners know how they could manipulate his capital for their own profit, and similar expressions of intention abound in the letters the scriveners received from their clients. If they were uncertain about particular clients' demands for their capital, they knew that the gentlemen's rents forming the bulk of their reserves came into their coffers in a predictable pattern. The agricultural year culminated in late summer and autumn, at the slaughter and the harvest. Tenants were in the best position to pay their rents then, though rents dribbled in all through the winter and the spring. Clients were apt to draw upon their deposits during certain fixed times, such as the meetings of parliament, the legal sessions and the period of the London 'Season.' When Sir Peter arrived unexpectedly at another time for money, the scriveners could rob Sir Paul's account to cover the loss, making certain that these irregularities never appeared in the ledgers kept in the shop. This discrepancy between the time country rents arrived in London for deposit and the time clients withdrew their capital favored the banker's manipulation of his reserves. The impediments which made the transport of capital to London so difficult also prevented the rerouting of capital back to the countryside in a convenient fashion, thus tending to bottle up deposits in London to the advantage of the scriveners. It is no accident that scrivener-banking was formed around the agricultural economy, rather than the mobile, urban world of commerce and industry where shrewd merchants were unlikely to leave their capital on deposit for long periods.

Moneylending was another activity of bankers, though, interestingly, the few definitions of banking in the seventeenth century did not include moneylending as a distinctive feature. This is correct, as far as it goes, for moneylending was not the sole preserve of bankers. There were, presumably, goldsmiths and scriveners whose cash-keeping roles were so undeveloped that they never became loan-brokers. Those who made the transition to the lending nexus, it could be argued, had specialized another aspect of cash-keeping, and the general definition need not include all the services which bankers rendered as cashiers. Moneylenders were tainted

[76]Sir Richard Newdegate to C. & M., February 16, 1676, Clayton Mss A.1/3, Buc. R.O.

with usury, and those who wished to give the new profession of banking a good name might hope that criticism would abate if the public regard of moneylending was confined to loan-brokerage, a fee-paid service such as other bankers offered. But through their role as investors, which money-lenders are, bankers were drawn into problems of credit, directing their attention beyond the walls of their banks; this, in their benign, insulated role as cashiers, they had never done.

Two separate kinds of moneylending were involved in this connection, placing bankers into entirely different relationships with their clients. When bankers arranged loans for their clients but did not themselves put up their capital for the loan, they acted as loan-brokers. This was the most lucrative service clients stood to gain from their bankers. Under the best conditions client-lenders reaped the maximum legal interest rate on their investments. Bankers, acting as brokers, in these negotiations received a fee of 0.25 per cent of the loans, limited to this amount in the Usury Acts. By the seventeenth century the role of brokers expanded to a greater capacity than merely finding debtors for their clients. The money-scriveners were the first bankers to become conveyancers. As conveyancers both groups of bankers assumed responsibility for drawing up the covenants for the loans and registering copies of the covenants on the Rolls once the loans were sealed. The Usury Acts recognized this distinction between brokerage and conveyancing, and allowed 12d. for the making of bonds and counter-bonds.[77] Brokerage and conveyancing fees were thus limited to prevent other interest charges being disguised under those labels. In all these stages brokers were servants to their lenders and debtors, following their clients' instructions and executing conveyancing skills which lawyers could exercise just as well.

The second type of moneylending common to banking in the seven-teenth century was personal lending by bankers themselves. When they placed their own capital out at interest they were entitled to the maximum legal rate of interest, though many thought that bankers charged in excess of that amount by illicit practices. The personal moneylending of bankers was a far more profitable activity than loan-brokerage, and different in function, as it appeared to be unconnected with the cash-keeping process. If a merchant, for example, loaned £100 out at interest, this transaction did not make him a banker, and so if a banker loaned £100 in his own name from his profits, this was a private venture seemingly separated from his practice as a cashier and loan-broker. By manipulating to his own

[77]See above, pp. 10–11.

advantage capital which was not his own, a banker like Clayton could make a fortune unlimited either to the fees and other transaction charges assessed to his clients or by interest derived from lending his profits. Legal interest and brokerage restraints did not circumscribe his wealth to that of an ordinary moneylender, if the banker's wealth did not, by and large, derive primarily from the constant reinvestment of his fees, charges and interest, but rather from the clandestine investment of his pool of clients' deposits. In this way the role of the cashier and the role of the moneylender were integrated, though in a way partly concealed from his clients. In one instance a banker might act as a loan-broker for his clients in an outward and honest way, putting out on loan a portion of the deposit. In another instance – the private role of the banker in lending capital in his own name – he surreptitiously expropriated another part of the same deposit.

As cashiers and moneylenders bankers offered services to their clients vital to the banking process at its base, its deposits. When they paid interest on their deposits, for which they gave their notes, bankers borrowed money from their clients under contract. This factor of interest-bearing deposits is taken to be the magnet compelling clients to place their deposits with bankers. If instead of offering interest to their depositors, bankers perform certain services for their clients, the contractual process of borrowing is broken. However, the principle remains the same, that in exchange for deposits the banker gives something in return, either his services as a loan-broker, or cashier, or both. Both functions were powerful attractions to landowning clients, needing cash-keepers and brokers in London, and they might regard both services rendered by their bankers as a trade-off more profitable than a low rate of interest for their deposits.

These common characteristics of both groups of private bankers changed in the course of the century. The bank of Clayton and Morris became an enterprise distinct from Robert Abbott's foundation, acting in capacities more extensive than John Milton père and Hugh Audley. The goldsmith-bankers of London in 1700 were a different breed from their forebears of the Commonwealth and the Restoration, and the differences lay in their roles as cashiers and moneylenders. Clayton's bank fits no convenient example of the period, but what models there were, for example, the goldsmith-bankers in 1676, were temporary. The common characteristics of goldsmith-bankers and money-scriveners – in certain stages of their growth, subject to several changes throughout the period – cautions one to believe that no single class of banker was predestined to capture the private banking market, which, as it happened, fell to a small group of goldsmiths by the eighteenth century.

CHAPTER 2

THE MASTER SCRIVENER
AND HIS APPRENTICES, 1610–58

———————— • ————————

No one could have known at their births that one day a provincial joiner's
son and an orphan would some day dominate the private banking world
in London. What was to follow was not quite the rags-to-riches story
Clayton's contemporaries imagined, though undoubtedly their lives were
exceptions to the general patterns of social mobility in Stuart England.
Only a few biographical facts remain to describe the early lives of Robert
Clayton and John Morris before 1658, but this period of their lives is not
silent, and there is no doubt as to what promoted their early success.
Clayton and Morris were not self-made men; they were second-generation
partners in a bank founded by Clayton's uncle. Even before the bank
began, a web of patronage, reaching back several generations, interlaced a
series of episodes culminating in the bank's creation. This chapter recounts
the early lives of Clayton and Morris, and, necessarily, the career of the
man who made their fortune possible during the dislocated middle years of
the seventeenth century.

The Claytons came from old Northamptonshire peasant stock recorded
first in the late fifteenth century as small farmers in and around the village
of Bulwick.[1] During the next hundred and twenty years the leasehold
acreage held in the senior Clayton line quadrupled. The Claytons acquired
small pieces of land they farmed themselves or let to families in the village.
William Clayton, the grandfather of the scrivener, left his eldest son
Richard forty-four acres of assart lands called Cleydons Dubbens in

———————————————

[1]Northants. R.O., Tryon of Bulwick MS 24/4.

Bulwick.[2] As the lands around the village became enclosed, many small farmers were dispossessed of their livings. At the same time, the village expanded with wheelwrights, blacksmiths, carpenters and other craftsmen associated with agriculture. From 1524 to 1670 the population of Bulwick increased from more than three hundred to more than four hundred people,[3] a significant expansion for a place with only a local importance. In 1609 William Clayton's heir Richard sold half his inheritance and settled most of the remaining acres on his daughter just before her marriage.[4] Before the final terms of the settlement were made, he acquired a blacksmith's shop in Bulwick.[5] His two younger brothers turned also to the craft trades in the village.

The first brother became a carpenter while his younger brother worked with him as a joiner. In 1627 the elder brother died,[6] leaving his five children for his brother to support. This man, named John Clayton, was the father of Robert Clayton.

In their father's generation the Claytons gave up their landholding, but there is no reason to believe they were poorer after they became artisans in the village. In the later part of the century Le Neve wrote that John Clayton had been a carpenter or joiner, a 'poor man of no family.'[7] As a joiner John Clayton would have made furniture, as well as the interior fittings of buildings. With his brother's help this had been a sideline of a greater enterprise in building. Later, John Clayton's younger son William took up the carpentry side of his late uncle's business. In a growing community such as Bulwick there was a livelihood to be had in the woodworking trades which the Claytons offered. The demands upon John Clayton's business were great enough after 1649 to induce him to contract with the naval commissioners for the tops and boughs of wood felled in Sherwood Forest.[8]

The Claytons were not victims of enclosure, but as the younger sons became landless, their situations changed in each generation, as do those of the dispossessed. All the sons of John and Alice Clayton left Bulwick to settle eventually in London. The Claytons were not *declassé* before the middle of the century, and after that time their fortunes began to improve

[2] *Ibid.*, MSS 176, 291.
[3] P. A. J. Pettit, *The Royal Forests of Northamptonshire*, Northants. Record Society, XXIII, 144, Table XX.
[4] Northants. R.O., Tryon of Bulwick MS 290/1; *ibid.*, Peterborough Consistory Court Wills, D.303.
[5] *Ibid.*, typescript catalogue of the Tryon of Bulwick Collection (1953), 129.
[6] *Ibid.*, Peterborough Consistory Court Wills, D.303.
[7] *Notes & Queries*, fourteenth series, CLX (1931), 406.
[8] *C.T.B.*, Part I (London, 1931), 1171.

dramatically. Robert Clayton was the first of his family to leave the village – some time between 1630 and 1647 – a period of relative stability, when the enclosure movement had generally ceased to press the population from the soil. Like his brothers who followed him after the Restoration, he left his birthplace for certain opportunity in London.

Alice Abbott Clayton, the mother of Robert Clayton, was the daughter of Thomas Abbott, a copyholder in the manor of Gretton, several miles from Bulwick. The Abbotts were a family on the rise. By the beginning of the seventeenth century Thomas Abbott, Alice's father, had established himself as a small farmer in the county. At the time of the revolt against enclosure in 1605, he held enough land to be charged with arms and horse to put down the insurgents in Huxloe Hundred. From 1613 to 1619 he was a member of the trained bands at Stanwick.[9] In 1619 his name appeared for the first time in the court roll at Gretton.[10] The move there and the date – 1619 – marked a turning-point in Thomas Abbott's fortunes. By that time his ambitions were intertwined with the aspirations of the Tryon family to become established in the county, and this connection set off the chain of events that brought his son, and, later his grandson, Robert Clayton, to London.

The Tryons fled to London from Flanders during the late sixteenth century, as victims of the Duke of Alva's persecutions.[11] In their new home they flourished in foreign trade, until the outbreak of the Thirty Years War threatened to interrupt the commerce between England and Flanders. After the war began, Moses Tryon began gradually to reinvest his mercantile fortune in land in the Midland counties. Over a period of forty years he spent more than £41,000 acquiring four manors and the land connecting them. In 1619 he bought the estates of Harringworth and Bulwick, and from 1624 to 1660 he and his son Peter bought up fifteen freeholds connecting the two manors. In 1646 Peter Tryon acquired three manors in Seaton, giving the property a northern extension into Rutland. On its Harringworth–Bulwick frontier the Tryon estates followed, roughly, the assart lands of Rockingham Forest, where the Claytons had recently given up their land.[12] The southern boundary of their holdings was the most troublesome to acquire, for it was formed by the recently enclosed manor of Gretton. This property had changed hands in 1616, when Sir Robert

---

[9] *Montagu Musters Book A.D. 1602–1623*, ed. Joan Wake, Northants. Record Society, VII (Peterborough, 1935), 6, 10, 29, 60, 74, 86, 105, 118, 141, 158, 185.
[10] Northants. R.O., Finch-Hatton MS 554.
[11] *Early History of the Tryon Family* (London, 1931), 9–10.
[12] Northants. R.O., Tryon of Bulwick MS 276.

Rich sold the property to Sir Christopher Hatton. The new owner was in possession of the lordship in the 1650s, for it was he, rather than the Tryons, who compounded for the estates.[13]

Thomas Abbott began to acquire leases as soon as he arrived in the manor. There are gaps in the court roll from 1633 to 1638 and again from 1641 Henry and Ellen Pressgrave were issued an order of trespass and ejectment from their copyholds by the Hattons, whereupon Thomas Abbott copyholder described in the court roll as an attorney. This implies that Abbott held a degree of trust in the village. At Michaelmas 1628 Robert Beridge surrendered two acres of pasture and a ditch to Thomas Abbott, who on January 3, 1629, resurrendered these lands to Peter Tryon.[14] In 1641 Henry and Ellen Pressgrave were issued an order of trespass and ejectment from their copyholds by the Hattons, whereupon Thomas Abbott intervened. Pressgrave took the copies of his leases over to John Clayton in Bulwick, and he conveyed them to his nephew Robert Abbott in London. By 1641 Pressgrave had transferred the leases to the name of Robert Abbott, who represented what were then his own interests in the Court of Common Pleas.[15] At least thirteen acres of land in Gretton came to Thomas Abbott's son in this way.[16] In 1645 William Walker, a yeoman of Bulwick, engaged Robert Abbott to act for him in the Bulwick court.[17] The same tribunal issued a warrant to Abbott to appear for the husbandman John Crane, threatened from another source with an order of trespass and ejectment.[18] This suggests that Robert Abbott's career as a scrivener in London supported his father's interests in Gretton and the ambitions of the Tryons by preventing the leaseholds in the area from reverting to the lordship of the Hattons.

Robert Abbott was born about 1610.[19] No records of his life survive from the date of his birth until after his arrival in London at the close of his apprenticeship. Who paid the fees for his training we are not told. If the lad's future bore a relationship to the interests of his father and the Tryons, suspicion points to the influence of the squire. Whoever promoted young

[13] H. J. Habbakuk, 'Landowners and the Civil War,' Economic History Review, second series, XVII (1965), 135.

[14] Northants. R.O., Tryon of Bulwick MSS 276/2, 276/3.

[15] Ibid., Clayton MS 80; Henry Pressgrave to Robert Abbott, Eng. MS 959, fol. 201a, J.R.L.

[16] Northants. R.O., Finch-Hatton MS 554.

[17] Ibid., Clayton MS 37.

[18] Ibid., Clayton MS 38.

[19] P.R.O., Town Depositions C.24/804/51. For biographical details of Abbott's life see J. A. R. Abbott, 'Robert Abbott, City Money Scrivener and His Account Book 1646–1652,' Guildhall Miscellany, No. 7 (August 1956), 31–9.

Abbott's departure from Gretton did so with the assurance that no future as a farmer awaited the man at home. His two sisters left for London also. One sister was married to a man named Barron; the other, Magdalen, married Richard Southwell, who became an ironmonger in the City.[20] Following another destiny away from home Robert Abbott left for London, probably during the 1620s, to begin his training as a scrivener in the shop of Francis Webb. The years the young apprentice spent learning 'scrivener's law' and writing out indentures are unrecorded, but one brief glance at the industrious student learning his craft appears in a document surviving from Francis Webb's business. From December 1633 to June 1636 Abbott kept for his master a cashier's book, a record of receipts and disbursements made at the counter of the shop. Abbott's notebook reveals something of the prosperous years of the Stuart Scriveners' Company. In the eighteen months covered by the account 1,278 people came into the shop to deposit money. Many different names of humble people appear in these entries, suggesting drovers, servants and other country folk bringing money to be deposited for their masters. Their collective efforts brought £33,059 into the money chests of Francis Webb.[21]

Abbott completed his apprenticeship and became free of the Scriveners' Company in 1635. Upon leaving the household and business of his master, he established in the parish of St Michael's Cornhill his own scrivener's shop, the Flying Horse, site of the bank's headquarters until its destruction by fire in 1666.[22] Then, in 1637 the young scrivener managed to marry into the cream of London merchant society. His bride was Bethiah Chapman, daughter of Jasper Chapman, a wealthy grocer with connections in the East Indian trade. Chapman settled upon his daughter jointure and dower rights in 122 acres of land near Colchester. When he died in 1653 he left £2,600 to his four Abbott granddaughters.[23] The smaller bequests made to Robert and Bethiah suggest that even larger sums of capital had been settled upon them earlier, and at a rather early stage in their married life. No such gifts appear in Abbott's records after 1646, when the first of his surviving ledgers begins. The year after his marriage Abbott was rated for a tax of £20,[24] along with the other wealthy men of his parish, just three years after he had begun a business with no other discernible source of capital to begin his brokerage operations.

[20] See below, p. 70.   [21] Buc. R.O. MS A.1/6.
[22] T. C. Dale, ed., *Inhabitants of London in 1638* (London, 1931), 145; see also references for 1640 in *Misc. Genealogica et Heraldica*, second series, II (1888), 107.
[23] Northants. R.O., Clayton MS 39; G.L., MS 2931, fol. 36r.
[24] See above, n. 22.

By the time of the outbreak of the first civil war there had come into the bank as an apprentice a man who was to be a cornerstone of the operation for the next forty years. This was John Morris, who was unrelated to the Claytons and the Abbotts. Morris was born in Abingdon, great nephew of a baker there also named John Morris. Before his death in 1628 Morris adopted his nephew John Hall, or Hales, as the name appears in the parish register. In 1633 Hall, alias Morris, died, leaving three sons who became paupers of St Helen's parish.[25] In 1641 the eldest son John Hall, son of John Hall, alias John Morris, deceased, was elected to a Bennett's scholarship in Abingdon School.[26] The young scholar, known in the town as Hall, was almost certainly the same as the apprentice who signed a bill of lading for his master in London in the summer of 1642 under the name his father had assumed, John Morris.[27] When he died, Morris left bequests to the Abingdon School and to Pembroke College, Oxford, where scholars from the school had gone for many years.[28] The outbreak of the first civil war interrupted Morris's education and forced him to London, shortly before Abingdon was sacked by royalists. Morris was to be Abbott's oldest associate in his business, for it was not until 1647 that the name Robert Clayton appeared in his uncle's records (as a witness to a legal deposition),[29] the first evidence of his connection with the bank.

When civil war interrupted his career, Abbott was caught in a plot which almost cost him his life and kept him under the suspicion of the government until 1655. The abortive Waller Plot of 1643, aimed to rescue the king from Oxford, exposed Abbott along with two other conspirators, Tompkins and Challoner. Abbott's own role in the affair was murky. Clarendon does not mention the scrivener in his account of the plot. Abbott's own defense of his implication was that his guilt was only in knowing about the conspiracy. While he was absolved of these charges, the taint of treason colored Abbott until his death. His lands were sequestered at the time of the plot and not redeemed until July 25, 1645, for the fine of £100. In 1646 Abbott withdrew from the City to Bow, following the government's order to all delinquents to leave London. After

[25] *Index to Wills Proved and Administrations Granted to the Court of the Archdeacon of Berkshire*, ed. W. P. W. Phillimore, British Record Society, Index Library, 8 (1893), 122.

[26] Bod. Lib., MS Top. Berks. b.7, fol. 1.

[27] 'John Prettyman's bill of sale of the moiety of goods aboard the *Peter and Andrew* in the Custome House . . . ' (August 1642), Box P, I.U.

[28] P.R.O., Prob. 11/371.

[29] 'Henry Ford's warrant to Confesse a Judgment to Mr. Holly's lands' (August 4, 1648), Eng. MS 959, fol. 96a, J.R.L.

Penruddock's Rebellion in 1655 the scrivener's lands in Lincolnshire were seized and not released until November 1656.[30]

Far from ruining his prospects, Abbott's politics marked him as a royalist money-scrivener, a survivor under constant harassment. As a consequence the royal party came to do their business at his shop in Cornhill. Abbott's banking success, as John Evelyn noted, was rooted in the disaster which royalist landowners suffered through the punitive policies of the government.[31] As local credit in the countryside dried up, desperate royalist landowners turned to London for loans to protect their estates. This encouraged more fortunate men to put their own capital up for loans. Abbott's success as a broker in this traffic was astonishing. His first extant ledger begins in 1646, while he was exiled at Bow. From then until Michaelmas 1652 he received on deposit £341,364. When the new interest rate took effect at Michaelmas 1652, Abbott began a new ledger – much stouter than the slim volume preceding it – in anticipation that his business would increase likewise. Loans became cheaper when the legal maximum interest rate dropped from eight per cent to six per cent. Abbott's deposits soared. During the next three years £1,137,646 came into his hands.[32] Abbott grew rich as the broker in loans negotiated from this capital, and, in another capacity, through the short-term loans put out in his own name.

The clouded first decade of Robert Abbott's business career is poorly documented. His business records surviving before 1646 are sparse. Abbott's first known transaction is a bond signed in 1638 by Richard Haddon, acknowledging a debt to the scrivener of 60s.[33] The next series of records relates to Abbott's intervention in the manorial courts of Gretton and Bulwick rather than to his moneylending in London. Nevertheless, Abbott the banker becomes more perceptible in his role as Abbott the attorney. By the early seventeenth century it was the practice for all money bonds to be signed by a citizen of London, if the parties to the contract did not live in town.[34] This in turn brought loan brokers into the legal consequences of the contracts, when they gave their signatures as the third party. This meant no more than the broker's signification that the terms of the contract conformed to legal practice; the broker might then protect the

[30] Abbott, 'Robert Abbott,' 33–4; *Calendar of Proceedings of the Committee for Compounding, 1643–1660* (1890), 893.
[31] G.L., MS 2931, *passim*.
[32] Taken from G.M.R., MS 84/1/1, *passim*.
[33] 'Richard Haddon's bond' (1638), Box H, I.U.
[34] J. M. French, *Milton in Chancery* (New York, 1939), 101–2.

contract further by seeing to its registration. If the contract was jeopardized, the broker was in a position to perform another legal service beyond ordinary notarial work, if as an attorney he represented the interest of the party in the courts. One example illustrates this connection. Sir William Courteen sent the scrivener in 1648 a warrant from Leghorn authorizing him to collect in the Court of Common Pleas on his behalf a bond which Abbott had negotiated upon finding a borrower for Courteen.[35] Thus, the man asked the scrivener to act in three capacities – as broker, conveyancer and attorney.

These traditional, fee-paid services were customary to simple brokerage. Intersecting all four roles of cashier, broker, conveyancer and attorney, Abbott then acted to secure use of his deposits for his own investment as he performed each of the brokerage functions. Interplay of these operations is not apparent in a single, actual case-study; here it is described by an entirely imaginary reconstruction, composed from various references in the two generations represented by this bank.[36] Sir Barnaby has put out several small loans in the country, but he knows no one himself to trust with a large-scale loan, which must be conveyed in London with the proper legal work. A broker in the City seems just the person to find him a debtor, and at the same time he needs someone who can receive some of his profits in London and to pay his expenses in town. He arranges to deposit money with the bank in Cornhill, though he is uncertain what the actual amount will be. Not until his drover sells his sheep at Smithfield will he know what money he has to leave with the scrivener. After the first deposit is received, the scrivener agrees to find a suitable debtor for a portion of his deposits, though he warns the squire that this may take some time.

Since the squire does not know what his expenses will be when he is in

---

[35] The warrant is the postscript of a letter to Abbott, dated May 28, 1648. Box 4, L.S.E.
[36] G.L., MS 2931, fol. 150r (March 21, 1650 and May 3, 1650); *ibid.*, fol. 171v (July 22, 1650); G.M.R., MS 84/1/1, fol. 1r (August 6, 1651), fol. 12v (December 27, 1651 and January 30, 1652) and MS 84/1/1, fol. 161v (June 1, 1655), fol. 3r (October 30, 1655); 191v (November 7, 1655 and August 24, 1655); fol. 200v (January 14, 1656 and July 16, 1656); warrant to Robert Abbott by Thomas Widdrington and William Sydenham, January 18, 1656, Eng. MS 986, fol. 1, J.R.L.; Edward Heath to Robert Abbott, July 8, 1657, *ibid.*, fol. 3, J.R.L.; G.M.R., MS 84/1/2, fol. 3r (July 20, 1658), fol. 5r (December 24, 1658), fol. 146r (April 15, 1659); grocer's bill paid for Mr Stafford, 1658; apothecary's bill; 'Bought for the use of Squire Greene for Stoke house, *c.* 1660,' Clayton MS A.6/1, Buc. R.O.; 'Mr. Cox's bond to M. for giving an account of Lady Starling's rents . . . 1672,' Box 4, L.S.E.; George Pitt to M., April 13, 1673, Box P, I.U.; Sir Thomas Abdy to John Morris, November 2, 1675; Sir Richard Newdegate to C. & M., February 16, 1676, Clayton MS A.1/3, Buc. R.O.; Robert Parkhurst to Peter Clayton, July 21, 1677, Box 10, L.S.E.; Henry Powle to C., October 26, 1677, *ibid.*; John Meredith to Mr Garrett, Box M, I.U.; Sir Thomas Peyton's warrant, June 12, 1682, Box 10, L.S.E.

town for the session of parliament, he is hesitant to lend out a large sum just yet. The scrivener offers to augment his account by collecting the rents of the squire's tenants in the Minories and placing those charges on deposit in Cornhill. In the spring Sir Barnaby finally arrives in London and inspects his accounts with Abbott. He instructs the scrivener to find a debtor for £500 of his deposits. In the following November Abbott has found such a borrower – one Thomas Church – but he cannot come to London until after Christmas. In February Church arrives in London to sign the indentures Sir Barnaby signed a fortnight before. Rather than carry so much gold on his person, Abbott argues, Church should agree to buy on credit in London, directing his creditors to his account in Cornhill. This will free his rents in the country to meet his needs there.

Meanwhile, Abbott has taken pains in Sir Barnaby's affairs. The squire's London tenants refused to believe that he had the authority to collect their rents until the scrivener obtained a warrant delegating such authority to him. One of the tenants is a brewer who paid his rent in ale. Two lodgings were deserted and the scrivener had to find new tenants. Then, for the two months Sir Barnaby's family planned to be in London, Abbott had to find suitable lodgings for them and arrange the furnishings. When the squire and his family arrived and ordered goods from tradesmen in London, they instructed Abbott to pay their bills and arrange the shipment of the articles to the country. As the scrivener becomes familiar with the patterns of the squire's life and his finances, the squire entrusts more of his affairs in London to his agent there, his banker, the money-scrivener Robert Abbott. To cite an actual and extreme example of how close a banker could become to his clients' affairs, in 1671 the Lincolnshire landowner Dymock Walpole asked Clayton to keep his eye out for a rich bride for his son ('you have all the money and women at London').[37] The outcome of this request is unknown, but shortly after, another client, Sir John Bramston, asked the same favor and was told that Clayton 'spoke as if he could propose a convenient match.'[38]

Simple brokerage operations were a different form of business from the more extensive financial enterprises of the money-scriveners. In simple brokerage the broker acted also as conveyancer and attorney, and for each of these services – brokerage, scribal and legal – he charged fees. In the more advanced operations of the money-scriveners the banker performed all the functions of simple brokerage also and assessed fees, but his range

---

[37] Quoted in J. W. F. Hill, *Tudor and Stuart Lincoln* (Cambridge, 1956), 198.
[38] Bod. Lib., MS Eng. Lett. c.14, fol. 17.

of services was more extensive than mere brokerage and he charged no fees as such for his time and labor in his clients' affairs. A crucial issue in banking history was whether or not the money-broker could escape the tight chains of the usury laws binding the role of brokerage. This he did in part by extending his range of services, fee-paid and otherwise, and in another capacity by circumventing the usury laws to become a direct moneylender himself. Robert Abbott, rated among the wealthiest men in Cornhill in 1638 and 1640, did not achieve that eminence merely by charging fees as a money-broker. In this transition from simple brokerage to a more complete stage of moneylending, banking in Stuart England acquired richer definitions.

Bankers seldom charged their clients fees for their additional services, but they rarely paid them interest on their deposits. In lieu of interest the money-scriveners, and the bankers succeeding them, rendered a range of non-fee-paid services, inextricably related to the deposits their clients placed with them. The advantage to their clients was obvious, complementing the opportunity their bankers now acquired in manipulating these deposits to their own advantage. These two strata of business were recorded as separate transactions, regarded at the time as being distinct operations. Using an imaginary reconstruction again helps explain the two-sided nature of the process. Soon after Sir Barnaby's drover leaves a deposit of £400 with the scrivener, Abbott lends £100 of this money out on a six-month penal bond. This is not the loan he promised to find for Sir Barnaby; the loan is made in the name of the scrivener. By the spring the money has been repaid and the interest credited to Abbott. The account books in the shop never show the loss of this money from Sir Barnaby's account. The transaction is recorded in the journals Abbott keeps upstairs under lock and key. By the time Sir Barnaby arrives in town in March Abbott cautions him to buy on credit rather than deplete his capital, for Abbott promises to find a lender soon for the squire's capital. Abbott gains new confidence and increased capital with Sir Barnaby's commission to collect his rents in the Minories. In May the scrivener lends £100 of the squire's money out on another six-month loan. In late August the drover appears with another deposit from the stock sales, this time for £300. By this time Abbott must keep the trust he has with the squire to find a debtor for his money. He actually found an excellent prospect in February, but he has held Thomas Church at arm's length, his temptation being too great not to use Sir Barnaby's money again. With the new deposit from the squire's drover Abbott arranges another secret loan in his name, this time for £300, to be repaid before Christmas. By the time Sir Barnaby's loan is arranged in February, all the capital Abbott diverted for his own profit has been returned to the squire's account. Thomas Church follows the scrivener's advice not to take his money from the shop, meaning that for several months more Abbott can use that capital to exploit for his own purposes.[39]

All parties concerned are the beneficiaries of this arrangement. Sir Barnaby makes interest on a loan he could not have placed himself and has found an agent in London to perform a range of services beyond the capabilities of his drover and his other servants who go occasionally to town for him. Thomas Church has found a loan he could not come by in the country. Having first established credit in London with the scrivener, he will more easily arrange another loan, put money on deposit and become a lender like Sir Barnaby. The several small lenders of Sir Barnaby's money in Abbott's name have found capital hitherto unavailable to them. And Robert Abbott has made interest by lending money which was not his own.

Throughout the process – on both sides of the counter – there is an apparent form which was brokerage and in reality a greater function which was banking. This was the dual character of seventeenth-century banking: a character recorded in the two consecutive ledgers surviving Abbott's career, one for the period 1646 to 1652 and the other following from 1652 to 1656. These two volumes were shop ledgers open for clients to inspect their own accounts. Sir Barnaby would find no record in his account of the scrivener's use of his capital, but elsewhere in the ledger the scrivener was obliged to record the transaction. All the loans of the bank were recorded in the journal. When Thomas Church repaid his loan, the scrivener would duly record this entry under his own, or 'proper' account, in the same ledger. Sir Barnaby would never have reason to inspect the scrivener's 'proper' accounts, but had he done so, there would have been no record that Church's loan came from his capital.

In the manner the ledgers were recorded there was no reason to believe they represented anything more than the records of a money-broker. From 1646 to 1652 Abbott received money on deposit from 186 clients. Interspersed among these accounts are his 'proper' accounts, a record of all his income expenses, household expenses being interspersed among his own business records. Each account is kept with the credit entries on one page, facing the debit entries on the other. The entries follow chronologically, and alongside each entry a brief note describes the type of transaction.

[39]See n. 36.

Frequently these jottings are so vague as to leave doubt about the nature of the transaction. At first inspection of the accounts there is no apparent relationship between the scrivener's personal finances and those of his clients, other than those loans he made directly from his own purse into his clients' hands, as well as the brokerage fees they paid him for his services.

When the same entries are rearranged into categories taken from his own entry descriptions, a banking record appears of the scrivener's affairs. From 1646 to 1652 Abbott's gross capital in his 'proper' accounts was £12,671, and from this amount he made loans in his own name and recorded in his debit account of £5,267. But in the period covered by the next ledger, 1652 to 1656, Abbott recorded that £19,271 was repaid as loan principals into his credit accounts. His actual loans (£19,271) were far greater than the figure he showed in his accounts to represent these investments (£5,267), and even greater than his total gross credits (£12,671).[40] His only other access to capital was his clients' deposits. From that source we must assume he had redirected capital to lend in his own name, as in the hypothetical example of Sir Barnaby and Thomas Church. Barring a run on the scrivener's reserves, he could replace this capital from other sources if his clients called for their deposits before his lenders repaid their loans.

In the following accounting period covering the years 1652 to 1656 Abbott continued to manipulate the lending capital of his clients. His gross credits were £38,795, including the £19,271 repaid into his accounts as loan principals. He had at some point to repay a minimum of £14,004 into his clients' accounts, leaving a net balance of £24,791 before his expenses were paid. But from his proper accounts he put out loans to the amount of £27,726. The ledger is missing for his next accounting period, 1656 to his death in 1658; there is no way of knowing how heavily he drew upon his clients' reserves for his own purposes.[41]

Throughout these two distinct operations another strand was woven into the process. In modern banking deposits are pooled to form a reserve of capital from which loans are made in the name of the bank. Before the advent of true limited liability laws, loans were made directly between each client-cum-lender and his debtor or the banker and his borrower, if the banker happened to put up a private loan in his own name. In the latter instance the banker controlled all the terms of credit. When he acted as a broker between parties, his role in determining credit was much less certain, dictated as it was by the credit terms of the lender and his own right

[40] See Appendix 2.   [41] Ibid.

to fees due him as broker. Merely as broker he hovered around each loan to make certain he realized two aspects of the transaction. First, in addition to the arrangement of the loan to the satisfaction of all parties, the broker insisted that his clerks wrote out the conveyances and that he provided the legal advice and sealed the covenants in his shop. Otherwise, these scribal transactions could just as well be completed in lawyers' chambers as in a scrivener's shop. Secondly, the broker stipulated in each contract that the loan must be repaid at a certain date at the shop of the scrivener, who thus tried to prevent the parties settling their contract behind his back.

Ordinarily a broker was a scribe and a passive intermediary between lending parties. If his position changed so that he was able to offer credit between parties to a loan which was not his own capital, he then assumed the character of a banker. Under the best circumstances for his own interests the broker ascertained credit to the loan with expertise peculiar to his craft. When the broker controlled entirely the process of the loan through his own domination of credit, the transition from brokerage to banking was complete. The most likely situation for credit arose when the lender delegated to his broker the matter of finding a debtor for his deposit and, subsequently, determining the credit-worthiness of the man. Credit meant surety, the gage or pledge of the lender, defined by four separate types of security. During the reign of Edward I merchants were allowed to register their loans before the mayors of London, Bristol and York, where the mayoral courts were empowered to enforce the collection of these debts. Then, in 1606 an Act of parliament broadened the regulations of the courts of requests in London by extending to all freemen, were they trades-men, merchants or victuallers, the privilege of small-debt registration, other than debts[42] of real contract. By 1647 the court of the Lord Mayor registered conveyances for any sum. Both in his court and the courts of the two sheriffs the debtors appeared to settle their debt at the dates deter-mined in the contract. If they could not pay their debt, they were imprisoned.[43]

The disadvantage of this type of loan lay with the lender, for if the debtor fled from the City or Middlesex, his recognizance had no validity elsewhere and the sheriffs could not arrest him beyond their own juris-diction. To overcome this limitation and to register lenders who lived in the country, another type of recognizance was used, the money bond

[42] 3 Jac. I, c. 15.
[43] The City Law . . . (London, 1647), 2, 53–4; see also P. E. Jones, 'The City Courts of Law,' The Law Journal, XCIII (September 18, 1943), 302.

(accurately, the conditioned penal bond), which was registered on the Rolls. Under this arrangement the lender agreed that if his debt was not repaid at a certain date, he would forfeit a large penalty, being sometimes as much as two or three times the amount of the loan.[44] This fine was the distinctive element of the money bond, for with the loans registered in the City courts the debtor was only obligated to pay the amount of the loan and principal. In both recognizances the debtor stood surety as the pledge for the worth of the contract. No security had to be given up during the life of the loan, as it would in the contracts of pawn and mortgage.

Public loan registers offered the broker the chance to command greater space in the lending process. After searching the registration records he was in a stronger position to judge whether his clients' credit was reputable. He could make or break the loan when he could persuade the lender of his potential debtor's credit. Through his knowledge he could weave his own interests into the negotiations, being commonly his demand that all the original indentures be kept in his shop until the loan was canceled. This gave him control of the process of the loan during its life, though it gave him no more control of the credit than he was able to determine in the registers. The broker had no reliable way of knowing what debts men owed to tradesmen. If he inspected his clients' personal accounts, he could no more be certain that these records told the whole story than he could pretend that his own shop ledgers could be taken at face value.

These loopholes closed when loans were secured with land. Land was specific credit in a way personal security was vague, relying on draconian penalties to resolve the inability of the lending parties to determine credit before the loan was signed. Land and mortgages followed different legal definitions from penal bonds. Determining credit for mortgage loans was a long, tedious matter, and ordinarily it was not worth the effort to secure a small loan with land. Land held its own finite value, and once the credit survey was completed, the security was freed from the risks characteristic of the penal bond. The loan could be calculated at approximately the value of the land.

Mortgages held two other attractions for both lenders and debtors. Unlike penal bonds, mortgage loans are inherently large-scale and long-term debts. A borrower under penal bond is likely to trim his loan to a small amount, less than his credit, to counter the possibility that he might

[44] A. W. B. Simpson, *A History of the Common Law of Contract: The Rise of the Action of Assumpsit* (Oxford, 1975) 118–22. H. Trevor-Roper, 'The Elizabethan Aristocracy: An Anatomy Anatomized,' *Economic History Review*, second series, III (1951), 279–98.

lose two or three times the amount of the loan in penalty. Since penalty diminishes in a mortgage, the loan could be set at the value of the land, varying with the amount of land the borrower could put up for security. The advantage of a penal bond was its efficiency, for penal bonds were simpler to arrange than mortgages. The life of a mortgage depended upon the way rents accrued from the land. Multiples of rent-charges were attached as the security, and the loan was repaid as the rents were paid in. For example, if land with an annual rental income of £100 per annum is loaned under mortgage for £500, the life of the loan is five years; whereas under penal bond the life of the loan was commonly six months or one year. The borrower in a mortgage contract spreads his debt over a longer period; the lender is able to invest his capital in a loan greater than that which is otherwise available to him.

Mortgage security necessarily changed the process of moneylending once it came into banking practice. In neighbor-to-neighbor lending, lender and debtor agree on what the land is worth and control the credit. Local factors governing land value diminish when land enters a banking context, for banking breaks down direct negotiations between lender and debtor once the banker puts together parties unknown to each other. Value and price of security depend upon an objective estimate of the land, taken as being more reliable than the estimate of the landowner, who is naturally suspected of asking too much. As valuation is removed from the borrower, the axis of credit changes. If either the borrower or the lender hires professional agents, such as lawyers or surveyors, credit rests with the testimony of these men.

Mortgage assessment is a more complex credit endeavor than determining personal security. Land valuation must bridge the space between London and the countryside, often to remote areas, while the process of penal bonds is completed within the small area of the scrivener's shop or lawyer's chambers, and the registers. Unless the broker can resolve the problem of access to accurate land assessment, his credit functions are confined to personal security. During the civil wars and Interregnum lines of access to the country were ruptured, and this hiatus affected the valuation of land in mortgage negotiations. In 1656 one of Abbott's clients, John Lewys, proposed to borrow from another client £31,712, secured for sixteen years with seven manors in Yorkshire. Lender and borrower agreed to resolve the terms of credit between themselves, though they turned to Robert Abbott for an objective estimate of the land. With no means of traveling north himself, he found at home another solution to the problem. In London were the records of the parliamentary commissioners who had valued the estates when the lands were sequestered. From the rent rolls in these papers Abbott prepared an abstract to use as the basis of his clients' negotiations.[45]

As this example shows, the broker handled the assessment of land only if the parties commissioned him to do so; in all the other stages of mortgage negotiation the broker's role was likewise dependent upon specific authority delegated to him. At his least intrusive the broker handled the conveyancing of the contract and the collection of rents, but performed none of the actions of credit. To cite such an example, in 1656 John Croke approached Abbott on behalf of a friend with a security worth £2,000. Abbott's role was limited to a twofold charge: to find the lender a debtor, and to collect the rents of the secured lands, which were near London. Lender and borrower would agree on the value of land and the contract would remain in the lender's hands throughout the life of the loan.[46]

In another instance Abbott was asked to provide an estimate of the security. Ordinarily this meant that he assumed control of the credit unless his charge initiated difficulties he could not easily resolve. Some time before 1652, for instance, Abbott reserved the rent roll of the profits of Moulsey Matham and Moulsey Pryor manors in Surrey as the terms for a mortgage security of £6,000. He then returned the copy to the potential borrower with corrections and questions. He struck out 'accompt' in the heading and added 'particular.' For 'the profits' he substituted 'yearly rents,' which later he deleted also, as his query became more substantial. His first interest lay in having an accurate account of the annual rents of the two manors. The notes he made in the margin of the vendor's draft pointed at a weakness greater than his instructions were likely to remedy. 'What about Brice's twenty acres' and 'how much of Beckford's 104 [acres],' he asked.[47] From some other source Abbott knew that the owner had concealed two leaseholds from his proposal. Until the valuation became based entirely upon evidence gathered at the site by the broker or his agents, credit for the negotiation did not lie within the broker's hands.

Once he acquired the right to inspect the lands for the contract, the broker's role in the negotiations grew to the point at which he was no longer a third party somewhere distanced from the lender and borrower.

[45] Brotherton Collection, MS C.cr.76; Ex. R.O., MS D/DAc (16–18). See also a copy of the survey made by the parliamentary commissioners of the manor of Ellercombe, 1651, in Brotherton Collection, Yorkshire Deeds, Manor of Ellercombe (1651), as well as 'Mr. Wolsthenholme's particular of Rotherhithe marshes, 1652,' S.R.O., MS 61/5/45.

[46] John Croke to A., January 9, 1656, G.M.R., MS 84/1/1, enclosure.

[47] G.M.R., MS 3/3/18; ibid., MS 3/3/19B.

The survey of lands to be mortgaged and the way bankers brought this inspection under their control was a critical stage in the development of banking. During Abbott's time, however, the evidence is lacking to prove that the scrivener mastered the valuation of securities. At the end of his career – the year before his death – Abbott made one further stage foreshadowing the control of the mortgage credit process which Clayton and Morris developed several years later. In 1657 the Cornhill scrivener hired one John Tunstall to survey the manor of Jenkin Maldon in Essex, with instructions to measure by acres, roods and perches all the leasehold lands and similar divisions in the meadow. Tunstall's report to the scrivener was a field survey, a rough estimate of the arable lands in the demesne with no attempt to measure the woods and pasture.[48]

Had he made the transition to mortgage-based lending, his loans would have been larger in scale than they actually were. During the ten years 1646 through 1656 Abbott granted from his own capital only one loan as great as £1,900 and four loans of £1,000. All his other loans were less than £800, and in most instances considerably less. During the period 1646 to Michaelmas 1652 the average amount of loan he put out was £83. During his next accounting period, 1652 to 1656, the interest rate decreased and loans became cheaper; as a consequence the size of the scrivener's loans increased. Abbott made 211 separate transactions in his own name during this period, of which the average loan amounted to £124.[49] These were not small-scale loans, but with several exceptions neither were they comparable to the large-scale loans secured with mortgages that Clayton and Morris were to negotiate so successfully after the Restoration.

Abbott's extraordinary success was fixed in the crisis of the Interregnum, which he realized would pass some day to more tranquil times when landowners would no longer need extraordinary loans to pay compounding fines. After Cromwell crushed Colonel Penruddock's rebellion in 1655, the scrivener purchased an estate in Chigwell, where he began to build a mansion.[50] He did not dismantle his banking operations before his death, but his testament made clear that he did not expect his heirs would follow his own success in banking. A codicil added on his death-bed provided for the rapid consummation of a decision made a year before, to call in all his loans and to liquidate his other assets in London.[51] When his will was probated shortly after his death in June 1658, the government had

[48] Ex. R.O., MS D/DAc 155.
[49] Based upon Abbott's own private accounts, G.L., MS 2931, *passim*; G.M.R., MS 84/1/1, *passim*.
[50] See G.M.R., MS 84/1/2, fol. 28v.   [51] P.R.O., Prob. 11/277.

every reason to believe that the power of this royalist bank was broken, and Cromwell ceased his final act of persecution against the scrivener's heirs.

The veil upon the operation protected the clandestine events that followed. Whose decision it was to ignore the late scrivener's plans is unknown. Whether Bethiah Abbott or her husband's executors saw the great opportunity of continuing the bank's business in the royalist underground now that the Protector's suspicion was averted is unclear. Abbott himself had estimated that it would take three years to settle his affairs, and if anyone noticed the comings and goings in the Cornhill shop during the next two years, they could be excused with the knowledge that to dissolve a bank was not a matter to be hurried. Whoever directed the bank's operations had to depend upon the clerks in the shop to manage the daily affairs of the business. At this point Clayton and Morris become visible in the business of the bank; their years as scribes had changed. Abbott bequeathed £100 to Clayton and £10 to Morris;[52] beyond that he could make no provision in a business he planned to disintegrate. Without a patron his apprentices' skills meant little in the narrowing world of the scriveners and the trading recession of the time. The dangerous game Clayton and Morris played for the next two years was one of gambling for stakes in a financial world unlikely to become theirs otherwise.

The main financial problem facing the scriveners after Abbott's death was committing their deposits to new loans. Several days after Abbott's funeral, on June 17, Morris and Clayton loaned to the Bishop of Rochester £3,037 10s. 9d.[53] This was the first of many subsequent reinvestments whereby new loans were made upon the old loans paid in. If the two men were to expand their lending capital beyond the loans paid in, they must increase their money on deposit. This predicament in the summer of 1658 – finding new depositors – brought the two men into the arena of the royalist underground. First they turned to the East India Company. In 1657 the Third General Stock of the company was founded. Six men who had subscribed to this undertaking all agreed to place money on deposit in the Cornhill shop.[54] These traders, all shrewd financiers, did not let their ordinary deposits sit long in the hands of the scriveners, who consequently had little opportunity to manipulate the funds for their own benefit. But through a collateral connection they received two large deposits over which they had greater leverage. Two of the East Indian mer-

[52]*Ibid.*   [53]G.M.R., MS 84/1/2, fol. 90r.
[54]G.M.R., MS 84/1/2, fols. 8v, 68r, 211v; East India Company Library, Home Misc. MS I, *passim.*

chants, Robert Abdy and Andrew Riccard, had become trustee and guardian respectively of the heirs of the late John Gayer.[55] On July 23, 1658, Riccard transferred into his own account with Clayton and Morris £10,400, the marriage settlement received by his ward Christian Gayer.[56] Later, between November 12, 1658, and July 2, 1659, Abdy and the other trustees for John Gayer placed £5,862 13s. into the scriveners' hands.[57]

During the time these deposits were made the scriveners acquired another client, who was later to come together with this East Indian interest. Between June 8 and 10 Clayton and Morris opened an account for General Monck for £5,000 7s. 6d.[58] When he made this deposit in London, the government's round-up of conspirators was at its height and Monck himself was not above suspicion.[59] On July 4 Clayton and Morris entered in their ledgers a new account with Lord Fairfax with two deposits, one being a loan for £5,000 transferred from Monck's account, the other being a cash deposit of £4,000 from the Gayer trust, made by Andrew Riccard, the East Indian merchant.[60]

Since 1650 Fairfax had retired from military affairs. And until the late winter of 1659, when Monck and Fairfax joined forces to march upon London and disperse the Protectorate government, Fairfax was politically neutral, unknown to have had any dealings with royalists or roundheads. If he needed money, it was a dangerous time to become obligated to Monck, especially for one who had gone out of his way to steer clear of political associations. Fairfax was in London during the summer of 1658 to secure the release of his son-in-law the Duke of Buckingham.[61] Monck was still in Scotland. Even though Clayton and Morris were brokers for his loan, they did not promote the transaction. Often it happened that lender and debtor were brought together by the middlemen, but in this instance the scriveners' accounts are clear as to who procured the contract. John Rushworth – once secretary to Fairfax – was the liaison between Monck

[55] John Gayer, a member of the Fishmongers' Company, was Treasurer of the Levant Company, 1630–2, and Deputy-Governor of the East India Company in 1639. He died in 1649. Robert Abdy was his son-in-law (A. B. Beavan, *The Alderman of the City of London* [London, 1908–13], Vol. II, 63; *D.N.B.*, Vol. VII, 970–2).
[56] G.M.R., MS 84/1/2, fol. 132r.   [57] *Ibid.*, fol. 142r.   [58] *Ibid.*, fol. 71r.
[59] W. C. Abbott, ed., *Writings and Speeches of Oliver Cromwell* (Cambridge, Mass., 1937), Vol. IV, 844.
[60] G.M.R., MS 84/1/2, fols. 42v–43r, 70v. Riccard's account showed a debit balance until July 23, when he transferred the Gayer wardship into his own account. Riccard's loan to Fairfax was possible only after the transferral had been made (*ibid.*, fol. 132r).
[61] Since he had married Mary Fairfax to regain that part of his confiscated estates which had been bestowed on her father, the Duke of Buckingham was suspect. When he broke the house arrest in London, Cromwell confined him to the Tower. Fairfax then tried to secure his release, which came the following winter (*D.N.B.*, Vol. XX, 339).

and Fairfax. A long-desired royalist aspiration had been that Rushworth's influence with Fairfax could bring the Lord General out of his isolation.[62]

The debt itself did not commit Fairfax to anything other than its repayment. Rushworth must have discussed with Fairfax at least the security for the debt as well as the terms of its repayment. Both the generals' accounts were interrupted by Cromwell's death. From July 9 until the day before the Protector died Fairfax paid out of his account £7,834.[63] Monck's account halted likewise, until October, when the flow of money began again.[64] After Cromwell's death Monck's position became stronger, as his accounts show. Some time between the death of Cromwell and the Restoration of Charles II in 1660 Monck made another loan to Fairfax, this time for £5,000.[65] Monck's accounts show only that the loan was repaid, not when it was granted.[66] Fairfax stood indebted to Monck for £10,000 before the winter of 1659, when Brian Fairfax went to Scotland to sound him out on the possibility of moving south to join the forces of his uncle.

On November 6, 1658, Clayton and Morris received a deposit of £1,200 into the general's account, transferred there from the chamberlain of London.[67] No form of security appeared alongside the scriveners' entry, which was the usual practice when money was credited as a loan.[68] This was not a clerk's error, for the City's payment was indeed not a loan. From then until 1663, when Monck's accounts with the scriveners were interrupted, no payment of any sort to the City was referred from his accounts. This grant was the first of several sums of money Monck received from the corporation before he crossed the Tweed in 1659. Unexplained donations such as this are at the least, gratuities and at the strongest, bribes. There is little doubt that these grants show how cognizant the corporation was of Monck's position.

Cromwell's death made little difference in the affairs of Clayton and

---

[62]H.M.C., *Portland MSS.* (London, 1891–1931), i.587; G.M.R., MS 84/1/2, fol. 43r.

[63]G.M.R., MS 84/1/2, fol. 42r. 'Mr. Jenkinson' received £1454 10s. 4d. In April 1658 Clarendon received word from G. Jenkinson that substantial loans for the royalist cause had been raised and he predicted that 'most part of the City will follow, if their expectations be quickly answered' (*Calendar of the Clarendon State Papers*, Vol. IV, 35). Routledge assumed that 'Jenkinson' was a pseudonym. If Clarendon's correspondent and Fairfax's debtor were Robert Jenkinson, a royalist who sat for Oxford in the parliament of 1659, Fairfax's loan is of unusual interest [E. L. Koltz and G. Davies, 'Membership of Richard Cromwell's Parliament,' *Huntington Library Quarterly*, VI (1943), 220].

[64]G.M.R., MS 84/1/2, fols. 70v–71r.

[65]*Ibid.*, fols. 41v, 160v.

[66]Apparently Monck kept another set of accounts for his personal finances in Scotland.

[67]G.M.R., MS 84/1/2, fol. 71r.

[68]In February 1659 Mordaunt wrote Ormonde that the City would lend money upon country mortgages (*Calendar of the Clarendon State Papers*, Vol. IV, 15).

Morris in the next six months. New depositors were hard to find in those unsettled conditions. But Monck and the East India merchants kept on their accounts with the scriveners. Gradually a sharper political focus emerged from this connection, when the East India connection aligned itself with royalists. The company had fallen into new straits by the spring of 1659. The monopoly which this organization acquired when the New General Stock was created in 1657 was effectively broken when Richard Cromwell approved the designs of interlopers into the East Indian trade. In the previous November the company had accepted provisions for the *Richard and Martha* which was due to sail to Bantam or Jambi the following March.[69] In March 1659 the company made a 'gratification' to the government in connection with this affair.[70] In the summer the government forced the company to lend the Exchequer £15,000, to be repaid from the customs duties charged upon the company's imports.[71]

Meanwhile, at the beginning of March the king revived plans for a royalist insurrection. The group of men commissioned to coordinate these plans was called the Great Trust, led by Lord Mordaunt. The Great Trust superseded an older core of royalist leadership, the Sealed Knot, though five of the members of the Knot were merged into the new group. Whereas the Knot had failed to lead various scattered rebellions to a successful conclusion, the Trust had essentially the same resources and objectives.[72] Timing was the chief difference between the two groups. Oliver Cromwell's death and the subsequent disruption between parliament and the army gave hopes that this time, a royalist rebellion carefully controlled by the Trust could succeed. Six months later, beginning on August 1, the plans of the Trust erupted in a rebellion known as Booth's Rising.

During the spring of 1659 alias surnames appear in the scriveners' accounts: until then, their clients' accounts concealed no such disguises. In the previous November Robert Villiers, a member of the Sealed Knot, opened an account under his Christian name. In the following spring he transferred most of his money to a new account in the name of his alias,

[69] In May 1657 the Dutch at Bantam seized the *Postilion* which was owned by Thomas Breton and other East Indian merchants. On June 25, 1658, Cromwell wrote to the States General, asking that the ship and cargo be released (Abbott, ed., *Writings and Speeches*, Vol. IV, 840). In the following November Monck loaned £1,000 of the City's payment to Thomas Breton (G.M.R., MS 84/1/2, fol. 71r).

[70] W. R. Scott, *The Constitution and Finance of English, Scottish and Irish Joint-Stock Companies to 1720* (Cambridge, 1910–12), Vol. I, 258.

[71] E. B. Sainsbury, ed., *A Calendar of the Court Minutes of the East India Company 1655–1659* (Oxford, 1916), xxxi–xxxii.

[72] D. Underdown, *Royalist Conspiracy in England 1649–1660* (New Haven, 1960), 234–53.

Robert Danvers.[73] If at that time the scriveners did not recognize that Danvers and Villiers were one and the same person, the use of other overt pseudonyms by the spring of 1659 betrays something of their own realization that a conspiracy was in the making.

The Earl of Peterborough opened an account under his title, but beside this the scriveners recorded 'et aliase.' What was this for? Peterborough took no part in the conspiracy, and there is no reason to assume that he required an alias unless this device was a red herring. Payments were drawn from the account in the name of 'Mr. Beasley.' Was this designed to conceal the unquestionably treasonable activities of Peterborough's brother, Lord Mordaunt?[74]

On April 30 the most important of these concealed accounts was opened at the same time that most of the deposit – £4,000 – was paid out again. This sudden transfer of funds (which was not a loan) went into the hands of an active conspirator, Colonel Richard Arundell, a member of the Great Trust in the West. In the same week the rift between the army and parliament came to a show-down, when Richard Cromwell dissolved parliament. Moderate opinion could now be expected to swing to the royalists after this *coup d'état*. The timing of Arundell's support was precipitous.[75] Who was behind it?

The account itself was in the name of 'James Butler.'[76] No one in the royalist retinue was ordinarily called by the name. But James was the Christian name of the Earl of Ormonde, now in exile with the king and serving as liaison between the court and the royalist leadership in England. Ormonde had not been in England for over a year when Clayton and Morris received the money which they transferred to Arundell.[77] If he did not appear himself in Cornhill to hand in these funds, the person whom the scriveners held accountable for the money was Ormonde or his circle. The timing and recipient of the transaction all point to the court and its direct links with the Great Trust, though there is no proof that the scriveners knew definitely about this core of the royalist leadership or the actual details of the rebellion.

[73]G.M.R., MS 84/1/2, fols. 209r–210v.
[74]*Ibid.*, fols. 86v–87r. For John, Lord Mordaunt's role in the conspiracy, see Underdown, *Royalist Conspiracy*, 234–53.
[75]G.M.R., MS 84/1/2, fols. 173v–174r; G. Davies, *Restoration of Charles II, 1658–1660* (San Marino and London, 1955), 82–96.
[76]The total of £4,024 went through 'Butler's' account from April 30 to June 17, and the payment to Arundell was made the day the account was opened: G.M.R., MS 84/1/2, fols. 209r–210v.
[77]Ormonde was in London in January 1658. According to the official sources, he did not return until just before the king's arrival in 1660: *D.N.B.*, Vol. III, 509.

It was no surprise that the king supported the Trust. But did this financial support actually arise in England? Two subsequent entries in the accounts tie the East India Company to the conspiracy. On May 12 Alderman William Vincent, a member of the Company and Deputy-Governor of the Levant Company, deposited £4,000 in the account of Villiers.[78] In spite of his history in the Sealed Knot, Villiers had been excluded from the Trust. But acting under his pseudonym, he was nevertheless a plotter at this time, expected to use his influence in East Anglia when the signal was given for the general uprising.[79] Then, on May 21, Alderman John Langham, another member of the East India Company, transferred £1,000 into the account of the Earl of Lincoln, who, two days later, turned over £500 to his son-in-law Sir George Booth, the leader of the projected rising in Cheshire.[80]

Altogether, this means that in the three-week period after Richard Cromwell dismissed parliament, two fledgling scriveners transferred significant financial support to three areas of the projected conspiracy: to Arundell in the South-West, to Villiers and his satellite support in East Anglia and to Lincoln and Booth in the North-West, who, as it turned out, became the most stalwart of the rebels. Did the East India Company or its merchants provide the money for 'James Butler' and Arundell? All the members of the company were affected by the political climate, which was far more critical in the spring of 1659 than it had been in the previous summer. It seems likely that if the company's members were willing to support two regional plans for the uprising, then they must have known about the Trust, the core of the rebellion. And who brought the rebels and merchants together, through the services of two obscure scriveners in a shop in Cornhill?

As long as the army failed to join its plans, the design never had much chance of success. Through its informers the government knew that a plot was afoot and was rounding up conspirators before the uprising was due to begin. The power struggle between the Sealed Knot and the Great Trust was never resolved, so that the bands of local rebels were never led into an effective pattern of action. Sir George Booth in Cheshire held out a few days longer than the other rebels, but only because he seized the moment on the day planned for the uprising, unaware that his chances of success were already doomed.[81]

---

[78] G.M.R., MS 84/1/2, fols. 111r, 177v–178r.
[79] Underdown, *Royalist Conspiracy*, 269–70.   [80] G.M.R., MS 84/1/2, fols. 177v–178r.
[81] J. S. Morrill, *Cheshire 1630–1660: County Government and Society During the English Revolution* (Oxford, 1974), 300–28; A. H. Woolrych, 'The Good Old Cause and the Fall of the Protectorate,' *Cambridge Historical Journal*, XII (1957), 133–61.

Months before the rebellion was over, however, another factor had damaged the plans for the uprising, evidence which comes again from the scriveners' records. Much of the money allocated by the friends of the Trust never went to support the uprising. A few of the chief royalist leaders had in mind purchasing land as much as they did restoring the king. Villiers spent one-half of Alderman Vincent's loan towards the repurchase of his family's estates, and on the day after Booth's rising had been foiled, he borrowed through Clayton and Morris the money to buy the other half of his lands.[82] Of Richard Arundell's allotment at least £800 – one-fifth of the entire amount – was spent on land purchases. Other payments were assigned to persons too obscure to trace.[83]

After the failure of Booth's rising Monck and Fairfax were the most likely sources of a restoration, though neither man had yet committed himself on that point. The king stood much to lose with a restoration promoted by a man on horseback. Charles II asked Monck to join the uprising as late as July 21,[84] but long before then Monck had decided not to take part. Before the end of April 1659 he had informed the government of the treachery of Sir Richard Willys, a member of the Sealed Knot whom even royalists could not trust.[85] There were too many open holes in the plans for Monck to become involved, even if his inclinations at this time were in agreement with the royalists, and that is uncertain.

In Monck's retinue was Sir Peter Killigrew, a mysterious figure even in this age of subterfuge.[86] 'Peter the Post' carried messages between parties who were loath to write out their intentions. He had been the liaison between Monck and the scriveners, at a time when he was also in touch with Colonel Russell and Fairfax. He visited the shop in Cornhill after

[82]G.M.R., MS 84/1/2, fols. 110v–111r.

[83]Ibid., fol. 170v.

[84]P. Barwick, The Life of the Reverend Dr. John Barwick . . . (London, 1724), 194–5. Between May 30 and August 8 the scriveners made no other payments to the Sealed Knot or Great Trust. On June 12 the king asked Barwick to enlist the aid of Colonels Clobery and Redman (ibid., 189–90). Monck surely recognized that the king's bid for military support was a sign of the fragmentary state of civilian royalism.

[85]Cal. Clarendon State Papers, Vol. IV, 189. Monck's revelation implied a commitment at this juncture to the royalist cause, which is unsupported by other evidence. 'When Willys was suspected, no one was safe' (Underdown, Royalist Conspiracy, 289). If Monck's accusation helped to fragment the Knot, he thus supported his own political purposes. See also D. E. Underdown, 'Sir Richard Willys and Secretary Thurloe,' English Historical Review, LXIX (1954), 373–87.

[86] In May 1660 Killigrew was carrying letters between Monck and the king (Diary of Samuel Pepys, ed. R. Latham and W. Matthews [London, 1970–83], Vol. I, 132, n. 2; Nicholas papers, Vol. IV, 208), but he served Monck rather than the court.

'Butler' had paid Arundell.[87] More than likely the scriveners informed Monck through Killigrew of the financial support for the plot.

That was not the same thing as the actual details of the plot, which Monck did not know until the king asked him to join the conspiracy.[88] If he and the scriveners were ignorant that the Great Trust was coordinating the plans for the uprising, they could nevertheless surmise that the uprising would include only paltry resources and that any general rebellion would necessarily include in some capacity the members of the Sealed Knot. The Knot, especially, interested Monck. One of the former members of the cabal, Colonel John Russell, had borrowed £5,000 from Monck as long back as September 10, 1658[89] – just after the death of Oliver Cromwell. Russell did not rise in August 1659, and he remained in Monck's debt until just after Charles II had arrived in London. By late April 1659 Monck had informed the king of the perfidy of Willys,[90] another member of the Knot, which helped to isolate him from the court's support for the rebellion. For other reasons Sir William Compton and Lord Belasyse reneged on their loyalties to the Trust and failed to join the plotters.[91] Most important was Villiers, whom Monck and the scriveners knew to have spent half the support given to him for the uprising. With the Knot fragmented and unreliable, Monck and the scriveners must have realized that the rebellion was ill-fated long before it actually occurred.

After Booth's rising Monck's personal financial fortunes soared. On September 17 the City transferred another payment of £1,344 into the general's account.[92] On November 28 George Oxenden and others who were probably East Indian merchants like himself paid Monck £1,128 10s. 0d. for procuring money.[93] The amount of the loan is unrecorded, but the gratuity fee is great enough to suggest that Monck had substantial influence over a great deal of private money.[94] From October 16, 1660, to September 20, 1661, Clayton and Morris retained the account of Monck, who by then had been created Duke of Albemarle. Into his account they received £11,729 6s. 8d. in interest and repaid loans, all

[87] G.M.R., MS 84/1/2, fols. 70v–71r.

[88] Monck's kinsman William Morrice joined the rising in the West, but there is no evidence that from this connection the general learnt any of the details of the plot (M. Coate, 'William Morice and the Restoration of Charles II,' *English Historical Review*, XXXII (1918), 367–77.

[89] G.M.R., MS 84/1/1, fols. 228v–229r.   [90] See above, p. 63.

[91] Underdown, *Royalist Conspiracy*, 270–1.

[92] G.M.R., MS 84/1/2, fol. 71r.   [93] *Ibid.*, fol. 19v.

[94] A month later Mordaunt wrote the king that Monck had arrived in England with £50,000 (*The Letter Book of John, Viscount Mordaunt, 1658–1660*, ed. M. Coate (Camden Society, third series, Vol. LXIX (London, 1945))).

of which had been granted before the Restoration; this amount did not include the loan to Oxenden.[95] Monck's personal financial accounts have not survived. But from the data and implications in the scriveners' accounts it is clear that on the eve of his invasion into England, when one might have expected him to use all the financial resources at his command toward the military and political objectives at hand, Monck was lending out large sums of money unconnected with the king's Restoration.

After the Protectorate dissolved, Clayton and Morris changed the peculiar position they held with the generals and the Trust. Obscurity and secret services were no longer virtues in a business planning to attract new deposits in the new regime. But from Monck the scriveners were due a favor. Abbott's Irish affairs were unsettled at the Restoration. During the Interregnum he had become a co-partner in a mining project at Enniscorthy, County Wexford. In 1662 the surviving partners drew up a draft proposal to the king, requesting confirmation by royal patent of their investment. Bethiah Abbott was mentioned as one of the seven participants, and Morris and Clayton as agents for the arrangement.[96] At this point the scriveners presented a gratuity of £42 13s. 10d. in silver plate to Killigrew,[97] who was still in the service of Monck. With his influence the Enniscorthy operation was included in the Irish Settlement Act of 1662, in which the scriveners' position was changed. Bethiah Abbott's rights were excluded entirely. The Abbott interest was vested in the late scrivener's son, a minor whose interests were looked after by Clayton and Morris. As full partners in the arrangement, the scriveners were given legal seizin of the lands at the same time they became the trustees for the other partners.[98] This new arrangement was the last chapter of Monck in his relations with Robert Clayton and John Morris from July 1658 to January 1660.

This episode in the history of the king's return to his throne restored also the business prospects of Robert Clayton and John Morris. Their fears that the bank would dissolve according to Abbott's directions receded. If they could prosper in the underground maze of the late Protectorate, even greater prospects seemed in store for the open parterres of the Restoration. The two men had proved themselves to the royalist vanguard who had been the mainstay of Abbott's clientele to be discreet gamblers. When Evelyn observed that all the royal party followed Clayton and Morris after

[95] G.M.R., MS 84/1/3, fol. 138r. Nor did it include those loans paid off before the Restoration.
[96] Public Record Office of Ireland, MS D.3655.
[97] G.M.R., MS 84/1/3, fols. 85v, 89v.
[98] 14 & 15 Car. II, c. 2, clxxi [Irish Statutes].

1660, he was perhaps unaware of their dare-devil exploits preceding the king's return. But his remark points to the continuity of the bank's clientele through adversity and prosperity. Just as the cavaliers of Charles I came to the Cornhill shop to save their lands, so also the cavaliers of his son would flock to its new leadership for the capital to restore their neglected properties.

CHAPTER 3

THE SCRIVENERS' BANK

—————— • ——————

During nearly half a century of its operation the firm of Abbott, Clayton and Morris changed out of all context from its foundation in Cornhill where Robert Abbott first displayed the Pegasus sign in 1638. Traditions of the enterprise stemming from the Jacobean scriveners waned over this period. From a shop associated with a craft, the business of Robert Abbott changed in the next generation to a brokerage house specializing in mortgage loans. Traditionally it was from the wisdom of the master scrivener that his apprentices acquired the skills and petty legal knowledge to enable themselves one day to set up their own shops and perpetuate the craft. Before Abbott's death the demands placed upon the business strained the skills of the master. After his death the new proprietors broadened the services offered to their clients, forcing a reorganization of the staff in the City and creating an entirely new level of the bank's operations in the country. Realizing that their own training was inadequate to handle the demands placed upon them, Clayton and Morris sought the advice of specialists, none of whom were other scriveners. As the firm separated itself from the craft, 'money-scriveners' seems a less meaningful label than 'bank,' since in many respects their business resembled the banking houses of the eighteenth century. These changes, the bank's reorganization, personnel and the sites and buildings of the headquarters in the City of London, are the subjects of this chapter.

The bank had three different sites. The first, a small shop that Robert Abbott established in the parish of St Michael's Cornhill, burned to the ground during the Great Fire of 1666. Clayton and Morris with their families and clerks then moved to a building spared by the blaze in Austin

Friars. During six important years of the bank's history the firm executed its function in cramped, makeshift quarters owned by the Drapers' Company,[1] while a site was found and a building constructed for the final location of the organization. In 1672 the bank relocated again, this time in the Old Jewry, in a splendid mansion set back from the street in a court-yard. Abbott's messuage and outbuildings in Cornhill never kept more than his family and several apprentices. Clayton's mansion in the Old Jewry was a much larger establishment, the heart of an operation with extensive contacts in the country. The scriveners' headquarters displayed in its setting none of the characteristics of the shop which Abbott's clients had patronized. The name and symbol of the 'Flying Horse,' which had hung outside the shop in Cornhill and Austin Friars, disappeared after 1672. The great mansion of the alderman and Lord Mayor Sir Robert Clayton, set at a distance from the goldsmith-bankers in Lombard Street and Cornhill, was too imposing in its own right to require the identifi-cation of a sign. Visitors entered the courtyard through iron gates, which protected the bank from the street. Once inside the building they passed in the great hall iron chests containing the scriveners' capital, in which, incidentally, certain of the goldsmiths used to deposit their reserves during the runs on their banks in 1672.[2] Solidity and security were the aura of this organization, for which the 'Flying Horse' seemed an inappropriate mark.

Upon their union in 1658 the two apprentices described their associ-ation in new business terms. Although referred to as 'John Morris and Partner,' 'Robert Clayton and Partner,' or even 'Morris and Clayton and Company,'[3] no contract was ever registered outlining details of the Clayton–Morris corporation. Account ledgers make clear that the profits of the company were never divided along the recognized proprietary rights by which a true partnership is constructed. Since so little of their own capital had gone originally into the business, neither man could claim a portion of the profits which was his own investment. More important to the nature of their enterprise was a grip of family relationships. John Morris never married, set up an establishment of his own or otherwise felt compelled to separate his fortune from Clayton's. From his arrival in London he lived with the Abbotts, and then with Clayton after the latter's marriage. In the City, Morris and the Claytons resided within their head-

[1] C.L.R.O., Ass. 292; A. H. Johnson, *History of the Worshipful Company of Drapers* ... (London, 1914–22), Vol. IV, 285, n. 1.
[2] See F. T. Melton, 'Sir Robert Clayton's Building Projects in London, 1666–72,' *Guildhall Studies in London History*, III, No. 1 (Oct. 1977), 38–9.
[3] See for instance, G.M.R., MS 84/1/3, fols. iii, 82–99; G.L., MS 6428.i, fols. 100–19.

quarters, along with their apprentices, clerks and several advisers. Clayton paid all the household expenses from his own accounts. Aside from the help he gave to his brothers and their children, Morris never spent large sums of money for his own entertainment. The loans they gave were made out in both their names, with their joint heirs or assignees as residual legatees. It was an amicable arrangement, and at his death Morris left Clayton his claims to all their mutual enterprises, as well as his capital, after bequests had been paid to his family and servants. On a more poignant note, he left Dame Martha Clayton his largest diamond and his ruby ring for having nursed him through his last illness.[4]

The third major person in the bank's operation was Clayton's wife, who ran the household in the headquarters. The scriveners' bank in London was at all times a residence also. In 1659 Martha Trott became the bride of Robert Clayton.[5] She was not rich, but then the groom was only an apprentice in a business slated for a prompt dissolution. Martha's father was Perient Trott, a merchant in Vine Court, near Bishopsgate, trading to Bermuda.[6] Upon the marriage he ceded to his new son-in-law one share of his stock in the Somers Island Company.[7] This seems to have been the sum total of the new Mrs Clayton's dowry. While Perient Trott was conspicuous in mercantile circles in 1659,[8] he does not appear to have been especially wealthy. Over the next twenty years his fortune increased. From 1666 to 1673, along with two other men, he secured the farm of the Hearth Tax.[9] By 1671 he had taken a warehouse in St Botolph Without Bishopsgate.[10] Another son-in-law, John Wyse, was a merchant in Smyrna trading in buffalo hides,[11] and two of Trott's brothers-in-law were members of the Merchant Taylors' Company.[12] His own son Samuel was also in the Bermuda trade at the time Trott made out his will in 1679 leaving him seventy-five acres of land in Hamilton.[13] If Robert Clayton's career in banking had not developed soon after his marriage, he might have found another livelihood in the trading circles of his wife's relations.

---

[4] P.R.O., Prob. 11/371.
[5] D.N.B., Vol. IV, 474.
[6] A True Relation of the just and unjust Proceedings of the Somer-Islands-Company; In Relation to 20 shares of Land that Perient Trott bought of the Rt. Honble the late Robert Earl of Warwick the 22th of February 1658 . . . ([London,] 1674), 26.
[7] Ibid., 4–5.
[8] C.S.P. Dom. 1658–59 (London, 1885), 565.
[9] C. R. Chandaman, The English Public Revenue 1660–1688 (Oxford, 1975), 92.
[10] Mentioned in an indenture of March 10, 1671 (G.L., MS 5386).
[11] John Fowke to John Wyse, October 25, 1686; ibid., March 17, 1687, Box 4, L.S.E.
[12] P.R.O., Prob. 11/360.
[13] Ibid.

The young bride moved into a male household, including, besides her husband, Morris and the other apprentices Abbott had taken on before his death. Bethiah Abbott and her children had left the shop in St Michael's Cornhill and retired to Stratford-at-Bow. When the Plague hit London in 1665, Robert Clayton and his pregnant wife fled from the City to Sir Robert Vyner's house in Middlesex.[14] Clayton's cousin John Southwell left an interesting account of Cornhill during the pestilence. An ironmonger hoping to sell shot to the navy during the Dutch war, Southwell was willing to risk a trip into the infected City, and Clayton persuaded him to look in on his own shop. Most of the master scriveners of the shops in Cornhill were dead, he reported. Bethiah Abbott had returned to the 'Flying Horse' to guard the premises, and she lay ill inside when Southwell arrived. He refused to enter the infected building and was unable to inspect the ledgers to answer the questions Clayton had anxiously asked him, 'to know what is due, or what is owing.'[15]

No clue appears in the Clayton papers about Bethiah Abbott's failure to obey her husband's wishes to dissolve the operations in Cornhill. If she paid even scant attention to the affairs in the shop, Clayton and Morris's management could only have impressed her. But when the widow Abbott died in 1666 without leaving a will, her death solved the question of whether or not the business would be dismantled or the Abbott fortune withdrawn from the capital which Clayton and Morris now controlled. In 1670 Robert Abbott the younger contested his father's will, though his efforts to restore his father's fortune were in vain.[16] In 1673 the young man was married to Morris's niece Susannah,[17] and after this convenient match had taken place, the couple were sent off to live as country gentry at Hambledon Manor in Buckinghamshire, to meddle or complain only to themselves. The next generation of the bank had fallen into the hands of Clayton and Morris in 1658, and the death of Bethiah Abbott consolidated their position with what amounted to the exclusion of her children from the firm.[18]

[14]W. H. Godfrey, *Swakeleys, Ickenham*, London Survey Committee Publication 13 (London, 1933), 13.

[15]John Southwell to C., September 12, 1665, Eng. MS 986, fol. 11, J.R.L. Bethiah Abbott died the following year: *Parish Register of St. Michael Cornhill, London*, Harleian Society Registers VII (London, 1882), 256.

[16]G.L., MS 6428.i, fol. 87 (September 5, 1670).

[17]January 2, 1678, in the marriage register of the parish of St Peter Le Poer (G.L., MS 4093/1); Thomas Langley, *The History and Antiquities of Desborough, and Deanery of Wycombe in Buckinghamshire* (London, 1797), p. 257.

[18]Bulwick parish register, Northants. R.O., Microfilm 47.

However uncertain their own futures might have been after Abbott's death, Clayton and Morris took care as soon as they could to provide for their poorer brothers in the country. John Clayton (*c.* 1632–75) was the second son and already established as a farmer when his brother's position made it possible to bring their younger siblings to London. In 1659 Henry Clayton was bound as an apprentice to Edmond Warcup, a member of the East India Company. At this time his brother Robert presented him with a set of nautical instruments, and after that his name disappeared from Clayton's records.[19] John Morris's younger brother Robert was sent off to sea also about the same time, after he was made free of the City of London in 1658.[20] Clayton's other brothers eventually came into his business operations. Thomas Clayton (*c.* 1635–1707) helped manage his brother's extensive holdings in Leicestershire and Northamptonshire until 1675, when he came to Marden Park to oversee the Clayton properties in Surrey.[21] William Clayton, born in Bulwick in 1641, was married and a father before he came to London. He had moved to the City by about 1670, and it was he who oversaw the construction of the mansion of the Old Jewry. He did not end his life as a carpenter, however. Sir Robert Clayton's last son died in 1674, ending the possibility that his fortune would descend through his own stock. When Robert Abbott the younger died in 1684 and Hambledon Manor reverted to Clayton's hands, William Clayton, his wife and family were established there. Thus the carpenter became a country gentleman through whom the Clayton fortune and a line of baronets descended.[22]

Peter Clayton (1649–85) was the only one of the scriveners' brothers who worked for his entire career in their establishment. The youngest of the Clayton brothers, he was thirteen when he arrived in London in 1662. Peter was never apprenticed as a scrivener, though he was the only one of the Claytons who appears to have received any education. After schooling for a year in London, he was sent off for two years to study privately with Nathaniel Croocher in Bishop's Stortford.[23] In 1666 he had returned to

[19] G.M.R., MS 84/1/2, fols. 135v, 189v (September 16, 1659).

[20] G.M.R., MS 84/1/2, fol. 72v (December 18, 1658).

[21] Thomas Clayton's order to Peter Clayton to pay Edmund Hoskins £9 was addressed Marden Park, March 4, 1675, Clayton MS C/DE, Buc. R.O.

[22] George Lipscomb, *History and Antiquities of the County of Buckingham* (London, 1847), Vol. III, 571.

[23] G.M.R., MS 84/1/3, fol. 247v; MS 533/2, MS 533/3, University of London Library. Possibly this was Nathaniel Crouch, who under his pseudonym P.B. published *The Apprentice's Companion* (London, 1681) and *The Young Man's Calling, Or the Whole Duty of Youth* (London, 1685): *D.N.B.*, Vol. III, 466–8.

London, keeping the scriveners' account ledger. From this time until his death in 1685 he lived in their quarters, and in 1680 he married John Morris's niece Lydia.[24] First he kept the scriveners' account ledgers, and as the years passed, he handled much of the correspondence of the firm.[25] He issued notes in the scriveners' names and wrote checks where there was no proper form for the discharge. Like the clerks who assisted him he wrote out conveyancing forms.[26] In the clerical side of the business there was no other person more skilled or knowledgeable than Peter Clayton.

As the two partners began to expand their business after 1660, they encountered complicated legal problems relating to the new operations. Clayton had an early practical experience with the law as well as knowing the terms and forms of conveyancing instruments. Between 1653 and 1659 he was in the sheriffs' courts, enrolling judgments for small loans.[27] He knew the traditional legal methods of foreclosure, ejectment and matters pertaining to the administration of wills.[28] Morris occasionally handled affairs arising from *nisi prius* cases in the assize courts.[29] He and Clayton did not act as attorneys, as Abbott had done when he represented his clients' interests at courts of law.[30] There the procedures were carefully defined and each plea limited to such a concise judgment that their clerks could handle these matters. In Chancery, however, the legal process was more intricate and ill defined. 'No man should dare to undertake to be a Sollicitor, either in Common Law, or in Equity, unless he had for five years before at least been of some of the Inns of Court, or Inns of Chancery,' Thomas Manley wrote in 1663.[31] As the scriveners' financial ventures carried them into uncharted legal territory, they needed a properly trained adviser who could represent their interests in equity and who could also be given the power of attorney to carry out financial matters. In the early Restoration years one of the most promising young lawyers in Chancery came into their employment and remained with them for over twenty years.

This man was Anthony Keck (1630–95), the fifth son of a landowner in

[24] Joseph Foster, *London Marriage Licences, 1521–1869* (London, 1887), 289.
[25] See below, p. 77.
[26] William Hardy to M., September 25, 1672, Foster Library, Lincolnshire Archives Committee; enclosure in William Hardy's letter, June 19, 1683, *ibid.*; William Hale to Peter Clayton, June 9, 1676, Box U, I.U.; John Clutterbuck to C., July 29, 1676, Box 4, L.S.E.; C. to Peter Clayton, 1677, Clayton MS A.1/3, Buc. R.O.
[27] William Hardwick to C., May 16, 1686, Spec. MS Coll. Buckingham, C.U.
[28] C. to M., July 19, 1676, Clayton MS D/CE, Buc. R.O.
[29] Daniel Sharpe's letter, April 30, 1674, Box 11, L.S.E.
[30] See above, pp. 43, 47.
[31] Thomas Manley, *The Sollicitor* . . . (London, 1663), 102.

Oxfordshire and Gloucestershire. He was admitted as a student in the Inner Temple in 1653 and was called to the Bar in 1659. Of all the men who worked for Clayton and Morris, Keck acquired the greatest reputation beyond the confines of their bank. In 1677 he was elected Bencher of the Inner Temple and in 1684 Autumn Reader. On March 4, 1689, he was appointed second commissioner of the Great Seal, an appointment which he held until May 14, 1690.[32] In the scriveners' service the earliest judicial opinion of Keck's to survive is dated March 27, 1666, and concerns his opinion about the administration of a legacy.[33] He arranged the assignment of leases and arbitrated legal matters out of court.[34] Like Peter Clayton he was given the power of attorney to issue notes in the scriveners' names.[35] Keck's advice helped the scriveners to define law where legal definitions were lax or non-existent. His ideas and influence lay behind *Dove* v. *Prettyman* and attempts to seek legal protection for the scientific surveying of land.[36]

Keck was a public figure, with quarters in the Temple which the scriveners' leased for him in 1672,[37] but his private counsel to the scriveners brought him to the bosom of the scriveners' household. In 1678 Keck was listed in a poll tax assessment as a resident in Clayton's mansion in the Old Jewry.[38] It is entirely possible that he lived in with the scriveners as early as 1660 until 1682, when he married Sir Robert Clayton's niece. In that year someone made a copy of the legal notes he had kept for Clayton from 1660,[39] suggesting that he moved from Clayton's quarters in 1682, to set up his own establishment with his new wife. The notebook he began at the Restoration recorded legal decisions relating to mortgages and trusts, along with the various decisions affecting the parts of these contracts, such as leases and bonds. Each legal term new cases were added, and these decisions were faithfully recorded in his book for twenty years, until 1680.[40] In 1697 these notes were published as *Cases Argued and Decreed in the High Court of Chancery from the 12th year of King Charles II to the 31st,* and became one of the law reports. To this extent Keck under the directions of Clayton and Morris helped to define the law for future gener-

---

[32] *D.N.B.*, Vol. X, 1184.
[33] Rylands Ch. 3757, J.R.L.
[34] Thomas Dove to Thomas Linden, August 16, 1672, Eng. MS 959, fol. 34r, J.R.L.; Sir Francis Fane to C., April 28, 1672, Clayton papers, 1672 Mar.–Apr., Osborn, Yale.
[35] G.M.R., MS 84/1/4, enclosure.
[36] See below, pp. 138–9, 178.
[37] G.L., MS 4400/2, fol. 21; MS 6428.i, fol. 115v (May 14, 1672).
[38] C.L.R.O., Assessment Box 11 (Coleman Street Ward).
[39] B.L., Stowe MS 406.   [40] *Ibid.*, 407.

ations of lawyers and bankers. During the years the notes were kept, however, many correlations can be made between the decisions in equity which he recorded and the policies which Clayton and Morris took in their lending activities. As a guidebook of one of the pioneers of English banking Keck's notes are of the greatest importance.

Several years after Keck came into the firm, the scriveners employed Stephen Monteage (1623?–87) to handle increasingly complex accounting methods with the bank's growth. As a young man he was apprenticed to the merchant James Houblon,[41] but after the Restoration he came into the service of the Duke of Buckingham. For several years he held a position comparable to a steward in the duke's financial household. In 1663–4 Monteage signed three discharges for the duke, but in 1664 Brian Fairfax took charge of Buckingham's household finances.[42] In the same year Monteage witnessed a bond for the duke drawn by the scriveners.[43] By this time Clayton and Morris used their own employees to witness bonds signed in their own quarters, so that Monteage's signature on this document might mean that by then he had come into their service. The precise period that Monteage left the duke's service to work for the scriveners cannot be fixed, as there is no evidence that he actually lived in the scriveners' quarters, where his son Deane Monteage later resided.[44] In 1670 he was living in Broad Street, and in 1677 in Winchester Street.[45] From 1678 until 1681 Monteage was said to be acting as steward to Sir Christopher Hatton, but it is clear from the correspondence of the two men that Monteage was still in the service of the scriveners, though to confuse his position still further, his name appears in a letter of attorney as 'merchant.'[46] Serving two masters at the same time was not only possible but perhaps even preferable when the masters themselves were debtor and creditor to each other. Hatton's finances were so bound up with Clayton and Morris that it is probably more correct to view Monteage as their agent in Hatton's affairs. When Monteage published *Instructions for Rent-Gatherers Accompts* in 1683, he dedicated this work on accounting

[41]B.L., Add. MS 29557, fol. 39.

[42]Dated October 10, 1663, October 17, 1663 and March 16, 1664. Buckingham Letters 1639–95. Fairfax Collection.

[43]Duke of Buckingham's bond, 1664, *ibid.*

[44]The ledgers for 1663 to 1669 are missing; otherwise it would be possible to note if Monteage was paid a salary by the scriveners. In 1671, when the scriveners began to handle the trust which the duke had created, Monteage's name never appeared as one of his servants, though the trustees later employed him as one of their agents (G.L., MS 6428.ii, fol. 247v).

[45]C.L.R.O., Assessment Box 11, MS 7.

[46]B.L., Add. MS 29557, fols. 39, 122, 254, 263, 361; Northants. R.O., Finch-Hatton MS 3180 (n.d.).

to Clayton, who, he wrote, approved the system which Monteage described. Only after many years of close involvement in all aspects of the scriveners' elaborate hierarchy of financial operations could Monteage have written about a system which he had known as Clayton's agent.

What caught the partners' eyes in 1664 was Monteage's expertise in accounting practices. Some time between 1659 and 1661 he wrote a treatise on double-entry bookkeeping intended to circulate in manuscript among his family and friends. In 1675 this essay was published as *Debitor and Creditor made Easie* ... Most of the writings on accounting then available were written for rich merchants, he wrote, who kept a variety of journals, ledgers, cash books, petty-charge lists and invoice registers. Monteage's redress was written for men of ordinary means and was based upon two accounts to serve a more modest purpose, a 'waste' book and a ledger.[47] The former was a thin notebook which could be slipped into a saddle bag or the deep pocket of a greatcoat. As money was spent or collected the items were jotted down one after another with brief explanations of each charge. Later all these recordings were transferred to the ledger, under appropriate debit and credit items.

Monteage never kept the Grand Ledgers in the bank. His contribution was to work out a system whereby the network of agents and bailiffs and even their underlings could be held accountable for all their expenses and receipts. At the bottom of the establishment the shepherd Richard Boddily kept an account book which shows Monteage's influence. The sale of his stock was itemized by beast, and he was made to record all his expenses for hedging and ditching.[48] Monteage devised the system of accounting for the trustees of the Duke of Buckingham's estates. Each bailiff kept an account along the lines of highly specific entries. Newman Williat, for instance, listed the money he laid out for Biddlesden, Bucks., in 1677–8 in eight categories: wages, taxes, rents, woods, repairs, abatements, incidental charges, and rental arrears. All the bailiffs' accounts were then transferred to another ledger for John Morris, who acted as receiver-general for the trustees in 1677–8.[49] From these accounts a general report was compiled and submitted to each of the trustees,[50] who approved the year's financial history. Monteage coordinated all these reckonings.

Keck and Monteage were men trained in certain professional skills who stood just below the partners in the chain of command. Peter Clayton was

[47] Peter Clayton kept a 'waste' book, which is now in G.M.R., MS 84/2/1.
[48] G.L., MS 6428.ii, fol. 334r.
[49] Buc. R.O., Clayton MS A.2/1.
[50] E.g., Dr Thomas Sprat to C., November 4, 1676, Clayton MS, A.1/3, Buc. R.O.

on the same level, no less skilled in the range of scribal functions he performed, and he was trusted with the same degree of responsibility. Below these men in the hierarchy were apprentices and clerks. Abbott had taken on four apprentices – Henry Avery, Thomas Browne, William Daynes and Thomas Goodwin – who stayed on in the business until 1666. Their fellow apprentice John Wotten was caught stealing from the cash box in 1660, and after the scriveners had retrieved their loss from the bond his father had put up, he was dismissed.[51] Clayton and Morris took on no new apprentices. The Scriveners' Company was in decline and no man could assume that his years in training would one day enable him to leave his master to set up his own shop.

In the place of apprentices Clayton and Morris hired several clerks, salaried scribes expected to remain with the bank as long as they were honest and competent. The clerks were not expected to leave the bank after a period of training to set up their own establishments. William Belke, a relative of John Morris, came to work in their shop in 1659 and remained with them until his death in 1674.[52] In a legal deposition of 1666 he stated that in 1663 he had taken over from Thomas Browne the posting of entries in the Grand Ledgers. His chief duty was to keep the till – to receive and pay money[53] – though this was probably in the shop, in connection with keeping the books.

John Burton came into their service at about the same time as Belke. His father was a Leicestershire knight, Sir Thomas Burton, who left his second son £200 to bind him as an apprentice to be paid by his executors when he became fifteen and £1,500 when he reached twenty-one, likewise to be paid by his executors. Upon these conditions Burton joined the scriveners' service, but the money was never paid, even though the executors were sued for the terms of the will.[54] Burton was never made free of the company, and before he died – some time before 1671[55] – he never became more than a salaried clerk in the company.

Belke and Burton, and a few years later, Simon Beech and William Chamberlayne, joined the scriveners for careers as clerks, unlike the apprentices, who had been there only long enough to fulfill their training. When the Great Fire in 1666 destroyed the scriveners' quarters in St

---

[51] G.M.R., MS 84/1/2, fol. 205v.

[52] G.M.R., MS 84/1/2, fol. 158r (March 1, 1659); Mary Harfleet to William Belke, May 23, 1672, Box H, I.U.; George May to C., November 19, 1674, Box M, I.U.

[53] Affidavit of William Belke, May 25, 1666, Spec. Coll. Buckingham, C.U.

[54] L.R.O., MS 35'29/296.

[55] Thomas Burton to C. and M., 1671, Box B, I.U.

Michael's Cornhill, the apprentices left the business. For about six years the bank was housed in makeshift quarters in Austin Friars where space was too cramped to include all the personnel and their families who had been housed in the messuage and outbuildings in Cornhill.[56] By the time the new mansion was completed in the Old Jewry, the apprentices taken on long before by Robert Abbott – Henry Avery, Thomas Browne, William Daynes and Thomas Goodwin – had all left the bank of Clayton and Morris and set up shops of their own.[57]

Thomas Browne, however, was not forgotten by Morris, who was his kinsman.[58] From July 1673 until November 1685 Morris commissioned Browne to write out conveyances for 1,472 separate transactions. Four other scriveners outside the firm in the 1670s were hired to do similar piece-work for 2,012 negotiations. During the ten months from November 1672 to August 1673 Peter Clayton himself wrote the indentures for 266 transactions, at the same time that he accomplished his other duties in the bank. Over one five-month period he wrote eighty-six letters concerning Sir William Hicke's account.[59] Mortgage finance swamped the scriveners' affairs with paperwork.

The work of the clerks was no different from that of the apprentices. They received money in the shop (but not in the country), and they kept accounts. Generally they did not correspond with the clients. They did not perform any legal action in the scriveners' names, nor were they given power of attorney to issue notes. The men who kept the Grand Ledgers issued receipts when money was paid in, and they authorized the discharges for money paid out of accounts.[60] One of the checks received by the bank was covered with letters addressed to Morris and Clayton or Peter Clayton.

Primarily the apprentices and clerks were scribes who copied out conveyances and other indentures. The scriveners' apprentice Thomas Goodwin left a record of the forms he wrote from February 1662 until August 1663. He copied out 276 separate transactions, comprising 1,516

---

[56]Indenture, dated March 21, 1664, Box M, I.U.; Indenture of Robert Pierrepoint, December 16, 1664, Box P, I.U.; David Loggan's receipts, April 6, 1665 and February 18, 1671, Box L, I.U.

[57]C.L.R.O., Assessment Box 19, MS 7 (Broad St Ward); Assessment Box 11, MS 21 (Cornhill Ward).

[58]Richard Coxeter to M., April 24, 1676. Spec. MS Coll. Buckingham, C.U.

[59]Peter Clayton's 'waste' book, G.M.R., MS 84/2/1, *passim*.

[60]See the receipt which William Belke gave Philip Barrow and, on the same form, the discharge addressed to Belke which authorized him to pay the same amount to Thomas Woodcock on November 14, 1664 (Bod. Lib., MS Eng. Lett. c.12, vol. 69).

pages.[61] Many of these copies were made to be presented for registration with the Master of the Rolls. Unless he made multiple copies someone else would have to write out at least two other copies – one to remain in the scriveners' archives, another to go to the client. With a multi-party transaction, each client would have his own copy.

Familiarity with the procedures of registering documents brought the apprentices and clerks to another task, that of checking through the Rolls for indentures and conveyances enrolled for other contracts. In this line they were a vital link in the process of ascertaining credit. Each title to a security had to be cleared of all prior encumbrances, and the clerks' task in the Rolls was to determine exactly what the liens were. One negotiation dragged on for five years because Clayton and Morris were not satisfied that an indenture of 1653 had been fully cleared.[62]

At the beginning of a negotiation the borrower placed all his writings pertaining to the property he wished to mortgage on deposit with the scriveners, and for this he was issued a receipt for his papers.[63] These bundles were then separated and a brief list was made of the various leases. This was given to the clerks who then searched the titles in Chancery. When Peter Clayton was considering purchasing the manor of Rotherby, Leics., someone made up such a diagram. A clerk then wrote in 'Besides the evidence of these things abstracted and made up in bundles as aforesaid, I find notes of some deeds enrolled in Chancery to this effect,' and proceeded to list the discrepancies between the abstract and what he had discovered in the Rolls.[64] In another instance, Sir Thomas Foot wrote to Morris in 1675 about some lands he had just purchased, and he mentioned that Thomas Browne knew of all the judgments on the land, for some years before he had made the search for the title in Chancery.[65]

Once the various deeds and indentures pertaining to the security had been arranged, the clerks prepared a history of the ownership and alienation of the property. Circulating among clients separate from the particular, the abstract of title was often a bulky document referred to occasionally as the 'paper book.'[66] The abstract which a clerk prepared for Sir Robert Thomas's lands in Glamorgan in 1626–76 survives today in a

[61] Thomas Goodwin's charges to C. and M. for writings, 1662–3, Box 7, L.S.E.
[62] See below, pp. 139–40.
[63] See below, pp. 117–19.
[64] L.R.O., MS 35'29/94. See also a clerk's notes on his search for John Thompson's title (n.d.) in N.R.O., MS 3324.
[65] Sir Thomas Foot to M., December 21, 1675, Bod. Lib. MS Eng. Lett. c.201.
[66] Thomas Dolman to C., December 4, 1672, Clayton MS A.1/2, Buc. R.O.; Hopton Shuler's letter, April 11, 1674, Box 11, L.S.E.

booklet as three folded sheets sewn together. The debts on the properties as well as the money owing to Sir Robert were included in the schedule.[67] Then, once the loan had been sealed, a clerk returned to Chancery with a copy of the contract to be registered on the Rolls, thus marking another item in the history of the property to be added to the copy of the abstract in the bank if the land came up again for sale.

All the scribes worked more or less interchangeably at these several assignments, but one man was given particular status. In 1669 Thomas Leman was put to keeping the Grand Ledgers,[68] the task that Browne, Belke and Peter Clayton had been assigned when they entered the business. Three years later Peter Clayton almost died from a serious illness.[69] In the event that a similar misfortune should happen again in the clerical side of the business, Thomas Leman was singled out from the other clerks as Peter's successor. His name was enrolled as a 'younger member' of the Scriveners' Company, and in 1677 he was granted the freedom of the company.[70] This promotion came his way primarily because of his family connections, for Leman was married to Rachel Trott, a sister of Lady Clayton.[71] After his advancement – if one can call it that – he received a few letters from clients, probably in response to the ones he wrote. He handled several petty legal matters, tended to the arrangements for William Gulston's trip on business to Norfolk and audited the account of the bailiff William Read.[72] In 1675 Daniel Sharpe, Clayton's agent in Norfolk, sent three inland bills to Leman,[73] who would have gone to the traders in London to collect the cash before placing it to account. The clerks collected bills also, and we can assume that most of Leman's time was spent, like their own, copying indentures and conveyances and handling other tedious scribal duties.

Other names appear for brief periods in the scriveners' records of men who might have assisted the clerks with their business. In the poll tax assessment of 1678 Clayton listed eighteen people in his household,[74] ten of whom are not accounted for in the records of the bank. These persons

[67] Glamorgan Record Office, CL/Deeds II/3559. See also George Pitt to M., October 4, 1673, Box P, I.U.

[68] G.L., MS 6428.i, fol. 1.

[69] U.L. MS 553/4.

[70] *Scriveners' Company Common Paper 1357–1628*, pp. 125, 127.

[71] Foster, *Marriage Licences*, 835.

[72] John Rea to Thomas Leman, May 25, 1675, Box 7, L.S.E.; Thomas Leman to C., n.d., G.M.R., MS 84/1/1(2).

[73] Daniel Sharpe to Thomas Leman, January 26, 1675, Box 11, L.S.E.

[74] C.L.R.O., Assessment Box 11, MS 7 (Coleman Street Ward).

were undoubtedly household servants. But it seems likely that over the long period of the bank's history servants would occasionally be asked to witness deeds or run minor financial errands, such as collecting inland bills. Stray names that occur in Clayton's records do not necessarily denote a lower level of clerks or other employees in the structure of the bank. At some point the functions of the bank and the household overlapped.

By 1666 the two partners sat at the helm of the business, advised by their lawyer Anthony Keck and their expert on accounting, Stephen Monteage. These men determined policy. The vast, complex paperwork of the bank was searched and written by clerks, superintended by Peter Clayton and his successor Thomas Leman. Until Peter Clayton's death in 1685 the bank in London maintained this form.

When Clayton and Morris expanded their services in the countryside after the Restoration, the structure of the bank inevitably changed. In 1661 a Mr Stafford offered a security in Northamptonshire to Sir John Cutler, and he paid Clayton to prepare the conveyances. Before the loan was signed Clayton asked Thomas Barker to inspect the property, but he used the opportunity to ask his commissioner to approach a Mr Nute and a Captain Sherwood about their finances. Barker never made these contacts, for both men lived some twenty miles from his mission, though he noted that they were both members of parliament and could be reached in London.[75] There were deposits in the country, as well as the opportunities for investment, though no bridge existed from the country to Cornhill to exploit this situation. Gradually the partners managed to forge the necessary links from the City to the countryside. These operations outside London are another division altogether of the structure of the bank and in no respect a part of the business which Robert Abbott managed in the past from his small establishment in Cornhill. The bank in the country acquired its own structure, like the headquarters in the City, and no complete description of how the City bank functioned is clear without an account of how the bank in the country developed and what operations it performed.

The major function of the bank in the country was to win new clients, those who put their money on deposit and others who then borrowed the same capital. In about 1661 someone in the shop drew up a list of 107 landowners in Norfolk, probably either to tap these men for their rents or

[75] Northants. R.O., Clayton MS 16. Mr Nute was probably John Newton, elected M.P. for Grantham in 1667. Captain Sherwood was Philip Sherrard, elected M.P. for Rutland in 1660 and returned to the Cavalier Parliament in 1661.

to persuade them to make a loan.[76] In 1664 Morris sent Benjamin Portlock to Cheshire to inspect the estate of Sir Fulke Lucy, but before he left, Morris gave him a set of instructions to follow. 'What is the man?'[77] This was the most important question his agent sought, for the fountain of credit sprang from character. No amount of time searching titles in Chancery or the court rolls made a man so credit-worthy as his own repute. References to character appear occasionally in the letters sent to London. In the early 1660s Clayton received from Berkshire a report that two men under scrutiny in the counting-house were 'known men' in the county and also that Sir Francis Chokke was a good husband and a reliable man.[78] In 1671 Christopher Cratford wrote Morris from Gloucestershire about Sir Gabriel Lowe, whom he had known for twenty years – 'he has always had the repute of a very honest gentleman, and I never heard he was in debt, he has many children.'[79] Local gossip had its place in the determination of credit. Charles Dymoke had known a gentleman of Creeton who three times had sworn in Chancery that his estate was free of encumbrance, but his neighbors knew that his debts were as thick as his lies.[80]

Ultimately credit rested upon security rather than personal regard. The mortgage credit which Clayton and Morris perfected was based upon a form of professional land assessment. Through these surveys and the men who performed them their operations first began to reach out from London. Either through young lawyers who supported themselves by keeping manorial courts or by their own agents who were sent out for each commission, a connection – however tenuous – soon existed between the bank in London and the countryside. From about 1660 to 1670 lawyers seem to have provided the bulk of land assessments for the organization. After 1670 the scriveners were inclined to take this control away from lawyers and to entrust their own agents with these tasks, but these men were few in number, and the scriveners continued to use the services of lawyers alongside their own men to value land as well as to do other assessments. Nevertheless, the structure of the bank in its extensions in the countryside was different from the organization of the personnel in the

---

[76]N.R.O., MS 3210. Thirty-four of the names are ticked off, as if they had been compared to another list.

[77]Benjamin Portlock to M., December 28, 1664, Box P, I.U.

[78]Unsigned report beginning '£1500 from sixe to sixe months,' (n.d., early 1660s), Box 3, L.S.E. See also Sir Philip Tyrwhitt to C., August 23, 1673, Box 4, L.S.E.

[79]Christopher Cratford to M., August 21, 1671, Box 4, L.S.E.

[80]Charles Dymoke to M., December 24, 1674, MS 5226, fol. 12. Lincoln City Library.

City. Whereas in the City the bank developed an organized hierarchy of services, with professional men giving advice and salaries clerks carrying out scribal functions under close supervision, in the country the scriveners never obtained the same control over their servants. The lawyers who worked for them in the country did more than give advice, for they carried out specific commissions; but since they worked only when there was a particular job to be done, they were not paid salaries and were not subject to the same kind of dependence which characterized the position of the clerks. William Gulston wrote back to London on one of his assignments that it was understood that he was to have the profits of a court he held to determine a survey.[81]

Even greater independence of the bank in the country from the bank in the City occurred when mortgaged estates fell under their management. The bailiffs who managed these properties over a long period of time found greater opportunities to cheat the scriveners than lawyers who worked only briefly on a variety of estates. When the scriveners became trustees of the Duke of Buckingham's estates in 1671, they were presented with a spectacular situation of mismanagement and flagrant corruption[82] which, on a smaller scale, was commonly rife at the level of the bailiffs in their other operations. Humphrey Tompkins, Clayton's bailiff at Down Rossal in Shropshire, planted the fallow field with peas and sold the crop in Shrewsbury, so one of the tenants reported to Clayton.[83] To prevent a similar situation from recurring when he purchased an estate in Norfolk, Clayton appointed as bailiff there William George, who had worked in his London headquarters for years and had married his kinswoman. But before long a man had successfully blackmailed George for £10 with the threat that he would tell his master Sir Robert Clayton what he knew of his dirty dealings.[84] Where the scriveners inherited bailiffs on estates mortgaged to them or to their clients the problem was almost intractable.

By about 1670 the scriveners began to place more of this responsibility upon their agents, who managed estates which the scriveners had mortgaged, as well as performing assessments and other banking functions. Two different situations are discernible in this pattern. In the first instance Clayton bought or rented an estate where his agent resided and managed the tenants, but he could be called upon to travel beyond his own

---

[81] William Gulston to Thomas Leman, May 25, 1675, Box 7, L.S.E.
[82] See below, pp. 187–8, 199, 202.
[83] Humphrey Tompkins to M., October 11, 1673, MS Eng. Lett. c.201, Bod. Lib.
[84] See below, p. 93.

immediate territory to perform the scrivener's wishes in a larger context. In another instance, Clayton's agent resided in a certain place to execute a variety of his requests from London, though this agent was relieved from managing any of the scriveners' own property in the neighborhood. The two situations which are the most closely documented concern William Hardy, their agent in Lincolnshire from 1671 to 1683, and Daniel Sharpe, their agent in Norfolk from 1671 to 1675.

In 1671 Clayton sent Hardy a particular of Robert Newcomen's lands in Hanby, to be checked against the court rolls.[85] In the following year Hardy put the scriveners in touch with Lord Crafts, who wished to mortgage two houses near London.[86] Hogsthorpe and Orby in the Fens were in the scriveners' lease and they could present peculiar problems of their own.[87] In the winter of 1673–4 and again in 1681 the drains at Orby failed, and the tenants' lands at Ingoldmells were flooded.[88] Managing the tenants and returning their rents to London was Hardy's main task, though occasionally he performed other tasks as well, unconnected with these two farms. In 1673 he drew up a particular of the lands which Lord Sherard wished to mortgage,[89] and in 1677 Hardy dealt with the question of how the interest money on the loan should be paid.[90] In 1673 he recommended a neighbor of his to the scriveners as a good risk for a security.[91]

When Daniel Sharpe's name first appears in the Clayton papers, he was already busily at work for the scriveners. He lived at West Dereham during his employment. He never managed any of Clayton's own property in Norfolk, and in 1675, when Clayton bought one of Sir Robert Paston's estates, he made one of the tenants there the bailiff.[92] But through estates which the scriveners had mortgaged for their clients in the county, Sharpe covered more territory than Hardy did at Orby and Hogsthorpe. In valuing estates to be mortgaged Sharpe's work was extensive, and in several instances he seems to have carried out all the three parts of assessment which Manley outlined.[93] No other agent whose work can be documented worked so comprehensively and independently as did Daniel Sharpe.

[85] William Hardy's letter, October 27, 1671, Foster Library, Lincolnshire Archives Committee.
[86] William Hardy to C. and M., February 16, 1672, *ibid*.
[87] Same to same, March 27, 1673, *ibid*.
[88] Same to same, November 20, 1673, February 3, 1674, December 14, 1681, *ibid*.
[89] Same to same, June 28, 1673, *ibid*.
[90] Same to same, January 16, 1677, *ibid*.
[91] Same to same, November 20, 1673, *ibid*.
[92] Daniel Sharpe to Thomas Leman, December 22, 1675, Box S, I.U.
[93] See below, pp. 161 n. 7, 162, 165, 166 and nn. 36 and 37, 167, 176.

Another member of the staff working in the country was Thomas Clayton who acted as the bank's representative in Leicestershire and Northamptonshire, before he moved to Surrey to manage his brother's estate at Marden Park. On Sir John Prettyman's estate at Raunds, which was mortgaged to Robert Clayton, his brother wrote in 1666 and 1667 that the tenants were hard pressed by the bailiff Mr Eakins,[94] though he was never replaced. He collected the rents and returned them to London, all the while reporting the misrule in the manor. At Allexton also the tenants were having a bad time. There the Claytons' cousin Brian Northerne, a shepherd, acted as the resident bailiff in the manor.[95] Thomas Clayton's own particular province was the estate of Harringworth, where he could be called his brother's bailiff.[96] In 1673 he attended the Northampton assizes to report on the scriveners' interests there.[97] In 1669 he sent William Clayton a particular of the lands and woods at Gretton, but he does not seem ever to have received much guidance in valuing estates, for in 1685 he prepared a timber estimate but suggested that another opinion would be valuable.[98] In 1670 he wrote to William Clayton that he knew of a man to rent Loddington,[99] and his position gave him an advantage in filling leases that was certainly greater than is documented in his correspondence. But beyond his own estate at Harringworth, Thomas Clayton's main function was collecting the rents at Raunds, Pickworth, Tempsford, Allexton and Loddington.[100] Interestingly, he never seems to have been able to set up the arrangements to return this money to London by inland bills as did Daniel Sharpe, but then, he so desired to join the bank's operations in London that it seems likely that he did not search long for anyone else but himself to take the rents to his brother.

Below the level of agents like Daniel Sharpe, William Hardy and Thomas Clayton there are bailiffs who managed single estates for Clayton. Three different situations arose with these men. At Down Rossall, Shrop-

[94] Thomas Clayton's letters, February 4, 1666, February 2, 1667, Clayton MSS D/CE/20, D/C/23, Buc. R.O.

[95] Thomas Clayton's letter, February 4, 1667, Clayton MS D/CE/20, Buc. R.O.; Catherine Northerne to Dame Martha Clayton, August 13, 1675, Ry. Eng. MS 959, fol. 134, J.R.L.

[96] Thomas Clayton to William Clayton, February 28, 1669, Clayton MS D/CE/25, Buc. R.O.; same to same, December 25, 1670, Clayton MS D/CE/38, Buc. R.O.

[97] Same to same, March 2, 1673, Clayton MS D/CE/[pagination incomplete], Buc. R.O.

[98] Same to same, September 5, 1669, Clayton MS D/CE/27, Buc. R.O. Thomas Clayton's letter, January 29, 1685, Clayton MS D/CE/[pagination incomplete], Buc. R.O.

[99] Thomas Clayton to William Clayton, November 25, 1670, Clayton MS D/CE/37, Buc. R.O.

[100] See the account of Thomas Clayton, 1671, in G.L., MS 6428.i, fol. 55v.

shire, Clayton held the lease and employed Humphrey Tompkins as his bailiff who set leases, dealt with the tenants, managed the demesne and returned the profits to London.[101] On many estates, however, the bailiffs were not the employees of Clayton. By the terms of mortgage contracts their landlords were obligated to direct part of their rents to London to pay off their loans. Even though the normal relationship between the landlord and his bailiff was interrupted during the life of the loan, the landlord remained the bailiff's master, keeping direct control over those parts of the estate which had not been mortgaged. If Clayton had reason to suspect that these men were corrupt, he might replace them by special warrant with his own appointees, as he did at St Osith, Essex, in 1674.[102] But ordinarily the landlord's bailiffs continued in their ranks as figures outside the organization of the bank, though vital to its deposits. When an estate passed to a freehold trust, a third situation developed. Complete control of the estate went to trustees for the duration of the contract. The landlords were no longer the masters of the bailiffs, and the trustees might replace the bailiffs at their will with their own men. When Clayton and Morris handled trusteeships, these bailiffs then became their own employees.[103]

Bailiffs and other agents working for the scriveners in the country were likely to spend more than half each year out of touch with the City. More than any other of their duties binding them to the bank in London, almost in rhythmic patterns, was their collection of money. Rents returned to London from mortgaged estates to repay loans depended upon these men. The evidence of this system of transfer is the thousands of entries in the scriveners' accounts. It is easier to calculate the quantity of money returned than to discover how the system of transfer actually worked. Clayton seems never to have employed a man whose sole duty was to collect rents apart from managing the estates from which the rents were paid. Monteage's *The Rent-Gatherers Accompts* is a treatise on estate management, and contains little reference to the transfer of money to London. While the scriveners had their own means of bringing capital to London, many of their deposits were brought to them independently of their own control by the bailiffs and servants of their clients. In the two years after Abbott's death, from 1658 to 1660, £617,170 was returned into a small shop with no personnel of its own in the country. From 1660 to 1663 Clayton and Morris received £1,380,953 before they had made significant changes in their organization.[104] This can be attributed to the stable con-

---

[101]See below, pp. 187, 191, 193.   [102]See below, pp. 186–7.
[103]See below, p. 204.   [104]See Appendix 1.

ditions following the Restoration which allowed their depositors themselves to divert their money to Cornhill.

Taking up rents from the tenants and sending this money on to London were two separate operations. Clayton's own bailiffs might combine both responsibilities. Bailiffs working under landlords who were Clayton's debtors usually assumed no responsibility beyond their own estates, and on many estates there were no bailiffs. In this event another intermediary intervened to collect the rents from the bailiff or the tenants and then arrange for their transfer to London. George Powell was a lawyer in the West working for Clayton who worked out an arrangement with the assistant to the sheriff of Pembroke to remit the rents he had collected for the scrivener. At the quarter sessions Powell submitted his rents to the sheriff, who gave him his receipt and entered the sum in his records. After the sheriff had returned to Westminster and turned over his accounts and monies to the Clerk of the Pipe, Clayton took to Exchequer the receipts Powell had sent him and was reimbursed.[105] Likewise, in 1673 Clayton proposed to the sheriff of Buckinghamshire that he transfer his rents in the county, but he refused to do so for fear of a conflict of interests.[106] William Hardy asked the under-sheriff of Lincolnshire in 1674 for the same favor. If he refused, Hardy then planned to send the money by the first drove of bullocks which passed his way.[107]

From the late sixteenth century scriveners and others had depended upon drovers for their deposits. In our period drovers still continued to drive graziers' livestock to the London markets and deposit the proceeds from the sales with Abbott and later, Clayton and Morris. They could also be prevailed upon to transport money on their journeys. As the drovers tended to travel together with their flocks, each man with his own sticks, crooks and dogs, they were a daunting posse to bandits. There is a suggestion in the Clayton papers that the drovers extended partial credit for the money they transported. In early December 1676 William Hardy paid part of £100 to a drover who then promised to pay Morris £100 in London. Morris would have followed the practice of giving him a receipt,[108] and when he returned to Lincolnshire, Hardy would make up

[105] George Powell to C., October 21, 1671; same to same, October 28, 1671, MS 8472A, National Library of Wales.

[106] Robert Chapman to Thomas Leman, December 15, 1673, Spec. MS Coll. Buckingham, C.U.

[107] William Hardy's letter, December 6, 1674, Foster Library, Lincolnshire Archives Committee.

[108] William Hardy to M., October 27, 1671, *ibid.*

the difference. By the middle of January the drover had not reappeared and Hardy had spent a week at the Plow Monday market hoping to catch the man on his return.[109] But there are no other complaints that the drovers were untrustworthy. When they were on the roads, the drovers must have brought thousands of pounds with them to London along with their stock.

On the other hand, drovers had their limitations as money carriers. Their services could only be hired as a seasonal facility, during the late summer and autumn when they were driving their flocks to market. Bailiffs stationed away from the drovers' traditional routes had no access to their services. Under these conditions the scriveners depended upon different means to transport money. In the winter of 1676 Francis Colles, agent of the Duke of Buckingham's trustees at Burleigh, Rutland, sent to the scriveners by his own courier £320 in four bags, in which the coins were neatly separated by units.[110] In November 1671 Ralph Clinton paid in his Michaelmas rents by Richard Blagrave, who was described as a 'carrier' and who was paid £2 for his efforts.[111] Clayton's agent on Brownsea Island asked him to send him money by way of the excise men who sailed from London to Poole every six weeks.[112] Alternatively, there were ways of circumventing the flow of capital to and from the countryside, by assigning country rents to loans in locale. For example, in 1673 Hardy recommended a Mr and Mrs Battel who wished to borrow £1,300 or £1,400. If Clayton approved – and he did – Hardy suggested that £500 of the loan be credited to his own account, whereupon he would pay the couple this amount out of the rents he collected for Clayton in the country.[113]

The inland bill of exchange provided another means of transferring money from the country to London. By the middle of the seventeenth century domestic bills were in use by merchants.[114] The first mention of bills as a means whereby Clayton's agents transferred credit to London occurs in 1665. Through John Hinton in Bristol George Powell sent Clayton £69 19s. 4d. Hinton drew the bill on Thomas Andrews of London, but the request evidently made him uneasy, for when Powell next asked him to send £134 more to London, he wrote Morris to ask if the first bill had

---

[109]Same to same, January 16, 1677, *ibid*.
[110]Francis Colles's letter, February 9, 1676, Clayton MS 183, Fairfax Collection.
[111]Ralph Clinton to M., November 6, 1671, Box 3, L.S.E.
[112]Francis Draycott's letter, April 21, 1677, Box 4, L.S.E.
[113]William Hardy to C., November 20, 1673, Foster Library, Lincolnshire Archives Committee.
[114]For the history of the inland bill see J. M. Holden, *History of Negotiable Instruments in English Law* (Cambridge, 1955), 42–9.

arrived.[115] Powell was a Customs Comptroller in Milford and was able to utilize his contact in Bristol for the purpose of sending bills. In 1671 Powell sent another bill to Clayton, but thereafter the scriveners preferred that he sent the rents he collected through the sheriff of Pembroke.[116]

· In another part of the realm a few years later Daniel Sharpe also used bills to remit money to the scriveners. In 1671 from Norfolk he sent Peter Clayton a bill to be paid by Matthew Howard, merchant in Bow Churchyard. Over the next five years he sent five more bills to be paid at such addresses in London as the Black Lion in Bread Street, Star Court in Broad Street, the Black Bull in Cheapside and the Horseshoe in St Lawrence Lane.[117] Nothing is known about the men who issued these bills other than that they were merchants. Drovers, carriers and couriers were not merchants, and the men who issued the bills to Sharpe were not carriers, since they did not deliver the money to Clayton's bank. From other evidence in the Clayton papers it appears that there were London brokers speculating in cheese, butter and horses in Norfolk at this time,[118] and Sharpe drew his bills upon these men. In no instance does Sharpe mention that he sold commodities to them. Whoever they might have been, they transmitted Sharpe's cash as a service; when the money was handed over, they issued him a note. Sharpe then enclosed the notes in a letter to Clayton, and the scrivener or his clerks or servants collected the bills in London from the men who had now returned the money Sharpe had given them.

If the bill-drawers did not themselves live in London, they had to have some facility there from which the money could be collected. Thus, exchange which was more than a simple party-to-party transfer confused the process as far as the scriveners were concerned.

From the manor of Melbourne, Leics., Peter Wood returned £30 through Henry Churchill, a grazier from Buckinghamshire who could be found in London at the stables of Mr Gray, a horse-courser in Smithfield. When someone at the bank went to collect the bill at Gray's, Churchill was not there, whereupon Morris wrote Wood for an explanation. Wood replied that 'I thought [it] unnecessary to tell you before because 'tis usually understood' that men who gave bills gave also letters of advice to

---

[115] John Hinton to M., July 24, 1665, MS 11017E, National Library of Wales.
[116] George Powell to C., November 30, 1671, MS 8472E, *ibid.* John Powell's letter, September 12, 1674, MS 8472E, *ibid.*
[117] Daniel Sharpe to Peter Clayton, May 8, 1671, Box 11, L.S.E.; same to Thomas Leman, July 8, 1672, Box S, I.U.; same to same, June 18, 1673, *ibid.*; same to same, August 27, 1673, Box 11, L.S.E.; same to same, January 26, 1675, *ibid.*; same to M., February 21, 1676, *ibid.*
[118] See below, pp. 196–7.

their London agents to pay their bills in their absence. It would be less trouble to return to Smithfield to cash the bill than to pursue Churchill in the country, he added.[119] Inland bills were not a little trouble to the scriveners, who regarded the process suspiciously, but they had little choice but to accept this system of transfer in the absence of another.[120]

An unusual example of the extent to which reliance on bills could go was the case of money from their ironworks at Enniscorthy remitted to them occasionally by their agents through Irish bills.[121] Similarly, in 1678 Francis Draycott bought a load of copperas from a man in Lime and gave him a bill payable on himself at six days.[122] In the previous year his cooper on Brownsea Island had asked him to take a foreign bill he had for £30 and to write an inland bill payable on himself for the same sum. He honored this request only because he had a supply of Clayton's cash.[123] This is an exceptional example, for there are no other instances of Clayton or his agents extending credit in this manner or issuing bills as a service.[124]

The scriveners' clients frequently assigned their assets to London by bills. In 1664 Lord Loughborough received the bill of a man who returned his money to London. The lord then sent his servant Robert Guerard to town with the bill, and he brought the bill-maker to Cornhill where it was cashed.[125] In 1675 Lady Diana Dixwell paid £140 in the country to a Mr Nicholas Warren, a merchant returning to London. The bills were made out in the name of her sister. Morris was asked to find out where Warren lived in London and send word to the sister who would then collect the bills from him and put the money on deposit with the scriveners.[126] These intermediary stages in bill transfer made this method all the more dangerous. Where the bills had not been made out to a specific party or where

---

[119] Peter Wood to M., September 27, 1673, Box 6, L.S.E. Wood also used the service of Churchill to carry a letter which authorized the scriveners to deduct £30 from the money he held for the scriveners in the country. Same to William Belke, December 26, 1673, *ibid.*

[120] 'I do expect to receive some money out of the north by bill of exchange and so soon as it comes you shall not fail to have it and should have had it sooner if my tenants had not failed me . . .' (Henry Hilliard to John Morris, December 9, 1672, Box I, I.U.).

[121] M. to C., November 26, 1662; Clayton MS D/CE/8, Buc. R.O.

[122] Francis Draycott's letter, April 27, 1678, Box 4, L.S.E.

[123] *Ibid.*, October 8, 1677, Box 4, L.S.E.

[124] Likewise, paying a bill can mean honoring an invoice for which goods or services have been rendered, rather than, of course, paying a bill of exchange. In 1670 Thomas Clayton wrote William Clayton that he was returning £40 by a coachmaker and that when the money had arrived, the man was to be given Thomas Clayton's 'bill,' meaning a receipt for the money returned (Thomas Clayton to William Clayton, August 28, 1670, Clayton MS D/CE/32, Buc. R.O.).

[125] Lord Loughborough to M., March 8, 1664, Clayton MS A.1/1, Buc. R.O.

[126] Lady Diana Dixwell to M., December 2, 1675, *ibid.*, A.1/3.

they had been endorsed to other parties, the risks were even greater. In 1673 Clayton wrote the Duke of Richmond's agent that Sir John Banks had advised him that 'it was neither safe for him nor me to pay that without a hand,' meaning a bill without a specific payee, which could be negotiated to one or several parties unfamiliar in the scriveners' bank.[127]

Two functions were at work here at the lowest level of the bank's extensions, one of collecting money actively and another of receiving money passively. Where the responsibility for depositing money lay, with the clients and their servants or with the scriveners and their agents, is often impossible to unravel. Broadly speaking, it seems that the scriveners saw to it that the rents on estates mortgaged to them or their clients were returned by their own means.[128] For those clients who wished to place money on account which was not earmarked as security, the responsibility remained with the clients, using whatever device they chose, though the scriveners might intervene at the latter stages of the process, for example, by collecting bills in London.

Where the bank transferred money from the country it provided a valuable service which must obviously be recognized as such. Where the banker received money on account placed there by the efforts of his clients, he offered them a London base for their finances. From these receipts their tradesmen's bills could be paid, and they had a source of capital in London when they were up in town. These deposits established credit with one of the greatest loan-brokers of his time, and he might then use his contact to find a borrower for the money which lay on account. The investment potential at this end of the spectrum attracted scores of clients who were willing to find their own means to assign their money to London.

Not all accounts were investment-oriented, however, nor were all the scriveners' clients single individuals. In 1660 Clayton and Morris obtained the right to receive the rents in southern England of Brasenose College.[129] Behind the three men who farmed the Hearth Tax from 1666 to 1673 was a group of prominent merchants and financiers, including Sir Robert Vyner, who delegated the two scriveners to collect a part of the taxes.[130] When fire destroyed half the town of Northampton in 1675, Clayton proposed to the mayor and town assembly that he be granted the right to collect the money from the parish churches of London for the relief of the

[127]C. to Mr Henshaw, April 21, 1673, Box H, I.U.
[128]But there were exceptions to this. See Sir Richard Heath to M., December 18, 1674, Box H, I.U.
[129]G.M.R., MS 84/1/3, pp. 196, 228.
[130]Sheepscar Library, Leeds, MS 2653. See also Chandaman, *English Public Revenue*, 93.

sufferers. The mayor answered Clayton's proposal by inquiring whether or not he should then petition the Lord Mayor and aldermen of London for their advice. On December 23, 1675, the town assembly delegated Sir James Langham, Thomas Pilkington and Francis Raynsford to appoint persons to return to Robert Hesilrigge in Northampton the moneys collected elsewhere, and the Lord Mayor and aldermen deputed Clayton to receive the fire collections in London.[131]

In these commissions the scriveners followed instructions laid out in letters patent, which was the limit of their authority. Under receiverships – to use the word in a broad sense – the scriveners took in and paid out money for a specific purpose at the instructions of legal or quasi-legal officers, such as executors, receivers or trustees, whose powers were determined by law. After the Restoration the scriveners sought out testamentary executorships. But settling the estates of rich men did not prove profitable – the money did not stay on deposit long enough for them to manipulate it for their purposes – and before 1669 they had given up this type of account. Occasionally wardships and receiverships came under their management.[132]

Geographic references to most of the English counties, Wales and Ireland appear in some form in the Clayton manuscripts. The territory of the scriveners' own operations was more circumscribed than these papers suggest, however, for the partners had no personal interest in many of these transactions where they merely held the deeds and other indentures for safe-keeping. Where their own direct financial interest is clear, the territory of these operations was as far-flung as the ironworks in Ireland, farming in Shropshire and copperas mining on Brownsea Island. Clayton also held investments in the Royal African Company and the Hudson's Bay Company.[133] The profits from all these ventures were transferred to the bank in London and used to finance its moneylending. The tenants in Down Rossall whose rents were loaned out in London on mortgage to another man in another county were a part of the same enterprise. Rather

---

[131]Northants. R.O. Clayton MS 120–1. *Records of the Borough of Northampton* (London, 1898), Vol. II, 245. In the scriveners' ledgers the account is titled 'Sir James Langham and Clayton's account for the town of Northampton' (G.L., MS 6428, iii.242–3, 255–6, 290–1, iv.109–10, 181–2).

[132]'Account of money deposited in Chancery for Lady Lumley,' G.L., MS 6428.ii, fols. 133v–134r; 'account of Lord Grey's children,' G.M.R., MS 84/1/4, fol. 109; 'account of the estate of Simon Bennett,' *ibid.*, fol. 146; 'account of money deposited by order of Chancery for Sir John Corryton,' *ibid.*, fol. 183.

[133]G.L., MS 6428.iv, fols. 56r, 58r. E. E. Rich, *History of the Hudson's Bay Company*, Hudson's Bay Company Record Society (Toronto, 1942–6), Vol. I, 89, 94, 96, 152, 170.

than draw the widest compass of Clayton's influence, we need to know more about the smaller area where deposits came from and where the scriveners' agents executed land assessments and handled the management of mortgaged estates.

The partners' ordinary banking operations did not extend over nearly so great an area as the territory which included their private investments. The estate particular provides some idea of where their mortgage interests lay. These forms were only advertisements of securities and do not mean that the transactions were actually completed or that the scriveners handled the management of the property, if they succeeded in negotiating the loan. Properties could be mortgaged without being advertised, and the particulars in the Clayton papers are, of course, only those which have survived. No particulars have come to light for Suffolk, yet Clayton had extensive dealings in Essex and Norfolk, and it is unlikely that he would have avoided mortgaging the rich farming lands of High Suffolk. Nevertheless, from the evidence of the particulars, land assessment, and, by implication, the management of mortgaged estates, appear to have followed two patterns. For Norfolk the particulars fall generally within a fifteen- to twenty-mile radius of West Dereham, where Daniel Sharpe lived. For Kent the particulars lie just along the main highways of the county, from London to Dover and London to Hythe. So far as is known Clayton had no residential agent in the county – at least over a long period.[134] The scriveners who sent their agents out for many of these commissions seem to have been limited by the realities of communication. The particulars for the other counties follow no discernible patterns, unless they be diversions from the circuits which 'court-keeping' lawyers kept for landowners, pathways lost to the historian.

Estate particulars survive for Kent, Middlesex, London, Essex, Norfolk, Lincolnshire, Leicestershire, Northamptonshire, Warwickshire and Surrey.[135] Lease covenants survive for Oxfordshire, and the correspondence of George Powell reveals that he collected rents from mortgaged estates in Gloucestershire,[136] even though no particulars have survived for these counties. In Lancashire and other areas of the Duchy of Lancaster mortgage covenants would have to have been enrolled in Preston, where the scriveners had no base and where the records were in greater disorder than in London. This might account for the absence of Clayton's activities

---

[134] See the two brief evaluations John Mayne sent the scriveners from Kent (K.A.O., MS U214.7/25 and *ibid.*, E.7/63).
[135] See Appendix 4.
[136] *Ibid.* and above, p. 86.

there. But in Hertfordshire and Bedfordshire, where one might expect to find a flurry of mortgage investment, no such evidence has appeared in the Clayton papers. The bank had zones of different activity, which often did not coincide. The trustees of the Duke of Buckingham delegated Clayton and Morris to handle the duke's estates in Rutland, Buckinghamshire and Yorkshire,[137] though the two scriveners had no ordinary banking operations in those counties.

Once the bank extended its operations in the country, with personnel who never went to the headquarters of the bank in London, frauds appeared in the countryside, claiming to be Clayton's men. After one of Clayton's borrowers died in 1674, two impostors arrived at the house of his brother, claiming that Clayton had sent them to collect the dead man's debt. They presented a copy of the bond, inscribed with the dead man's forged signature. The brother became suspicious. He grabbed their money bag, as they called it, and opening it upon the table, he found that they had not been jangling coins, but the heads of horse-shoe nails.[138]

One anecdote suggests that scriveners traveled in disguise themselves, as a means of keeping their agents in line. In 1675 another impostor talked William George in Norfolk out of £10. 'He had a genteel habit when his riding coat was off;' he wore a black hat with a gold band and rode a black horse which he said was Clayton's. Who was the mysterious stranger Daniel Sharpe described to Thomas Leman on December 22?[139] William George had not been able to get a name from the man, who said he had lived with Clayton for twenty years.

Clayton had a long, severe illness in 1675,[140] and he is unlikely to have been traveling by horse on a cold winter's day in Norfolk. But the flim-flam man may have been John Morris, testing the gullibility of his new bailiff William George. After the incident had passed, villagers at the nearby inn remembered a stranger to those parts who matched George's description. When he took his wig off he was found to have fair hair, and one of his legs was larger than the other, as he suffered from gout, one of Morris's complaints.

Even in the close quarters of the counting-house the two partners held constant vigil over their staff. In 1674 Sheriff Robert Vyner reported to Clayton that he had found Anthony Keck in a whore-house, 'and therefore think it may not be amiss that you prevent any ill he may do you.'[141]

[137] See below, pp. 204–5.　　　[138] Henry Rae to C., 1674, Box 9, L.S.E.
[139] Daniel Sharpe to Thomas Leman, December 22, 1675, Box S, I.U.
[140] D.N.B., Vol. IV, 474.
[141] Sir Robert Vyner to C., 1674, Sir Robert Vyner's Original Papers 1657–84, Fairfax Collection.

Embarrassing incidents could occur when outright peculation was uncovered, if the guilty parties refused to leave the bank quietly, as John Wotten had done in 1660. In 1663 Clayton dismissed his clerk John Norgrave who then took the scrivener to court. The vengeful clerk managed to expose the partner's practices of keeping secret books of account and intimated that moneylending and usury were hidden under the guise of land sales.[142] However much responsibility Clayton and Morris delegated within the elaborate structure of their bank, they alone remained its guardians.

In summary, the difference between the scriveners' bank and their goldsmithing counterparts lies in the specialized role of loan-brokers which Clayton and Morris created for themselves. So technical and complex were the requirements of mortgage lending that the structure and personnel of the bank became organized around those demands more than any other. Neither the master scriveners nor their scribes could hope any longer to acquire by reading and writing conveyances the legal expertise necessary to protect their contracts. When the scribes in the City's headquarters became salaried clerks, displacing the apprentices, the bank lost its dependence upon the Scriveners' Company and the craft whereby all experience was transmitted through the master to his apprentices. Now the bankers took the advice of lawyers, on the changing nature of mortgage law as well as on the legal framework of the manor. As the new demands for accountability outmoded the bookkeeping experience of cash-keeping in the shop, Clayton hired an expert in accounting to lay down principles of accountability from the countryside to the City. The money-scriveners of the past were not dependent upon professional advisers.

The most original feature of these organizational changes was the way the bank extended its operations into the countryside. From the self-contained shop in Cornhill there emerged gradually a series of connections with the country, which upon development constituted a second level of the bank's structure. Relying at first upon private commissions given to lawyers in the country, the scriveners later trained their own residential agents in various places to perform assessments and manage mortgaged estates. Through a hierarchy extending from bailiffs' deputies to the scriveners in the City, the bank took its direction inward to the world of the squires rather than outward to the world of the merchants.

---

[142] Affidavit between John Norgrave plaintiff and Morris and Clayton defendants (1663), Spec. MS Coll. Buckingham, C.U.

CHAPTER 4

THE RECORDS OF EARLY BANKING

———————— • ————————

Banking cannot exist without credit, which is the deferral of monetary
obligations through time. Two separate applications of credit are
associated with deposit banking. The banker borrows money from his
clients and in addition lends money of his own and his depositors to others.
These two distinct activities require separate contracts. The first is a
bankers' note, the written promise to repay the money on deposit with
interest at some time in the future. The second is a lending contract made
between the banker or his client as one party, with a debtor as the other.
These agreements may take several forms – money bonds, promissory
notes and mortgage contracts.

At the same time, bankers must arrange to extend credit by transmitting
capital from one place to another by commuting capital to a paper form.
This transferral of credit over space is negotiability, and the proper instruments used are bills of exchange, checks, and, again, bankers' notes.
Negotiable instruments can also have the effect of inflating a banker's
reserves. Between the time that the money is deposited and the time that
the note or bill is collected at the bank, the banker may invest this money
to his own interest. As the owner of the instrument is reassigned each time
it is negotiated, the claim to capital shifts. Only in 1704 were all the parties
to negotiable contracts fully protected in the law, though for some time
historians have known that these instruments were in use before the practice was protected by the courts.

The records of credit and negotiability proper to banking do not appear
until some time after there is evidence that the first scriveners began to
accept money on deposit and some form of rudimentary banking began.

From the latter part of the reign of Elizabeth, when banking first appears, the records of credit are legal covenants rather than instruments devised by bankers. The first evidence of checks, inland bills and bankers' notes do not occur until the 1650s, some sixty or seventy years later. The first bankers were little more than cashiers and brokers who received money on deposit and then loaned at least a part of this money on behalf of their clients.[1] The first banking forms which have come to light from this early period are a series of rental receipts which Henry Garway, scrivener, issued from 1613 to 1621 to his depositor from Leicestershire.[2] Similar receipts, issued much later in Clayton's bank, were probably made to clients to assure them that their money had been collected, rather than to be a claim against that deposit. That claim lay as an entry in the scrivener's ledger.

The accounting ledger was one type of banking record that existed from these early times, even though no examples have come to light. Book-keeping manuals were fashionable by the reign of Elizabeth,[3] and the scriveners who took in money on deposit and paid it out again must have recorded this movement of capital in some accounting form. The first banking ledger known to survive was kept by Robert Abbott.[4] It seems clear that he did not issue for each deposit a corresponding receipt. The entry in the ledger was understood by both the depositary and his client to be a tacit receipt. Kept in the shop where clients might inspect their accounts, the ledger was considered to be a record of some importance and more than just the banker's register of the money which had been taken in and paid out. Calling upon the semi-public nature of ledgers, Serjeant Newdegate in 1678 asked Clayton to bring to court his copy of a deed and his ledger, or 'memorialls,' to prove by the relevant entries that Clayton in his role as broker had loaned money upon mortgage to a certain client.[5]

As an additional source of confusion in this early stage of banking, a banker might make unwritten commitments to his client. These were known as parole contracts. They usually referred to leases, but the same term could be applied to other types of contracts. This is dimly referred to in the Clayton papers, for during the careers of Robert Abbott and Clayton and Morris these obligations tended to be written down. The check and the

[1] See above, pp. 20–30.
[2] Sir William Hartopp's receipts, Box F, L.S.E.
[3] See R. D. Richards, 'Early History of the Term Capital,' *Quarterly Journal of Economics*, XI (1926), 329–38, 547–8, and *Studies in the History of Accounting*, ed. A. C. Littleton and B. S. Yamey (London, 1956).
[4] See above, pp. 50–1.
[5] Sir Richard Newdegate to C., 1678, Clayton MS A.1/3, Buc. R.O. and see below, pp. 107–8.

note were no more than house chits as far as the law was concerned, which meant that the oral pledge of the banker was as strong as his written word. At least, this was the theory, though in practice the informal inscriptions carried greater weight.

Nevertheless, there was an interesting and delicate tension between the two traditions of the written and spoken contracts. In 1672 Thomas Elmes sent his servant to London with a voucher to withdraw from his account £700, an unusually large sum. But instead of giving him gold, Morris gave him a note for the amount, saying that he 'did not use to re-send parcels but that it would have been the same thing, for he should have use for it,' through the interest-bearing note. This condition did not appear on the note, however, which was merely a promise to pay the sum deposited. In 1675 Elmes went to London to cash the note. The apprentice Thomas Leman took Morris's note, saying 'it shall no more come in judgment,' and in its place issued a new note, again in the form of a promissory note. Elmes demanded his interest, but Morris claimed that his deposit had not actually been put out on loan ('security is hard to be got . . . '). He returned his note – 'erased and imperfect' – a simple receipt with no obligation to repay the deposit with interest. The conversion of a check into a note (their decision and not their client's), the alteration of the note through erasure and the attempt to resist repayment were high-handed tactics, to be sure. But the loose distinction made between the forms and the chance attention for what was written on the paper indicate the scriveners' casual regard to the problem of paper forms and should be borne in mind in this examination of the refinement of what are the earliest records of banking.[6]

As the new paper instruments emerged, they still had unspecialized forms and labels which do not usually correspond to those in modern use. 'Notes' can be bankers' notes or promissory notes. 'Bills' are both inland and foreign bills of exchange, but the term can also mean notes, as well as a simple receipt. A 'receipt' means a bankers' note as well as a non-contractual chit. 'Checks' were known by that name (and original spelling) only after the partnership of Clayton and Morris dissolved. In the Clayton papers what are in effect checks are called 'vouchers,' 'discharges,' and 'orders.' The banking statement carries no labels whatsoever. The estate particular, which became the abstract of mortgages for sale, has the same label affixed to the parts from which it derived. Rent rolls, surveyors' field notes and terriers all appear as 'particulars.' Until the form of the abstract was set, 'particulars' meant merely 'details.'[7]

---

[6]Thomas Elmes to C., August 1675, Box E, I.U.   [7]See below, p. 161.

Even though bankers' notes and inland bills first came into use in the early 1650s, they and other banking forms grew in use with the birth of the postal system several years later. The mailing system established during Cromwell's second parliament in 1657 was reconfirmed by charter at the Restoration in 1660.[8] As the post reduced the need for couriers and the costs of transporting written communication decreased, the volume of mail passing between Clayton and Morris and their clients quickened. Certain instructions which before had been included in ordinary business correspondence now began to circulate as separate items in shortened forms. A form is an abbreviation of what before had been a more elaborate order or contract. Something had been left behind. But the reduction of command or agreement to its essence – a form – is a more powerful statement than its forebears. A form is inherently efficient and businesslike. Less personal than the older methods of negotiation, forms appeared when banking operations covered greater territory than they had reached during their first years.

Simplest to trace in its development as a business form is the banking check. The first written discharge in the Clayton papers was a legal warrant, which can be taken to be the ancestor of the check and which was addressed to Robert Abbott by Lord Windsor's trustees on February 10, 1653:

Wee the Trustees of the Lord Windsor doe desire you to pay the sume of Threescore and Tenn pounds p[ar]te of the five hundred pounds and all which remaines in yor hands upon our Conveyance of the Mannor of Tardebigg and Bordsley [Warwickshire] to Mr. Alderman Langham and for w[hi]ch wee have a Note under yor hand to be paid as wee shall direct. And this shalbe yor suffitient discharge for soe much of the said sume as remaines in yor hands given under our hands this Eight day of February 1652.

   The discharge was endorsed:

Received the same day of Mr. Robert Abbott the sume of Threescore & Tenn pounds above Menconed and accordinge to the Noate above Written to the use of the said Lord Windsor I say Recd.
   by me Jo: Christmas.[9]

More frequently these discharges appeared as parts of correspondence.[10] But on February 16, 1659, Clayton and Morris received their first abstract of a written order to pay, which was neither a warrant nor a part of a letter:

---

[8]H. Robinson, *The British Post Office: A History* (Princeton, 1948), 46.
[9]Warrant of Ld. Windsor's Trustees, February 10, 1653, Box 3, L.S.E.
[10]See n. 15.

London
16 Feb. 1659

> Mr. Morris & Mr Clayton
> Pray pay the bearer hereof Mr. Delboe or order ffour hundred pounds I say
> £400: ——: —— for
>   Yrs: Nic: Vanacker.[11]

With slight variations this form became the check. In practice checks were vouchers either mailed or sent by clients to servants or agents in London, who then presented these orders to the scriveners for payment. Through the natural processes of the new postal system the check filtered out from the letter and warrant as a distinct business form, which was sent from client to banker, often with no other instructions. Clayton encouraged the use of the new form. When Mr Crouch's servant appeared in Cornhill with a letter from his master, Clayton instructed his Clerk Thomas Browne to write out a discharge for the servant to sign before the money was paid to him.[12] In 1665 Sir Robert Howard wrote Clayton a brief letter asking him to send him £200, but before the money was released, the servant who bore his letter was made to sign a formal voucher at the foot of the letter acknowledging that he had received the gold.[13] By 1676 no payments were allowed from clients' accounts without duplicate vouchers, one of which remained in the counting-house.[14] But throughout the seventeen-year period when the check first appeared and when it superseded other forms of discharges, the same orders continued to appear as unseparated instructions in ordinary correspondence.[15]

Like other early banking forms these checks appear distinct and are clearly distinguished from notes and bills. From 1663 to 1665 the Duke of Buckingham drew twenty-five checks on account in his own name, while his servant Stephen Monteage signed two of the check forms.[16] But on January 9, 1661, Brian Fairfax, who was a factotum of the duke and kinsman of the duchess, wrote out an order that read:

---

[11] J. M. Holden, *History of Negotiable Instruments in English Law* (Cambridge, 1955), 210. Cf. the six checks drawn by George Pitt in June 1659 in Box P, I.U.

[12] C. to Thomas Browne, September 3, 1660, Box 11, L.S.E.

[13] Sir Robert Howard to C., January 24, 1665. Clayton MS A.1/1, Buc. R.O.

[14] William Hale to Peter Clayton, June 9, 1676, Box H, I.U.; John Clutterbuck to C., July 29, 1676, Box 4, L.S.E.; C. to Peter Clayton, 1677, Clayton MS A.1/3, Buc. R.O.

[15] John Percival to C. & M., October 19, 1659, Box 10, L.S.E.; Humphrey Gore to M. & C., January 30, 1666, Box 7, L.S.E.; Robert Gayer to M., October 2, 1664, Box G, I.U.; Edward Cooke to C., December 16, 1671, Box C, I.U.; James Buck to C. & M., September 7, 1671, Box B, I.U.; John Clutterbuck to C. & M., July 15, 1676, Box 4, I.U.; Robert Clarke to C. & M., June 14, 1679, Box 4, L.S.E.

[16] Buckingham Letters 1639–95, Fairfax Collection.

Sr

I desire yu to pay unto the bearer hereof the sume of Five hundred and Thirty pounds for wch I have taken a Receipt and pass it to Accompt.

On May 4, 1661, Fairfax signed a similar order for £100 in gold. These were check forms, and there would be no reason to assume that they served a different purpose if another form had not survived similar to them which read:

Jan. 6, 1663

Mr. Cleyton

I desire you to let me have 200 peeces of Gold upon this Bracelet of Diamonds . . .

for the duke needed gold to gamble with the king that evening. The duchess's jewels had already been pawned, for Fairfax redeemed them for one evening for the duchess to wear at a great ball at court.[17] It is probably safest to assume that the discharges of January 9 and May 4, 1661, were pawn tickets drawn against the jewels rather than checks, and fall within the development of lending contracts rather than the history of negotiability. This should serve as a warning against believing that the form alone is always what it appears to be.

From 1659 to 1665 Sir John Wolstenholme drew thirty-four checks made to order or to his assignees and one check to his servant Mary Brograve, making a clear distinction between which of these forms were negotiable and which were a mechanism to return cash from his account into his own hands.[18] But several other variations appear with the use of the check that confuse the distinctions Wolstenholme made. On June 20, 1660, John Walpole wrote a check to Thomas Walpole, who endorsed it with the instructions that it be paid to the bearer, his servant John Carter.[19] Since the check was assigned from brother to brother, both of whom were Clayton's clients, it would be stretching the point to cite this as evidence of negotiability. In another example and at first glance Matthew Johnson's check seems to carry an endorsement to a third party, but in fact the third assignee was the manservant to the agent who signed the first endorse-

---

[17]All these forms are in sequence, though unpaginated, in the Brian Fairfax Correspondence 1660–88, Fairfax Collection. The scriveners held also for the duke a set of crystal plates (Brian Fairfax to C. or M., July 29, 1663, Clayton MS A.1/1, Buc. R.O.).

[18]Clayton MS 172, Fairfax Collection.

[19]Lincolnshire Archives Committee, Hill MS 30 1.A/1.

ment.[20] Similarly, Peter Tryon wrote out a direction in the check form to Clayton and Morris to use their service to pay £12 16s. 6d. for all tithes due on his property in Middlesex.[21] Likewise, upon James Monteith's check in 1665 the scriveners wrote the charges due them, which they had deducted from the money given to the bearer, and included also a list of the deposits made to the client's account.[22] These instructions were extraneous instructions on the new business form – parts of a letter on the form of a check and a variation of the more common use of checks which were parts of letters. In 1665 John Wolstenholme drew an order upon his account to pay Anthony Hall of Oxford £60. On July 6 Hall endorsed £2 2s. 0d. of this amount to be paid to E. South.[23] Assuming that Hall and South were not Wolstenholme's agents, this is the last example of a check in the Clayton papers that can be considered to have been negotiable, even allowing for the several variations in form.

The bankers' note is more difficult to trace. The note was a two-party contract, unlike the check, which was not a contract at all. The bargain arose first from the depositary who agreed to pay to the bearer at a later date an interest-bearing sum which had been left with him. On the one hand, the note was a receipt, on the other, a loan agreement. The first bankers' notes known to survive in English history carried all the terms of the contract. Issued by the London goldsmith Feild Whorwood in 1654, these two notes were at the same time a receipt for the sum deposited, as well as a promissory note given by Whorwood to repay the sums with interest. One of these notes reads as follows (see also Figs. 3 and 4):

Recd. ye 16th [December] 1654 of Sam Tofte the some of Twenty five pounds w[hi]ch I promise to repay upon Demand I say R[eceived]
    P[er] me
        Feild Whorwood
interest of both £2–05–0.

So far as is known, these first notes were the only notes issued by Whorwood, and despite their antiquarian interest, they leave no indication

[20]Matthew Johnson's check, April 7, 1663, Hill MS 30/B7, Lincolnshire Archives Committee.
[21]Peter Tryon's order, August 21, 1660, Box T, I.U.
[22]James Monteith's order, 1665, Box 9, L.S.E.
[23]John Wolstenholme's order, 1665, Box W, I.U.

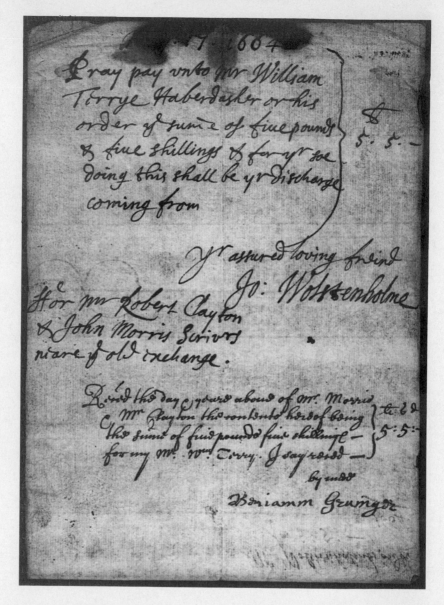

Fig. 2. Check (discharge) drawn by Sir John Wolstenholme, 1664. By permission of
the London School of Economics and Political Science

Fig. 3. Feild Whorwood's note to Samuel Tofte, December 7, 1654. By permission of the London School of Economics and Political Science

Fig. 4. Feild Whorwood's note to Samuel Tofte: endorsement, June 7, 1655. By permission of the London School of Economics and Political Science

of how that form evolved.[24] The same form of a receipt for the sum deposited with a promise to repay the sum with interest appears in a note which James Heron, goldsmith, issued to John Boate in 1665.[25]

Only one reference survives to a note which Abbott issued during his career, but since the document itself does not survive, it is unclear whether this was a fully formed note, such as Whorwood issued, or merely a receipt which was loosely referred to as a note. In June 1658 either Clayton or Morris wrote in their ledgers: 'Recd. of Mr. Reeve and Mr. Backwell for Mayor John Farmer and for which he has John Morris's note . . . £3400.'[26] Whether or not this was a receipt or an interest-bearing note is unclear. Some three weeks later the 'note' was paid off.[27] Or was the deposit collected at par with a receipt?

In late 1660 upon a receipt signed by Henry Jephcott, servant of Sir Richard Hopkins, there was written: 'Mr. Clayton gave a note or receipt for the payment hereof as my master . . . should appoint . . . '[28] If the terms were precise and distinct, then the note meant that Clayton and Morris issued both simple receipts for deposits and another form, a bankers' note. A simple receipt obligated them to repay the deposit at par. A note was a pledge for an interest-bearing deposit.[29]

The first bankers' note to survive from their house is dated 1663, in a form that is both a promissory note and a check. It is a variation upon the two characteristics of notes, as both the interest-bearing component and its endorsement appear in different forms:

June 8, 1663
> I doe hereby promise to pay unto Sir Thomas Hesilrigge's servant or to whomsoever he shall bring this note the sume of £4035 . . .
> I say upon demand the same sume . . .
>> John Morris.

---

[24] See F. T. Melton, 'Goldsmiths' Notes, 1654–55,' *Journal of the Society of Archivists*, VI, No. 1 (April 1978), 30–1. Upon Whorwood's death, Clayton became one of the executors of his estate and his financial papers came into the scrivener's possession. The third oldest bankers' note also survives in the Clayton papers:

> October ye 23rd 1657
> Recd. of Mr. Jno Taylor ye sume of One hundred pounds which is by ye order & for ye use of Walter Walker Doctr in ye Civil Law wch sume I promise to pay ye sd Doctor or his assignees on demand – I say – £100
>> for Sr. Tho. Vyner, Wm. Smythies & myselfe
>>> Witness J. Lewis   Robert Vyner
>>>> (Sir Robert Vyner's Original Papers 1657–84, Fairfax Collection).

[25] James Heron's note, 1665, Box H, I.U.
[26] G.M.R., MS 84/1/2, fol. 41r.   [27] *Ibid.*, fol. 40r.
[28] Sir Richard Hopkins's receipt for £300, December 5, 1660, Box J, I.U. On the same form the deposit was withdrawn with a discharge. *Ibid.*
[29] *Ibid.*

This was scratched out and beneath it was then written:

To pay to none without Mr. Robert Hesilrigge come with them in person.

There followed an order to pay the note, in the form of a check, rather than a simple endorsement of the note:

June 15, 1663
Mr. Morris
I doe order and appoint John Horton to assigne and dispose of the money in your hands, and desire you to pay it in unto him or his order.
        Thomas Heselrige.[30]

When Heselrigge brought in the note to collect all but £100, the scriveners then issued him a new contract. Written on July 3, 1663, it was a promissory note to repay the drawee £100. When the note was handed back to Heselrigge's servant John Horton to return to his master, he then wrote in that part of the agreement – the oral pledge – which the scriveners had omitted from the statement: 'To pay interest & 14 dayes interest to pay & money as to [be] abaited 14 dayes interest to wch is on demand.'[31]

In the following year William Belke wrote for Robert Clayton and Company a note to Philip Barrow or his assignees in much the same form as the note of the previous year – a simple promissory note with no mention of interest.[32] A note is referred to in a letter of 1665 and another note survives for 1666.[33] In 1672 the two men began issuing notes again, in the form of simple promissory notes which had been established in 1663–4, that is, merely to repay the sum which had been deposited, with no mention of interest actually written upon the note.[34] As late as 1684 the same form for notes was still used in the scriveners' bank:

1 March 1684

I promise to pay unto Mr. John ffowke or the bearer two hundred pounds upon demand I say ———————————————————
        for My Ma[r] Sr Robert Clayton
        Anthon[y] Keck.

[30] Sir Thomas Heselrigge's note, June 8, 1663, Box H, *ibid.*
[31] Sir Thomas Heselrigge's note, July 3, 1663, Box 7, L.S.E.
[32] Bod. Lib., MS Eng. Lett. c.12, fol. 69.
[33] Robert Gayer to M., September 22, 1664, Box G, I.U.; John Gouldby's receipt, February 16, 1666, Box 7, L.S.E.
[34] Between 1665 and 1668 the scriveners issued two receipts which were endorsed and circulated as notes (Nathaniel Herbert's receipt from C. & M., June 19, 1665, Box H, I.U.; John Gouldby's receipt for Sir Herbert Howard for monies paid in to M. & C. for £250, February 16, 1666, Box 7, L.S.E.). These represent the final separation in form of the receipt from the bankers' note.

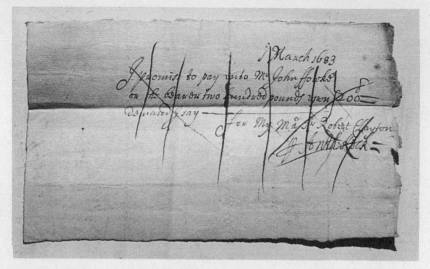

Fig. 5. Anthony Keck's note, March 1, 1683. By permission of the Surrey Archaeological Society

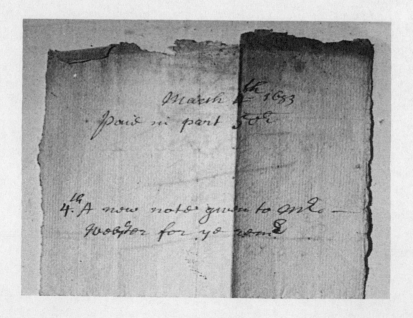

Fig. 6. Anthony Keck's note: endorsement, March 4, 1683. By permission of the Surrey Archaeological Society

The note was endorsed:

> March 4th 1683
> Paid in part £50
> 4th [March] A new note given to Mr. Webster for ye rem[ainde]r.[35]

This note is almost exactly the same in form as one the goldsmith-banker Francis Child issued in the same year.[36]

The bankers' note grew into its modern form first in the banking operations of Clayton and Morris. Their notes resembled bankers' notes of the eighteenth century. When the receipt left the note and it became merely a promise to repay a sum of money, no claims could be made upon the older notion that bankers returned the same funds as had been deposited with them. The discharge which Robert Gayer sent to Morris in 1664 to release £100 sealed up in a bag cannot be regarded as a check but rather as an order to release a valuable, as jewels or plate would have been collected.[37] The form of the note symbolized the change that had taken place in the deposit-lending nexus, that the money deposited into the scriveners' hands lost the one-to-one identification with the depositor. Deposits became fully the bankers'. The old age of sealed bags recalled as parcels was over, as Morris had daringly put the matter to Thomas Elmes in 1672.[38]

Their note took its form where there were no other records of the contract. It was not a receipt of the sum deposited, for that record lay already as a bookkeeping entry.[39] While the scriveners never inscribed upon the note the interest to be paid on the deposit, that agreement was understood to be a parole contract between Clayton and his clients. What John Horton wrote as a postscript to his master's note in 1663 was a bargain which the scriveners had already struck with the depositor.

Then, in 1672, these arrangements – the terms of the clients' loans – were written alongside each bookkeeping entry which was an interest-bearing deposit. This practice followed a decision in Chancery that interest

[35] G.M.R., MS 84/1/4, enclosure.

[36] Holden, *Negotiable Instruments*, 73.

[37] Robert Gayer's discharge, October 2, 1664, Box G, I.U. See John Tufton's order for his jewel, July 25, 1661, to collect a valuable which had been deposited with them rather than to redeem a pawn, since no money was transferred at the same time (Clayton MS A.1/1, Buc. R.O.).

[38] Thomas Elmes to C., August 1675, Box E, I.U.

[39] On April 8, 1663, the Duke of Buckingham signed a receipt for £1,000 for part purchase of Hartingdon Manor, Derbyshire. On April 10 he endorsed this receipt to the duchess, which probably means that the money was not actually paid to him and that the receipt was in fact the equivalent of a note (Duke of Buckingham's receipt, April 8, 1663, Clayton MS A.1/1, Buc. R.O.).

on a contract must be taken from the time the contract was formally made and not at any other time, such as an oral agreement between parties. This case, *Cornbury* v. *Middleton*, involved a trust, but the principle could be applied to bankers' notes and other parts of banking, and Clayton's lawyer Anthony Keck wrote the decision in his notes and returned the brief to his master.[40] In the following year, when Charles II stopped payments out of the Exchequer and the government began to clamp down on usurers, Clayton's ledger notations had already begun to inscribe what could no longer be in dispute. The full ledger entry of receipt and contract is the scriveners' equivalent of the early goldsmiths' note.

The discrepancy between the note and the entry arose as a practice in record-keeping. It prevailed for other reasons, which had to do with the use of the note in a wider context than the receipt it represented. As a contract for repayment obligated by the banker, the note was inherently monetary, and, indeed, from the moment they were first issued, notes were passed from party to party as if they were paper currency. Bankers consented to the assignment of notes just as they agreed to pay interest upon them. Negotiability was implied in the contract. Like any other interest-bearing loan contract, the note could be assigned to other parties, even though the signatories were not yet protected in the law.[41]

The opportunities for forging and altering checks and notes were greater now that they passed through the mail. Doubtful of the authenticity of his client's signature Morris in 1664 posted to his agent Simon Neale in Cumberland Thomas Stanley's voucher for £50. Neale then wrote upon it 'all that is above written I do know to be the hand writing and to be written by Mr. Stanley.'[42] Until the scriveners had assembled enough paperwork from their clients, there was no consistent method of verifying the names on vouchers or notes, for Clayton and Morris kept no signature-books. In the same year Sir Robert Abdy misplaced his note from Morris, 'and moreover he says that Cuntry his servant has left his papers in such disorder that he knows not where to find [the note], and therefore let this . . . desire you to use all diligence to find it out.'[43] In another instance in 1673 Sir Charles Wolseley sent his note to Clayton, with instructions not to honor it unless he should receive another letter ordering payment, 'for fear

[40] Keck, *Cases Argued and Decreed in the High Court of Chancery from the 12th year of King Charles II to the 31st* (London, 1697).
[41] Holden, *Negotiable Instruments*, 73–87.
[42] Bod. Lib., MS Eng. Lett. c. 16, fol. 12.
[43] Robert Gayer to M., September 22, 1664, Box G, I.U.

this should miscarry . . . '[44] In form the notes were usually made out to only one party, with no mention of assignees. Since they were unlike goldsmiths' notes, they were probably not known at large for what they actually were. The wide circulation of the scriveners' notes determined the restricted form which they carried.

Once the note had taken its shape, it worked in close conjunction with the check, first as a convenience. In 1659 Richard Webb wrote a discharge to be credited against a bill of the same amount (£9) which had been deposited in his account. Walter Long then endorsed the check but instructed that the bearer, apparently his servant, credit the amount of the voucher to his account with the scriveners.[45] In other examples, from 1664 to 1669 Sir William Glasscock deposited a series of notes and drew against them with discharges during the same period, as did Grace Garway from 1659 to 1663[46] and Henry Murray in 1664–5.[47] As the note assumed its form and became negotiable, inevitably the question arose as to whether or not the check had the same properties. In 1663 Sir Mervin Touchett wrote an order to be paid to the bearer, who was not his servant, but rather to Sir William Pulteney or his assignees 'for w[hi]ch this note together with a lease under his hand and sealed to me of the house wherein I now live shall be your sufficient discharge on the account . . . '[48] He wished to withdraw money from his account through a check, then to negotiate the same check as a loan. This use of the check Clayton and Morris did not allow.[49] Had they done so, it would have been competitive with their own money-lending. Their note offered clients the same option of investing deposits. Along the same principle, that clients could not themselves create their

[44]Bod. Lib., MS Eng. Lett. c.12, fol. 9; see also John Clutterbuck to C., July 29, 1676, Box 4, L.S.E.; William Hales to Peter Clayton, June 9, 1676, Box H, I.U.; Humphrey Gore to M. & C., January 30, 1666, Box 7, L.S.E.; Col. Fitzgerald to C., 1673, Box F, I.U.

[45]Richard Webb's discharge, June 11, 1659, Box 6, L.S.E. and see Edward Greville's receipt from M., May 4, 1659, and his voucher, May 24–October 19, 1659, Box 7, L.S.E.

[46]Sir William Glasscock's voucher and notes, 1664–79, Box 7, L.S.E.; Grace Garway's receipts 1659, 1660; her vouchers, 1661, 1663, *ibid.*

[47]Henry Murray's receipt from C. & M., 1664; his voucher, 1665; Box 9, L.S.E.

[48]Mervin Touchett to C., November 18, 1663, Box T, I.U. See also Gilbert Crouch to C. & M., June 14, 1659, U.L. MS 553/1; Edward Cooke's letter, December 16, 1671, Box C, I.U. In 1676 Sir Patience Ward wrote to C. that if the opportunity should ever arise to lend £500 from his account, his letter should be the warrant (Sir Patience Ward to C., 1676, Box W, I.U.).

[49]But see the brief letter, similar to a discharge of Sir John Talbot to lend Stephen Fox £1,000 upon a bond Clayton is to draw (Sir John Talbot to C., n.d., Clayton MS A.1/1, Buc. R.O.). See George Pitt's order to Clayton to pay off his loan to the widow of Sir Thomas Hatton, delivering up the writings of the contract as well as the principal (George Pitt to C. [1662?], Clayton MS A.1/1, Buc. R.O.).

own loans from their deposits, the scriveners were forced to forbid the use of checks as overdrafts. In 1665 Clayton's clerk John Burton returned Benjamin Portlock's check, unpaid, with a memo that if the discharge were honored, he would be overdrawn by £135.[50] In 1682 Clayton advanced Sir Thomas Peyton £160, after he had signed a warrant authorizing the scrivener to take back his loan with interest from the money to be collected on his share in the Coal Farm.[51]

Just as notes and checks were used by clients as a means of depositing and withdrawing credit by paper instruments, the question arose as to whether or not promissory notes and inland bills of exchange could be used as withdrawal instruments. The promissory note had a long history before the seventeenth century. At the end of the Middle Ages the bill obligatory was used by merchants as an informal way of assigning debts through a form which was neither sealed nor registered.[52] From this practice the form of the promissory note emerged. The first use of the promissory note in Clayton's operations occurred in 1659. On March 12 Eliab Harvey wrote out such a note to his brother-in-law Sir William Whitmore for £3,000. On the same day Whitmore endorsed this note to John Benet, who, two days later, appeared at the scriveners' shop to collect the note on Harvey's account.[53] This was the only instance of the promissory note being used in the scriveners' bank as a means of assignment and withdrawal, whereby clients themselves assigned and withdrew money.

Notes and checks emerged as instruments peculiar to banking, alongside two other withdrawal instruments peculiar to trade. These merchants' devices were promissory notes and inland bills of exchange, which had come into use before their correlative instruments in banking practice. The question inevitably arose as to whether or not promissory notes and inland bills of exchange could be used by merchants in their banking affairs. Would a merchant who held an account with Clayton and Morris be allowed to withdraw and transfer on his own initiative sums from his account by issuing these forms, or would the scriveners demand that all withdrawals from accounts be controlled through their own choices of notes and checks?

In spite of the attempts of merchants in 1663, 1669 and 1672–3 to persuade the House of Lords to put the endorsed promissory note on the same

[50]Benjamin Portlock's receipt, February 20, 1665, Box B, I.U.
[51]Sir Thomas Peyton's warrant, June 12, 1682, Box 10, L.S.E.
[52]Holden, *Negotiable Instruments*, 73–87.
[53]Sir Eliab Harvey's note, March 12, 1659, Box 6, L.S.E.

footing with the inland bill of exchange, the two instruments did not achieve the same status until 9 & 10 Will. III c. 17 and 3 & 4 Anne c. 9.[54] The promissory note was used primarily by merchants as a way of assigning debts on goods, and in Clayton's dealings this instrument was superseded by a similar form which is more proper to banking, the bill of exchange.

By the mid seventeenth century two different bills of exchange were in use in England. The foreign or 'outward' bill had an ancient past. The internal bill of exchange was in use by the 1650s.[55] In 1661 George Charnock sent Clayton his bill from the country, with instructions that it be used to pay his rents to Robert Greenwell – another example of a banking form embedded in a warrant.[56] In another example, in 1661 John Walbone received from John Machine of Bristol £500 for which he gave him his bill drawn on his banking account. Walbone then sent Clayton a voucher – still in the form of a letter – 'which I desire you will not fail to pay unto him or his order upon sight hereof according as you . . . certify me . . . ' Machine then endorsed Walbone's bill to Mr Blackwell, a draper in Watling Street, who collected the money from Clayton.[57] It was the accompanying check which validated this bill for the scriveners.

Among their clients the bill of exchange as a sovereign instrument drawn upon accounts was never accepted in their banking negotiations. Drawing bills of exchange were the privileges of the sender, as were promissory notes. It was this which restricted its use in Clayton's dealings. It lay too far beyond the scriveners' control. The check had only a limited negotiability, which restricted the flow of capital leaving the scriveners' coffers. To allow bills, as well as promissory notes, drawn at random on clients' accounts would have countermanded the development of the check. In 1676 Sir Thomas Peyton, stranded by storms in port at Great Yarmouth, drew a bill upon his account with the scriveners to Sir George England for £30. The scriveners refused to honor it, and after the bill had been returned to him, Peyton wrote Morris an indignant letter, protesting that his credit was impeccable.[58] Had he sent Clayton a check drawn to England, covered with a letter of advice, the scrivener might have honored that device.

[54]Fritz Redlich, 'The Promissory Note as a Financial and Business Instrument,' *Revue Internationale d'Histoire de la Banque*, III (1970), 277, 279.

[55]Holden, *Negotiable Instruments*, 30–52.

[56]George Charnock's warrant, July 20, 1661, Box 3, L.S.E.

[57]John Walbone to C., July 29, 1664, Box M, I.U.

[58]Sir Thomas Peyton to M., September 18, 1676, October 6, 1676, October 10, 1676, Box P, I.U.

In what soon had become a rivalry between inland bills and checks as withdrawal instruments, the scriveners won the upper hand by forbidding their clients to issue inland bills to transfer deposits. Similarly, when a Mr Salladine drew a bill payable on his account for £100 to Mrs Ann Smith, it was returned to him unpaid.[59] In 1671 Clayton and Morris were accused of ruining Sir John Cutler's credit by refusing to accept his bills from Ireland.[60] In another instance, John Hinton wrote to Morris from Wales, asking to draw a bill for six days for £15 payable to one William Wogan. Morris is the only person he knew who had money to command in this fashion, and he promised to repay the sum with interest when he came to London.[61] The difference between this request and the others is that the bill was to be drawn in the scrivener's name and not upon his own account. As long as requests for bills and notes were routed this way through their bank, the scriveners seem to have consented, but this was the same as taking out a loan or requesting a fee-paid service. And as long as the money was *paid into* their accounts, clients were free to use the option of bills and promissory notes.

The foreign bill of exchange had a somewhat different history in the scriveners' bank. On May 20, 1659, they paid a bill of exchange 'drawn upon Mr. Abdy by Mr. Robert Gayer from Amsterdam,' probably in connection with East Indian trade.[62] Several months later Walter Long inquired about the bill from Rouen which he had left with Thomas Browne for collection.[63] In 1660 Morris took in Humphrey Abdy's foreign bill for £200, to be divided between cash and a deposit for which a receipt was given.[64] By the following year they had stopped receiving foreign bills for collection at their own quarters. Walter Long wrote Thomas Browne to inquire about exchange rates in Hamburg, with the suggestion that John Colville, goldsmith, might handle these exchange transactions.[65] At about the same time the scriveners paid Colville for discounting other foreign bills.[66]

Then, much later, and only as a favor to a trusted client, Laurence Hyde, later Earl of Rochester, Clayton experimented with bills in sterling drawn on his own name, to be exchanged in the foreign market, covered with a

[59] Charles Courtnay, October 2, 1677, Box 4, L.S.E.
[60] *Stampe* v. *Heath*, MS 607, Crookshank Papers, Society of Genealogists.
[61] John Hinton to M., July 24, 1665, MS 11017E, National Library of Wales.
[62] G.M.R., MS 84/1/2, fol. 140v (May 20, 1659).
[63] Walter Long to M., October 10, 1659, Clayton papers, 1659 Jul.–Dec., Osborn, Yale.
[64] 'Humphrey Abdy's Bill of Exchange,' *c.* 1660, Box 4, L.S.E.
[65] Walter Long to Thomas Browne, 1661, Clayton papers, 1661 Jan.–June, Osborn, Yale.
[66] G.M.R., MS 84/1/3, fol. 83r (March 2, 1661).

letter of credit in his own name. Clayton made arrangements that his bills be accepted by John Moody and John Pargiter, English merchants in Danzig. But Clayton's directions to Hyde were based on several misconceptions as to how foreign bills were negotiated. Hyde found it

impossible for me to follow many of the directions you gave me at parting either in drawing it in English moneys, or informing you how the Exchange goes as to England, all which is heathen Greek to everybody in this place. But in what I have observed then in making it payable at a months sight (& that word Usance in this Country have several significations) & by sending 3 bills of the same date for the same sum for the rest, I have been fain to leave a blank for the number of gilders . . . because I know not what I must allow for my ducats, which are sometimes dearer & sometimes cheaper as our guineas are in England, but I have desired Mr. Pargiter and Mr. Moody to whom the bill goes first, to insert the number of gilders in the blank I leave, or have sent them word I would give you notice that they were to do so, that you might not wonder it was in another hand, & by that & by the Exchange, you will know exactly what you are to pay in English money for the said 950 gold ducats, which sum I mention in my bill as it goes from me, & is all the particulars I can specify. For the rest I must depend upon the honesty of my two Merchants at Danzig, & upon the account they will make. You will be pleased to comply punctually as to the payment . . . [67]

The following year Hyde was in Holland, where he found a merchant in Antwerp who promised to stand for Clayton's credit. But before long Clayton had written to another Dutch merchant to exchange Hyde's bills.[68] The Dutch money-men were well enough known in England for Clayton to establish these connections, though before the bills were drawn and the letter of credit was issued, Lord Brodrick put up his own security for £500 with Clayton for Hyde's credit. This is the last time that Clayton seems to have ventured into foreign banking.[69] Clayton and Morris were not merchants. They never acquired a focus on the world of international finance.

Several other types of manuscripts in the Clayton papers can be described as service forms. They were designed to clarify relationships between the scriveners and their clients and included bank statements, receipts for writings and abstracts of title, as well as a variety of papers dealing with

[67]Bod. Lib., MS Don. c. 69, fol. 13.
[68]Bod. Lib., MS Don. c. 68, fols. 19, 21, 23.
[69]Mr Brodrick to C., October 29, 1677, Clayton MS A.1/3, Buc. R.O. In 1674 Ld. Cornbury wrote that he had made use in Paris of all the credit Clayton had extended to him, but these details are too vague to know how the operation was handled (Ld. Cornbury to C., July 25, 1674, Box C, I.U.).

securities. Service forms were not contracts, such as notes, nor were they disbursement receipts, such as vouchers. They were forms designed to have no weight beyond the banker and his clients. The most common type of these forms was a variety of simple receipts – which Clayton and Morris issued and took in – for rents received, for annuity payments, for valuables, for legal writings, or for stock sold at Smithfield.[70]

The distinction is not always clearly drawn between service forms and other banking instruments circulating outside their house. There are several instances of forms that appear to be proper banking instruments but which in fact are no more than in-house transfers. In 1666 Christopher Cratford wrote out a bill on his account to John Lindsay for £33 and instructed Clayton and Morris to pay it, a favor which the scriveners ordinarily forbade.[71] In fact, Cratford was a lawyer working as an inter-

[70] See Mary Uphill's receipt, September 21, 1676, Box U, I.U.; Nathaniel Herbert's receipt, 1665, Box H, I.U.; Charles Chambers' receipt, 1661, Box 1, L.S.E.; Charles Carfield's receipt, 1660, ibid.; Sir William Turner's receipt, October 15, 1664, Box 4, ibid.; Ralph Wilde's receipt, 1664, Box 5, ibid.; Edward Checkeley's receipt, April 11, 1676, Box 3, ibid.; Christopher Cratford's two receipts, 1666, ibid.; Sir William Hecke's receipt, 1664, ibid.; Elizabeth Wingfield's receipt, 1672, Box 5, ibid.; Charles Whitaker's receipt, 1661, Box 6, ibid.; Elizabeth Huntley's receipts, 1661 and 1663, ibid.; Matthew Wren's receipt from M. for £2,600, June 26, 1662, ibid.; Sir John Wroth's two receipts, 1660, Box 6, ibid.; Edward Wroughton's receipt for interest, 1671, ibid.; George Wroughton's receipt, 1660, ibid.; Richard Wynn's receipt for interest due him and Lady Reynardson, 1665, ibid.; George Gosfright's receipt, July 3, 1663, Box 7, ibid.; Edward Greville's receipt from M. for £185, May 4, 1659, ibid.; Edward Greville's order to pay, May 24, 1659, ibid.; Edward Greville's order to pay, May to October 19, 1659, ibid.; Morris's receipt to Edward Greville, October 21, 1659, ibid.; William Gulston's receipt, September 22, 1676, ibid.; William Goodman's receipt, November 19, 1674, ibid.; Joseph Godden's receipt, November 25, 1663, ibid.; Henry Wayne's receipt, 1673, ibid.; Richard Glyd's two receipts, 1659, 1661, ibid.; Sir William Glasscock's order and notes, 1664–79, ibid.; James Gibbons' receipt, 1678, Box 7, L.S.E.; William Gibbes' receipt, September 29, 1676, ibid.; Richard Gawthorne's receipt, 1660, ibid.; Allan Garway's receipt, 1674, ibid.; Grace Garway's receipts, 1659, 1660, ibid.; Grace Garway's orders, 1661, 1663, ibid.; Robert Hyde's receipts, 1663–4, Box 8, L.S.E.; John Stone's receipt, 1664, ibid.; Frederick Howpert's receipt, 1655, ibid.; Sir Henry Hudson's receipt for £770, June 17, 1665, ibid.; William Hutchinson's receipt, 1660, ibid.; Henry Murray's receipt from C. & M., 1664, Box 9, L.S.E.; Henry Murray's order to pay, 1665, ibid.; John Seller's receipt, February 4, 1662; Deane Monteage's note to Dymock Walpole, July 1676, ibid.; John Parrey's receipt, 1663, Box 10, L.S.E.; William Pemble's receipt, July 13, 1682, ibid.; Thomas Pennington's receipt, 1665, ibid.; George Peryer's receipt, 1659, ibid.; John Pettiward's receipt, 1659, ibid.; Anthony Smyth's receipt, 1662, Box 11, L.S.E.; Simon Smith's two receipts, 1664, ibid.; Nathaniel Smith's receipts, 1662, ibid.; William Smith's receipts, 1664, ibid.; Samuel Smith's receipt, 1665, ibid.; John Skinner's receipt, 1663, ibid.; James Sherman's receipt, Box 11, L.S.E.; William Sherman's receipt, ibid.; Thomas Shippey's receipt, 1673, ibid.; John Sharpe's receipt, October 18, 1662, ibid.; Richard Segar's receipt, 1662, ibid.; George Sedley's receipt, October 2, 1659, ibid.; Jeremy Sambrooke's receipt, 1659, ibid.; and Jerome Salter's receipt, February 12, 1666, ibid.

[71] Christopher Cratford's receipt, January 2, 1666, Box 4, L.S.E.

mediary for a small group of goldsmith-bankers. His 'bill' of 1666, although written in the proper manner, should be regarded as an internal arrangement and form, rather than a proper inland bill. In another instance, in 1672 the scriveners' agent in Lincolnshire, William Hardy, sent money to them by a drover who forgot to wait for his receipt. Peter Clayton then sent Hardy by mail either a bill or a note for the amount.[72] In 1673 a grazier in the same county came to Hardy to ask for an advance of £80 credit on the sheep he was sending to London the next day, drawn on the scriveners, so that his accounts could be adjusted for the amount at the reckoning. Hardy then wrote out a bill in his own name, with an order restricting the negotiability to Clayton.[73] Again, this should be regarded as an internal transfer of credit rather than a proper bill of exchange, even though it has that form.

For some forty years before the banking statement of account evolved, clients who wished to know their balance with the scriveners appeared in the Cornhill shop to inspect their ledgers in person. Since no balance was drawn until the half-yearly reckonings – if then – the clerks had to interrupt their work to add and subtract the debit and credit entries. Added to the ordinary debits were charges for services rendered them by the scriveners, and these contingency fees could only be ascertained in the scriveners' ledgers. Clients probably had a rough idea of what their accounts held, even if they kept no precise record.

On March 12, 1662, one of their clerks noted beside the account of Mrs Judith Tryon, widow of the Northamptonshire farmer Peter Tryon:

This account is cast up here, for that there is an account in paper delivered to the Administratrix of all money received and paid from Mr. Peter Tryon's death to the 25 March 1662 which agreed with the account kept in this book.[74]

The following year Sir John Wolstenholme wrote in the margin beside his debit account

I John Wolstenholme Esq. have received under the hand of Mr. Robert Clayton an account this present 24th March 1663. The balance whereof being £239–6–6 agreeth with this book . . . [75]

In another example a duplicate of Dr Thomas Yate's debit account was

[72]William Hardy to M., September 25, 1672, Foster Library, Lincolnshire Archives Committee.
[73]Same to same, August 13, 1673, *ibid*. See also Hardy's letter to the Earl of Devonshire, June 19, 1783, *ibid*.
[74]G.M.R., MS 84/1/3, fol. 162v (March 12, 1662).
[75]*Ibid*., fol. 130v (March 24, 1663).

prepared and presented to him.[76] This is the last book memo to appear in the ledger noting that a complete account had been presented as a written statement to a client.[77]

Five copies of statements survive in the Clayton papers, the first compiled in 1667, from a loan contracted in 1664,[78] at about the time the scriveners discontinued the practice of making complete written accounts. To some extent the banking statement was designed to discourage personal written audits, though what emerged as the statement was not a complete reckoning, but usually selected entries of monies laid out to repay principal and interest on loans. Checks and receipts signed by clients for other withdrawals were not listed in these statements, nor were those contingency profits which the scriveners transferred for their own use. The wide sources of credit accretions do not appear in these accounts. William Calder's account of his loan to Clayton records the half-yearly payments of £25 principal repaid, together with the interest which declined over the three years as it was compounded.[79] Thomas Sturges' statement for the period 1664–7 recorded the numbers of days between the times that he repaid the principal and interest, which was in irregular intervals.[80] On Sir Henry Coningsby's debt to Sir William Hickes, which was to be paid off at once, at the end of nine years, the entire amount due was given.[81] The account of Fabian Phillips to Sir John Musters was arranged in a similar manner in 1675.[82]

These statements were schemes of loan contracts, and at the foot of Lord Yarmouth's account was written that nothing had been paid into his account for twelve years.[83] The scrivener sent a similar notice to Sir Christopher Wray in 1674 after he had written to London saying that he would not pay his debt until they had sent him their ledgers.[84]

This was the ploy of a client with an overdraft, who could not be nudged with this new breviate of his contract. Statements were prepared only upon the request of clients; otherwise no written account was submitted to

[76]G.M.R., MS 84/1/3, fol. 125v.
[77]With the possible exception of a list of Thomas Breton's credits and debts, 1667–71, which resembles a page from an account book, Box B, I.U.
[78]Thomas Sturges' Account (1664–7), K.A.O. MS U214, E13/1.
[79]'Mr. Will. Calder his account to me for interest' (1664–7), Box 3, L.S.E.
[80]See n. 78.
[81]'Sir Henry Coningsby's Statement of Account' (1661–9) contains both credit and debit entries of interest payments, Box C, I.U.
[82]'Mr. Fabian Philipps to Sir John Musters' (1675), Box P, I.U.
[83]Ld. Yarmouth's Account, July 26, 1677, Box 4, L.S.E.
[84]Sir Christopher Wray to C., January 23, 1674, Box 6, ibid.

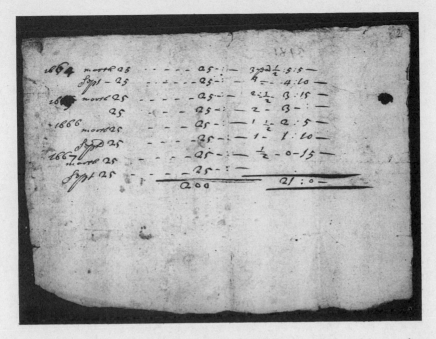

Fig. 7. William Calder's banking statement, 1667. By permission of the London School of Economics and Political Science

them.[85] No other bank of the period seems to have presented such a record, the ancestor of the more complete pass-book of the eighteenth century.

Receipts for legal writings, or, rather, 'writings,' were issued by the scriveners to acknowledge that these papers had been placed with them for safe-keeping. They are not to be confused with a form which is similar to the receipt, the bill for writings by which the scriveners charged their clients for scribal work which their clerks had completed.[86] Receipts recognized writings made outside the bank yet deposited within, while a bill was a charge for documents composed within the scriveners' counting-house. The receipt for writings is not a business form in any way negotiable or related to the transfer of capital, but since it is similar to other banking instruments and reflects another aspect of the control of credit in the transition between simple brokerage to banking, it deserves mention here.

The first such receipt was written in 1653, from writings deposited with

---

[85] See Henry Allnutt to M., June 28, 1675, Box A, I.U.
[86] See below, p. 138 and n. 48.

Abbott who planned to prepare an abstract of title that he could then circulate to prospective mortgagors. It carried the note 'A brief of some writings concerning the manor of Lowesby in the county of Leicestershire, deposited with Mr. Robert Abbott.' At the bottom was written 'upon the delivery both of these writings to take in my note given for the same,' and they were not released until the form was endorsed on January 9, 1663.[87]

Christopher Bernard's receipt of March 6, 1660, on the other hand, resembled a check:

Recd. of Mr. John Morris four parchment writings, two paper copies, the pattern and abstract thereof and the abstract of title all concerning the title of Hanslopp Park . . . I recd. the same writing by the order and appointment of my master for Christopher Bernard and to be returned to Mr. Morris.[88]

These writings were received and discharged with the same procedure as money on deposit. Mrs Faith Heneage left her writings sealed up in a box, much as jewels and plate were left with the scriveners for safe-keeping.[89] Large classes of these writings did not leave the bank with the same freedom as ordinary valuables taken in for safe-keeping. John Bendyshe's note recorded that the three deeds he deposited had been left in connection with his security to Mr Howland.[90] In 1672 Robert Pierrepoint, having previously mortgaged lands in Norfolk through the scriveners, who had taken in all his leases and deeds relating to the lands, then decided to sell a part of the mortgaged estate. 'I have had several proposals but could not conclude with any by reason your writings were not produced which has prevented my paying it in.'[91] In a similar instance Morris told Sir George Stonehouse that in the scriveners' custody his papers were kept only under 'friendly preservation.' By this time all the scriveners' mortgagees, as well as those of their clients, were required to deposit in the bank all the legal papers of the title to the security throughout the life of the loan.[92] When Mr Wall paid in the remaining £120 of his loan, his lawyer instructed the scriveners to deliver up to him the six conveyances which they had held from the time the loan had been negotiated.[93] Writings which had sealed

[87] L.R.O., MS 35'29/365.

[88] Christopher Bernard's receipt for writings, March 6, 1660, Box 6, L.S.E.

[89] F. Hampden's receipt, July 15, 1671, Box H, I.U.

[90] Ex. R.O., MS 68.D/DA(69).

[91] Robert Pierrepoint to M., July 11, 1672, Box P, I.U.

[92] Sir George Stonehouse to M., July 6, 1674, Box 5, I.U.; 'show the bearer hereof . . . the counterpart of my mortgage of Ashby. He will only peruse it in your presence . . . ' (Sir Christopher Wray to M., January 14, 1677, Clayton MS A.1/3, Buc. R.O.).

[93] Henry Powle to C., November 24, 1677, Box P, I.U.

the loan were already in the scriveners' care, and the receipt–discharge system applied ordinarily to deeds and leases of land which the mortgagee held until it became security.

The practice of mandatory deposits of writings bears a close analogy to the practice of partners putting their legal writings, or exhibits, in Chancery to support litigation while the case was in progress. In 1666 Keck found it pertinent to record the instance of Lady Baltinglass who had retrieved a trunk of her writings from the Master of the Court. To his regret no written discharges were made of what she had taken.[94] In 1681 John Walden signed a receipt for a mortgage covenant made between William Gyles and John Wyse in 1679, on the condition that Gyles submit to Clayton his counterpart of the contract until the borrowed document was returned.[95] The receipt for the papers deposited was one way of distinguishing what were properly the debtor's covenants and which papers of the transaction itself were the scriveners' own records, though this was incidental to the primary issue. As long as the scriveners held all the papers pertaining to the security, the debtor could not mortgage the lands to someone else. With the irregularities in the public registration of conveyances, Clayton's control of all the private deeds and leases of land gave him virtual control of the credit of his mortgagees, a position of knowing exactly where the papers to each loan lay. The files of the bank were as closely watched as all the capital which came in and left his coffers.

The greatest set of records in the history of the bank is a long series of account books, termed by Clayton and Morris the Grand Ledgers[96] to distinguish them from other types of registers which their agents kept and which were reconciled in the main records in the shop. There are gaps in the Grand Ledgers for the period 1656–8, 1663–9 and 1680–2. No accounts survive after 1685, but the balances in the ledger which ends in that year were carried over to another book, and it is likely that Clayton kept detailed accounting books for his estates and his business dealings – whatever they might have been after 1685 – right up to his death, for he was a stickler for such accurate accounting.

Alongside the Grand Ledgers the scriveners kept another set of accounts, which have not survived. In 1666 one of their clerks, William Belke, testified in a legal deposition that each night Clayton and Morris counted the cash in the shop and cast up an account.[97] These tabulations

[94] Keck, *Cases*, 66.　　[95] John Walden's receipt, Box W, I.U.　　[96] See Appendix 4.
[97] William Belke's deposition, May 25, 1666, Spec. MS Coll. Buckingham, C.U.

do not occur in the Grand Ledgers, which suggests that they kept systematically another set of accounts containing these notations. The practice of maintaining dual sets of accounts was common, so the bookkeeping treatises of the period relate.[98] The second set of records was referred to in the financial world as 'journals,' though they did not represent the same daily activity recorded in the ledgers. The scriveners' own private manipulation of their clients' deposits would appear in these records. When Sir Barnaby's drover paid in his £500, that sum would be written in the Grand Ledgers, as would all loans which Clayton, in the role of broker, arranged on his behalf. But when Clayton then loaned £200 of that money out in his own name, shrewdly calculated to be recalled before Sir Barnaby drew upon his account, that transaction would be registered in the journals, but not in the ledgers. If the journals survived to be compared with the ledgers, a more precise calculation could be made of where the capital in the scriveners' hands was actually invested.

Just after he left Clayton's service, Stephen Monteage explained to his new employer Lord Hatton how he had ordered his accounts to be kept. Every entry was written 'in an abbreviated manner, every sum with short expressions,'[99] and this could just as well describe the manner in which the scriveners' accounts were kept after 1652. Where the description was made out in the name of a person – and this is frequently the case, particularly in the accounts of his clients – it is impossible to arrange a category for that notation. Under Sir Barnaby's account we might find 'Paid Mr. Smith £100 for a loan,' but the same transaction could just as well have been written simply 'paid Mr. Smith £100.'

The accounts of the personal finances of the scriveners are somewhat more distinct than those of their clients, even though the two accounts were interspersed in the ledgers. Money received for deposits at interest is clearly marked as such in the scriveners' account in 1672, for by that time that entry became the most complete statement of the contract of the bankers' note. No secrets or subterfuges could appear in the Grand Ledgers, which were kept in the shop for their clients to peruse. In 1672, during the Exchequer crisis, all the ledgers containing the accounts no longer current were turned over for some time to Serjeant Pemberton, who was presumably looking for evidence of usury.[100] To no avail – all the evidence of interest payments adhered strictly to the maximum legal interest

[98] Littleton and Yamey, eds., *Studies in the History of Accounting*, 183, n. 7.
[99] B.L., Add. MS 29558, fol. 484.
[100] Robert Morris to M., July 16, 1672, Box 9, L.S.E.

rate, even though from other evidence it is clear that Clayton was charging in excess of that amount. Where the accounts are irregular and confusing they are obviously unhelpful, but where they are clear and seemingly accurate, there is so often a case of deception that the ledgers cannot be taken by themselves as the most reliable record of the scriveners' finances.

Two critical questions have already arisen with banking forms, namely the question of money on deposit and the practice of negotiability. In spite of the drawbacks which the ledgers present as evidence they do shed light on these two problems. In the two years after Abbott's death, 1658–60, when Clayton and Morris were acting on the orders of executors who might have dissolved the firm, the deposits of the bank sank to £617,170, a drop of 54 per cent from the amount Abbott had taken in from his clients from 1652 to 1656. Then, during the bookkeeping period which began in 1660 and ended in 1663, their reserves more than doubled, to a total of £1,380,953, the most dramatic increase in their capital during a single ledger period throughout their career. During this time they began paying interest on deposit, but only a total of £2,386 or 0.17 per cent of the money paid in by their clients. From 1669 until 1672, when their deposits reached £1,515,491, they paid out £22,806 for interest on their reserves, or 1.5 per cent of their deposits. In 1672 the manner of accounting for interest changed, so that all interest charges – on long-term loans as well as notes – were undifferentiated. Even so, during the period 1672 until 1675 they received a total of £1,763,085 on deposit and paid out a total of £21,894 in interest, or 1.2 per cent, of which the interest on deposits would be a much lower figure.

The Exchequer crisis ruined several goldsmiths who had paid money on deposit, thereby lessening the competition that the scriveners had in the market for deposits. But over the next ten years, as farming prices worsened, their own deposits suffered. From 1675 until 1677 their clients' deposits reached a peak – a total of £1,828,091 – but in the next four years, 1677–80, this figure dropped to a total of £1,324,912. The ledger for 1680–2 is missing, but from 1682 until 1685 their deposits improved to a total of £1,168,592. In these three accounting periods, 1675–7, 1677–80 and 1682–5, the scriveners paid out in interest less than one per cent in each period of the money taken in at the same time on all their deposits, be they interest-bearing or interest-free. The scriveners' deposits were never closely aligned to interest, even after 1675, when their reserves declined.

The cyclical nature of their reserves, as well as the difficulty of finding sound investments greater than interest paid on deposits, limited the scriveners' opportunity of making money by offering interest. Usually two reckonings were made annually in the Grand Ledgers, to conform to the traditional idea of the rhythms of the agricultural year. Many rents were set after the slaughter sales and later after the harvest at Michaelmas (September 29). Other leases were renewed at the beginning of the new year at Lady Day (March 25), which long ago had been the time that spring plowing began. In the late fifteenth century and throughout the sixteenth century the accounts of a depositary would swell during the autumn and winter, while during the spring and summer months his reserves would ebb. When farmers began to implement new techniques in arable husbandry – and these changes happened during the careers of Abbott and Clayton – the velocity of capital from the country to London lost its old predictable character. Spring plowing could begin as early as Plow Monday, and where three-crop rotation and sheep and arable husbandry were practiced, the agricultural year did not come to a halt in the winter. Many of the rents which were due at Lady Day were not actually paid until Michaelmas, for the harvest was the time tenants were most likely to have the money for their rents.[101] In many places at Plow Monday and Candlemas (February 2) there were markets where farmers and their families sold goods they had made during the winter after the harvest, so that those tenants in arrears with their Michaelmas rents might pay their debts in midwinter.[102]

Bailiffs often waited six months after Michaelmas before collecting their arrears and remitting them to London (and they were likely to insert an extra half-year's salary into their accounts, Monteage warned).[103] Even under the best conditions – abundant harvest with high prices for crops, followed by an early spring – many tenants were niggardly with their rents. The new season involved an outlay of capital which had to come from the profits of harvest and Candlemas, so that Lady Day tenants often had to beg off until the crops were harvested. But throughout the period agricultural recession was the rule, and even though there were ways to offset the slump, the old days of rising rents and the fairly predictable patterns of agriculture had passed.

Often there was a long time before the money which was collected in the country was actually paid into the scriveners' shop in London. Clayton's agents kept part of what they collected for repairs and improvements, and the accounts which they sent up to London for audit came in long after the

---

[101] See James Bryan to William Belke, June 9, 1673, Box B, I.U.
[102] Charles Dymoke to M., December 24, 1674, MS 5226, fol. 12, Lincoln City Library.
[103] Stephen Monteage, *Instructions for Rent-Gatherers Accompts* (London, 1683), 29.

rents they had returned. Peter Wood, for instance, submitted a list of expenses incurred by him on their land at Melbourne from Lady Day 1672 until Michaelmas 1673 almost one year later, on August 31, 1674.[104] Similarly, when William Chamberlayne's account was audited in 1674, it was discovered that he had kept back in the country £73 15s. 0d.[105] Also, Langley Gace submitted a half-year's account for the manor of Orby, Lincs., for 1689 only in January 1691.[106] These three lists survived only accidentally; probably there were many other instances of the lag between what was due on the accounts and deposits in London and what cash was actually on hand. The ledgers made no allowances for this discrepancy. Clayton knew what the harvest was likely to bring, for he had extensive contacts in the country, but there is no way he could have estimated with any precision what his capital on hand was likely to be for more than one season at a time.

Constant uncertainty about his reserves determined the way in which the paper instruments of Clayton's bank evolved. The non-negotiable check countermanded the practice of clients' drawing promissory notes and bills at random on their accounts. This interaction, together with Clayton's doubt about his cash flow, appears to be a more convincing reason why these forms retained a constricted use than does the lack of legal protection.

The bankers' note presents a different problem, however, since it was negotiable and had the property of inflating the scriveners' reserves, which he might have turned to when his deposits slackened. How many notes Clayton issued is unknown, though the number would seem to be small. In the ledger kept from 1672 to 1675 Clayton allowed forty-six persons interest on their deposits which ranged from £200 to £8,000. In 1673 Colonel Fitzgerald inquired of Clayton about two deposits he had made some time before and how he might then arrange to draw interest upon them, which implies that this had not originally been his motive in placing the money there.[107] Three years later Sir Richard Newdegate instructed his man to look over his deposits with an eye to investing at interest part of his money on deposit with the scriveners. Two thousand pounds was to be invested at four per cent for three months in his grandchild's name.

---

[104] 'A particular of the disbursements of Mr. Peter Wood,' Box 5, L.S.E.
[105] M.'s note of Chamberlayne's account, 1674, Box 6, L.S.E.
[106] Rylands, Ch. 2684, J.R.L.
[107] Col. Fitzgerald to C., 1673, Box F, I.U.

Another deposit of £1,000 was to be invested for about three months. Two other deposits of £400 and £500 were to be left until Easter but were not to be tied up in interest commitments.[108] Likewise, in 1672 Sir Robert Howard wrote to the bank on behalf of his servant Mary Uphill who wished to invest £300 at six per cent for three months. She had not been a client of the scriveners before, and they were to look upon this request as a special favor to him,[109] as, indeed, it was exceptional that the scriveners received deposits exclusively at interest from people who did not leave them other monies to manipulate in other ways to yield greater profits for themselves.

These interest-bearing deposits included bonds at interest, as well as deposits for which notes were given. Through a money bond Clayton promised to repay a certain sum on deposit at a fixed rate of interest at a certain day, so that in effect he was taking in a timed deposit, whereas a note was on demand. From Clayton's viewpoint a timed deposit was preferable to a deposit on demand, since with the former he had a precise idea of when the money with interest would be recalled. Yet the interest he paid on both types of account does not vary significantly. Between 1672 and 1675 he paid between four and six per cent for money on deposit, but the common and average figure was five per cent. Again, if notes were recalled with regularity, then their value to the scrivener, though they were less like money bonds, was not distinctive. Five per cent interest was a high rate to be paying out on short-term investments, and it was this fact, surely, which explains why Clayton inflated his reserves only minimally by taking in deposits at interest. The costs were too great.

Clayton and Morris were more than simple cashiers. Rather than being limited to the short-term use of capital by taking in and paying out their clients' deposits, they were moneylenders whose main innovations occurred in mortgage finance. Negotiable instruments played their role in their activities, but it was not around these credit instruments that their primary banking activities lay. On the whole, neither the check nor the note seems to have added significantly to the scriveners' money supply. Where notes and bonds held inflationary properties, these conditions were not essential to the scriveners' reserves. The note was a proper credit instrument in the limited use it had in Clayton's dealings. Until about 1665 the check at times was used as a negotiable instrument, though primarily as a means whereby clients claimed their deposits. Nevertheless, as a

---

[108] Sir Richard Newdegate to C. & M., February 16, 1676, Clayton MS A.1/3, Buc. R.O.
[109] Sir Robert Howard's letter, January 5, 1672, Clayton MS A.1/2, Buc. R.O.

means of transferring credit from one place to another the note, and to a lesser extent, the check, are banking instruments and place the role of Clayton and Morris in that tradition.

CHAPTER 5

LAW, PRACTICE AND
PROFITS OF THE
EARLY BANKING MORTGAGE

————————— • —————————

Unlike negotiable instruments which were unregulated by law during the scriveners' career, lending contracts were controlled by a welter of legal restrictions, constantly in flux. As soon as bankers arranged legal contracts, the morality of moneylending became legal questions which bankers must answer to the king as well as to God. Perhaps nothing so invaded the otherwise secretive milieu of the counting-houses of the seventeenth century as did equity law. The law regarding land had an ancient and respectable pedigree. During the sixteenth and seventeenth centuries, as land changed hands with increasing frequency, the laws governing real security changed accordingly. Bankers like Clayton and Morris kept abreast of these changes, but moneylending was so dependent upon law and lawyers that bankers could never themselves master the laws defining these spheres of their operations. By the eighteenth century lawyers had even greater control over bankers than in the seventeenth. For this reason early English banking never became its own self-contained profession, like the church or the army, with skills entirely peculiar to itself.

At every turn confusions arose between the law and the actual practice of mortgage financing. The courts could speak clearly about the legal nature of the mortgage and of the regulations surrounding contracts. However, the forms of contracts used for real securities were not nearly so distinct, and the courts did not answer the vexing question of what contracts securities must take. The convolutions of land conveyancing were so subtle that it was possible, for example, to arrange a lending contract having the appearance of a lease, for the distinction between the two types of conveyancing instruments was unclear. If the bargain was then seen as

126

constituting a loan, it would be regulated by the usury laws; if it was viewed as merely a leasing arrangement, it lacked such control. To complicate matters further, the courts considered mortgages to be private arrangements between two or more parties and not business contracts handled by middlemen such as the scriveners Clayton and Morris whose innovations placed them at times in advance of the law.

Clayton and Morris were subject to the criticism that their practices took advantage of loopholes in the law, partly because their role was unclear to people ignorant of the work in the bank. As brokers in land as well as money, they sat astride two aspects in the land market. Primarily they arranged mortgages as securities for loans. When all parts of the process of the negotiation fell under their control – the transfer of the loan itself and the arrangement of the security – they clearly fitted the role of moneylenders. Occasionally they acted merely as conveyancers in a contract in which the parties themselves devised the loan and the security. From this there arose the suspicion that they sold land apart from any considerations of moneylending, that is, that they were land agents. In 1663, for example, they were summoned to Chancery to clarify whether a series of documents they had negotiated constituted a land sale or whether the same indentures represented a mortgage.[1] The legal position of mortgage financing was recognized at the time as confusing. Shrewd bankers like Clayton and Morris thrived on the inconsistencies between mortgage law and land law, and they were not alone. Their lawyer Anthony Keck recorded the example of a case in Chancery in 1675 of a man who had required his tenant to sign a contract for collateral security to run concurrently with his lease, a set of joint contracts defying proper legal classification.[2]

Borrowers acquired a new protection in mortgage law in the latter half of the seventeenth century with the growth of the equity of redemption. With this proviso written into the contract the borrower who failed to repay his loan at the time specified in the contract might, under certain conditions, save his estates from reverting to his lender by extending the contract. The background to this innovation went back to the confiscations and sales of royalist estates during the civil wars and Interregnum. When Oliver Cromwell died, many of these estates passed back into the hands of the families who had lost them, and the period of transferral

---

[1] Deposition in *Blount* v. *Clayton* (1663), Box B, I.U.
[2] Anonymous (1675), in A. Keck, *Cases Argued and Decreed in the High Court of Chancery from the 12th year. of King Charles II to the 31st* (London, 1697), p. 261.

lasted during the royalist apogee of the early Restoration.[3] In these political circumstances the courts supported landowners reclaiming their land titles, and, by extension, the same protection began to apply in the future to those men who wished to mortgage their estates with the least risk of losing them. What had first emerged as a general sympathy of the courts came gradually to be referred to as a legal principle, the equity of redemption, which received its most precise form during the lord chancellorship of Lord Nottingham, from 1673 until his death in 1682.

Only if the proviso of redemption appeared somewhere in the contract was the borrower protected. As a consequence of an arrangement which worked to the disadvantage of lenders, many of the men who had put up their money for loans appear to have entered the estates of their borrowers at the time the contracts were made, quite commonly by the time of the Restoration.[4] As the courts handled the question after 1660 – and they were generally favorable to the equity of redemption – the real issue became not the time of entrance, but whether or not the lender was to be allowed to occupy the lands permanently. In other words, was the borrower to lose his land as a penalty for not paying off his loan in time, even though the principal and interest might be paid off later than the date which had been set originally? The safest way of protecting the borrower's security was to disallow the lender entrance into the land for the life of the contract, and even though as a practical arrangement lenders often did occupy these estates from the inception of the contract, the legal fiction was otherwise. Gradually mortgages which carried the proviso of the equity of redemption were recognized as mortgages for a term of years.

Mortgages continued to be drawn up throughout this period without the proviso of redemption written into the contract. The redemptionless mortgage was the original mortgage form. While the equity of redemption developed to the extent which seemed to set that form of real security apart from other mortgage arrangements, the older mortgage was recognized as the mortgage in fee. Under this arrangement the lender was guaranteed entry into the land at the time the contract was signed, and he continued his possession until the income from the land had repaid his loan. It was this characteristic of direct and immediate occupation of the land which set the mortgage in fee apart from the mortgage for a term of years as a legal

[3]R. W. Turner, *The Equity of Redemption*, Cambridge Studies in English Legal History (Cambridge, 1931); J. Thirsk, 'The Restoration Land Settlement,' *Journal of Modern History*, XXVI (1954), 315–28.
[4]Turner, *Equity of Redemption*, 90.

definition.[5] In practice the mortgage in fee was often applied to parts of entire estates. Specific leases were attached in the contracts, and these liens or rent charges, not the entire estate, became the security.

Under the equity of redemption the land was the security for the loan in the event that the loan was not repaid. This protection worked to the interests of the borrower. In a banking context the lender is more likely to lend his money when his own interests predominate in the contract. Under the mortgage in fee, immediate possession of the land by the lender or his agent guaranteed that the loan would be paid off through the rents which came to the lender during the life of the loan. Strictly speaking, the land was not therefore a security. Once the concept of penalty had disappeared with the equity of redemption and lenders occupied the land anyway, the mortgage for a term of years was similar to the mortgage in fee, in spite of what the law might read. Clayton's clients do not seem to have labored over the differences. For instance, Lord Peterborough's proposal for a mortgage just before the Restoration was only 'to have the tenants as to so much as will pay interest at term so that there shall be a good performance for £4000.'[6] In another example, a particular of 1660 advertising West-house, near Billericay, mentioned 'for security so much land as may resume the repayment of the £500.'[7] Likewise, in 1671 Thomas Stanley was willing to give as much land as security as was 'proportionable to the sum borrowed.'[8]

Different mortgages required different conveyances, though the question of which contracts to use was more complicated than the simple distinctions between kinds of loans. The tendency during the scriveners' career was for informal instructions and contracts to be written up as formal conveyances. In 1659 Lord Shrewsbury wrote to the scriveners for a loan of £50, and they honored his request by having his servant sign the letter, much as they would have done had the authorization been a voucher to pay a sum from his account.[9] By 1671 the preliminary procedures of their moneylending had changed to the point that now any prospective client was asked to make a written request for his loan, regardless of what details he had discussed before with the scriveners or their agents. When Lady Fanshawe approached Morris about a loan of £200, he consented,

[5] For these distinctions in mortgage law see E. C. Wilmot, *A Succinct View of the Law of Mortgages* (London, 1819), 11–12.
[6] Northants. R.O., Clayton MS 11.
[7] Ex. R.O., MS D/DAc 23.
[8] Thomas Stanley to M., July 26, 1671, MS Eng. Lett. c. 16, fol. 16, Bod. Lib.
[9] Gilbert Crouch to C. & M., June 14, 1659, U.L. MS 553/1.

with the stipulation that the loan be made from the account of Sir Edmund Turnor who had already asked the scriveners to find a suitable lender for his reserves. Morris then sent word to Turnor, who assented to the transaction when the proper contracts were signed. Morris, however, needed this written permission from the lender before his clerks wrote out the contracts.[10] In another instance, when Henry Hilliard borrowed £50 in 1675, he was made to sign a bond for the loan, though with a special concession which Clayton had granted sometime before. If he had not paid in the money a month or six weeks before the deadline, at the scriveners' warning he would then sign over property for the amount due, though without making an actual mortgage deed.[11]

Primitive forms of mortgage arrangements which are no more than instructions and which are more accurately termed proto-mortgages appear in connection with the scriveners' role as stewards for their clients' affairs. As they received rents and other deposits for their clients, they paid off their clients' tradesmen's bills, and as a part of the same service, their loans. In one instance, in 1652 Lord Warwick sent Abbott a list of lands he had set aside for the rents to pay off his son Lord Rich's debts.[12] In another example, shortly before he died Abbott heard from Sir John Prettyman:

In regard of my father's occasions for moneys at this time for payment of some bond debts . . . it is agreed between my father and myself, that there should be so much land out of Ash & Sandwich made over to me as will amount to £2200 at 17 years purchase, and I shall take care to pay off the Alderman his money . . . [13]

Likewise, several months later James Huxley endorsed his rental receipt due on his houses in Milk Street, London, and enclosed them in a letter which authorized Morris to collect this money to repay a debt.[14] To cite another example, some time between 1658 and 1661 Lord Peterborough sent the scriveners a copy of his rent rolls of the manors in Slipton and Islip, Northants., with instructions that they repay his loans in accordance with the rents from the Michaelmas and Lady Day terms of these properties.[15] Similarly, in 1660 a Mr Hon, though reluctant to give land in a formal contract as security for a loan, promised to send the scriveners a copy of his rent roll, out of which they would be able to choose their security as a rent

[10] George Weldon to M., Clayton MS A.1/2, Buc. R.O.
[11] Henry Hilliard to C. & M., February 11, 1676, Box H, I.U.
[12] Ex. R.O., MS D/DAc (70).
[13] Sir John Prettyman to A., May 12, 1658, Box P, I.U.
[14] James Huxley to M., July 19, 1658, Clayton papers, Osborn, Yale.
[15] Northants. R.O., Clayton MS 11.

charge.[16] Likewise, in the same year Mr Tuckey wrote that 'Upon the loan of £2000 [he] . . . will grant the premises.'[17] In another instance, at the bottom of his promissory note for £30 Sir John Prettyman wrote in 1666 'for repayment thereof with interest . . . the same shall be received . . . out of the rents and profits of the lands at Boothby and Willoughby, Lincs., which [Morris and Clayton] already receive for a greater debt.'[18]

Through direct possession rents could be delegated to pay off loans, but until these rents were formally specified as real security in contracts which set the terms of payment, there was little difference between rents used to repay loans and rents used to pay off tradesmen's bills. According to legal theorists, as long as rents were unpledged to specific loans, the transaction was a personal debt rather than a real loan, and so not subject to mortgage law.[19] In 1660 Chancery declared that 'a poll agreement after conveyance cannot make it a mortgage, if [it were] not so at first,'[20] which recognized this *de facto* and *de jure* difference in mortgage practice. As late as 1668 the scriveners received word that one of their clients was 'willing to mortgage for £1100 provided the mortgage may not take place . . . ,'[21] meaning that he wished to encumber his loan with rents, though not in a formal contract. Since informal lending arrangements were unregistered and had no certain legal validity, the scriveners by that time protected their lenders by urging them to make their loans with proper indentures.

Once the decision was taken to write up these informal agreements into proper mortgage contracts, the parties to the loan with their broker or lawyer had to decide which conveyancing instruments to employ. Of the guides to indentures during the period the greatest encyclopedia was Sir Orlando Bridgeman's *Conveyances: Being Select Precedents of Deeds and Instruments Concerning the Most Considerable Estates in England*, drawn from this Lord Keeper's papers at his death in 1674. Clayton and Morris never consulted this work in their banking operations, as the first volume was published in 1689. But they could hardly have missed in their own legal work the trend which Bridgeman summarized, that is, the merging of all parts of a legal contract into a single conveyance. Forty-one

[16] John Talbot to M., July 14, 1660, Clayton papers, 1660 Jul.–Dec., Osborn, Yale.
[17] K.A.O., MS U214, E.7/40.
[18] 'John Prettyman's Receipt . . . 1666,' Box P, I.U. See a similar agreement for real security in Mervin Touchett's discharge, June 14, 1663, I.U. Box T, and another as late as 1671 in G.L., MS 6428, i, fol. 107v (March 10, 1672).
[19] A. P. Usher, *The Early History of Deposit Banking in Mediterranean Europe*, Harvard Economic Studies, LXXV (Cambridge, Mass., 1943), 136.
[20] *Copleston* v. *Boxwell* (1660); Keck, *Cases*, 1–2.
[21] K.A.O., MS U214, E19/7.

examples of mortgage contracts appear in Bridgeman's work, all examples he found himself to be most reliable in the courts. All the parts of the lending process were integrated in these models into a single document, the transferral of the loan as well as the cession of land.

Reliable and innovative as it may have been among lawyers of the Restoration, the indentures which Clayton and Morris used on behalf of their clients did not fall into the same pattern. As the title implies, Bridgeman's *Conveyances* was designed for the cession of large estates rather than for the mortgaging of selected tenures only, which was the scriveners' specialty. Bridgeman included only one example of the mortgage in fee, while the scriveners generally preferred this form of the mortgage contract to all others. Clayton and Morris's conveyances were in several parts, the entire mortgage contract often running to many pages, the various parts being registered in separate divisions in the Rolls. Before the contracts were sealed, copies of the indentures were sent to both parties for their approval. For example, when Elizabeth Duke perused the draft copy of the assignment of Sir John Evelyn's mortgage to her brother in 1672, she objected that the sum was incorrect and that the document was worded 'as if you intended the same should be mortgaged again . . .'[22] In another instance, in the same year Morris prepared a copy of a deed which Sir Henry Bedingfield required in his loan to Jeffrey Cobb, and at the same time the scrivener asked Sir Henry for a frank appraisal of his debtor's situation. Cobb was careless about signing his indentures, which opened Sir Henry's eyes to more important questions concerning his slovenly finances.[23] It was not unusual that the transactions occurred in two distinct stages. The loan itself – or a bond obligation to that effect – could be signed, often in the country, while some time later, either in the scrivener's quarters or in lawyer's chambers, the deeds ceding the security were signed and sealed.[24]

Traditionally loans were transferred through money bonds, either simple money bonds or conditioned penal bonds. From the sixteenth century the courts had gradually refused to uphold the drastic penalties of the penal bond.[25] In 1663 Anthony Keck remarked in the notebook he kept for

[22] Elizabeth Duke's letter, 1672, Box D, I.U.

[23] Sir Henry Bedingfield to C., July 22, 1672, Clayton MS A.1/2, Buc. R.O.

[24] William Hardy's letter, February 3, 1674, Foster Library, Lincolnshire Archives Committee.

[25] E. Henderson, 'Relief from Bonds in the English Chancery: Mid-Sixteenth Century,' *American Journal of Legal History*, XVIII (1974), 298–306; A. W. B. Simpson, *A History of the Common Law of Contract: The Rise of the Action of Assumpsit* (Oxford, 1975), 118–22.

Clayton that henceforth Chancery would regard a bond on which more was due than penalty for principal and interest to be a worse security than the bond at par. This implied that the punishment of the penal bond must be no more than the interest rate, hence that all profits on the use of money were usury and limited in law.[26] Even after bonds were thrown into jeopardy in the courts, loans through penal bonds still remained, as one of their clients put it, a 'more speedier way' of obtaining loans than the more complex procedures of mortgage credit.[27] Nevertheless, Keck's notes on bonds in Chancery underlined the risk the scriveners took on conveying loans through penal bonds,[28] so that they were just as likely to use simple money bonds to transfer loans. Under this conveyance the borrower was liable for the principal and interest of a loan. If the loan had not been paid off at the end of the contract, the lender would expect no forfeiture. If a simple money bond was not honored, the lender could expect to spend time and money in the courts collecting only the money with interest he had put out on loan.

The harsh, punitive constrictions of bonds were their own guarantee that the loan be repaid on time. Lucy Weldon was so fearful of signing Alderman Holt's penal bond that she asked John Morris in 1672 to act as intermediary in the loan, to cushion the impact of the penalties if she should default.[29] To prevent their clients the trouble of going to court to insure that the loan would be repaid on time, bankers like Clayton and Morris then turned to rent-charges attached to the debt to pay off the loan by the end of the contract. These arrangements constituted the second half of the negotiation, in different contracts altogether. The advantage to the borrower in mortgaging his property rather than leasing it was that his lender ceded him a sum of money once the loan began; whereas in a leasing arrangement, his investment would only accrue gradually as the rents were paid at one date set in the contract, though in practice, through the leasing arrangements of the security, the loan was paid off intermittently as the rents came in. Clayton's lenders were likely to draw upon these repayments before the entire principal and interest had been paid in as impatiently as Sir Thomas Englefield, who could 'wait no longer than the loaf is putting into the oven . . .'[30]

The scriveners used three different sets of leasing arrangements to com-

---

[26] In the case of Crispe et al. v. Blake, in Keck, Cases, 24.
[27] Henry Montague to C., May 4, 1676, Box 9, L.S.E.
[28] Keck, Cases, 72, 77, 78, 94, 106, 184, 189.
[29] Lucy Weldon to M., October 1672, Clayton MS A.1/2, Buc. R.O.
[30] Sir Robert Howard to M., 1671, Clayton MS A.1/2, Buc. R.O.

prise the mortgage counterpart of security, each with a conveyance which placed the lender (at the same time, the lessee) into the possession of the land, as well as another conveyance by which the borrower (at the same time, the lessor) regained his land. The lease of Bargain and Sale with Feoffment was distinguished by two characteristics. It carried a term of one year and it did not have to be registered. If at the end of the year the loan had not been repaid, the scriveners were likely to require that the parties to the contract signed another set of indentures which would then be registered, a Lease and Release, which was scaled upon a 'life' of one to three terms, or what was known as years' purchase. This was the common form of lease in use in various parts of England by about 1670. Then, for a mortgage expected to last a considerable length of time, the indentures of Demise and Redemise for the required years were employed. In all three sets of indentures, however, the life of the lease was unimportant, as Chancery allowed the borrower to regain his land, even if the day written in the lease had expired.[31]

Unlike the gentleman who asked the scriveners for a loan to defray the costs of his election at Grimsby,[32] the scriveners' clients wasted little space in their correspondence justifying their needs for loans, knowing that what they offered as security, and that alone, was likely to attract the scriveners. No single security was necessarily fixed at the beginning of the negotiation. For instance, in 1674 John Neale wrote Morris that he needed about £2,000, and he proposed three different securities for the scriveners' selection. If a simple money bond was unsatisfactory, he would agree to a mortgage. He also suggested a third alternative, a Statute Staple, which was a recognizance or obligation of record.[33] In 1665 Clayton and Morris had loaned Sir Peter Heyman £4,160 on a Statute Staple sworn before Sir Robert Hyde, Lord Chief Justice of the Court of King's Bench, before the recognizance was enrolled,[34] a point of procedure repeated in a parliamentary statute in 1678.[35] As Neale's letter indicates, each debtor who signed a Statute Staple had to agree also to guarantee the loan with some form of real security such as John Neale was willing to offer, namely, his share in a brewing enterprise. As conveyances, a bond supported with leasing covenants and, alternatively, a Statute Staple strengthened with real

[31] See A. A. Dibben, *Title Deeds* (The Historical Association, London, 1971), 11–14.
[32] Dymocke Walpole to M., August 20, 1675, Hill MS 1.A/9, Lincolnshire Archives Committee.
[33] John Neale to M., August 26, 1674, Eng. MS 959, fol. 118, J.R.L.
[34] G.L., MS 5386.
[35] 29 Car. II, c. 3.

security, both appeared to be mortgages, distinguished by their different covenants. There was a difference, implied in a particular advertising two securities, one for £1,500 for six months to be secured either by a Statute Staple or a mortgage, 'as your counsel advise.'[36] In a letter Richard Marriott wrote Morris in 1664 he described the Statute as a short-term device. 'I had rather give you a statute than to trouble you and myself with a mortgage for six months,'[37] he wrote. In a proper mortgage the security was used to repay the loan throughout the contract. With a Statute Staple, it seems, the land was the resort of the lender if the borrower failed to repay his loan, made simpler to collect because the security was in a separate conveyance altogether and not subject to the equity of redemption.

Anthony Keck was careful to describe his notes for Clayton so that the legal decision affecting bonds and leases appeared under those categories – the two parts of Clayton's mortgage contract – apart from another series of Chancery decisions he noted regarding the general nature of mortgages. When the Clayton papers were dispersed in this century, the bond counterparts of the mortgage contracts became separated from their lease indentures with no indication on either conveyance that they formed only a part of a larger contract.[38] As these leases generally lie in archives today,

---

[36]'£1500 for six months . . . ,' Box 3, L.S.E.

[37]Richard Marriott to M., May 16, 1664, Box M, I.U.

[38]When the Clayton papers were rearranged for sale, most of the money bonds were sorted with other money contracts, such as checks, notes and receipts; the largest concentrations of these documents are in L.S.E. and I.U. During the same dispersals the leasing counterparts of money bonds contracts were grouped with estate particulars and other papers concerning land transferrals and were directed toward county and municipal archives. Once the archival integrity of these mortgage contracts was broken, it became extremely difficult to reconstruct individual mortgage contracts (but see L.R.O. MS 35'29, 172–7). First, not all the bonds and leases in the enterprise of this bank have survived, and there is no reason to assume necessarily that for each extant bond there is a corresponding lease in another archive, and vice versa. When each loan was repaid, the borrower reclaimed from the scriveners' possession the original bond and defeazance; copies of the leasing counterparts of the former contract were more likely to remain in the scriveners' archives. (But see the defeazance in Ex. R.O., MS 68.D/DAc 63, and L.R.O., MS 35'29, 173–4). Secondly, where the name of the same estate appears both in a bond and in a lease, there is no guarantee that the indentures are part of the same contract. The bond might refer to a primary loan where the original leasing covenants are now lost, while the leases which do survive might refer to a second mortgage on the same estate for which the later bond is missing. Or the leases might have been assigned as a new security for a previous loan, e.g., L.R.O., MS 35'29, 15. Thirdly, there is no apparent correlation between the size of the loan – set in the bonds generally in even amounts, such as £1,000 or £2,500 – and the annual rents of the leases which were irregular amounts, such as £253 10s. 5d. Fourthly, in unusual circumstances other mortgage conveyances superseded the bond-lease arrangements. In 1664 Clayton and Morris anticipated that if they mortgaged their half of the manor of West Thurrock, Essex, under a bond-lease, they would be sued. Instead, they transferred their interests for two years on security under a declaration of trust (Ex. R.O., MS Acc. 68.D/DAc 260–2). Occasionally the

it is possible to receive the false impression that Clayton was in the business of selling land, much as a modern estate agent deals in property. Even in Clayton's time the same confusion arose over the character of leases in a contract. If the owner passed over all his interest in the property to another person free of any claims of repossession at a future date, this transferral was termed in the law the 'absolute conveyance' of the land. To our modern way of understanding such things, the land would have been sold rather than leased or mortgaged. In the seventeenth century it was possible to attach to an indenture of land ceded by 'absolute conveyance' a proviso that the land be returned to the owner at some future date, that is, to revoke the character of sale made in the first part of the contract.

In 1676 Lord Nottingham addressed himself to the difference between a mortgage contract and an 'absolute conveyance' with a collateral agreement to reconvey, and even though he admitted that the distinction between the two contracts was great, he was unable to resolve the differences in the law. Most frequently, he pointed out, the practical difficulties arose at the death of the mortgagee, when the executor to his estate and his heirs were likely to make conflicting claims.[39] In 1664 Chancery had

---

transfer of capital is referred to in a bond now missing from the land indentures: *ibid.*, 378. The 'Provision of a security for money' of the manor and lordship of Writtle, Essex (*ibid.*, 378) implies that a bond accompanied the loan, though that conveyance is missing from the leases. (See another example in *ibid.*, 85.)

Where archivists preserved the Clayton leases and other estate muniments as a collection, the papers were usually arranged by the estates the scriveners mortgaged. In each file common documents recur, such as release conveyances for the leasing indentures and other deeds and covenants to levy fines. Often notations in the endorsements of the estate particulars clarify the precise nature of the transaction more than the fragmented conveyancing instruments; see, e.g., Northants. R.O., Clayton MS 75; *ibid.*, 109. Receipts issued to Lord Banbury upon the repayment of his loan identify the nature of the transaction in a way the indentures do not (*ibid.*, 99c). The bond indentures from these contracts are missing, but the types of documents associated with the surviving leasing indentures are not those which accompanied simple leasing arrangements. Copies of deeds and other indentures pertaining to the history of the property for many years prior to the beginning of the new contract were included in the transaction. From these documents the scriveners prepared abstracts of title, which indicated which muniments would accompany the cession of estates (see Sir Robert Howard's letter to one Slaughter accompanying an account of the descent of the manor of Chigwell from 1663, Ex. R.O., MS Acc. 68.D/DAc 87. See other examples in *ibid.*, 391–3; L.R.O., MS 35'29, 85–90, 93–4, 115, 118, 120, 125, 129, 130, 143, 152).

Clayton and Morris were bankers specializing in mortgaging estates. When their clients wished to purchase lands by leasehold or freehold, the scriveners might raise the money for these sales through mortgage. But they were not in the practice of selling land apart from a banking context. This character of their business is described in great detail in the correspondence in the Clayton papers, a more reliable index than reconstructing the nature of their financial transactions through conveyances.

[39] *Thornborough* v. *Baker* (1676), in Keck, *Cases*, 286.

declared that unless executors were actual parties to the contract, they had no title to the mortgage money and could not obstruct the heir's attempt to require a mortgagor to put up further security for the loan or to foreclose the contract.[40] As long as the mortgage remained a part of the real estate, that is, if it had the appearance of a leasing arrangement rather than a debt, the executor did not have a clear role to use the property to settle the debts of the deceased mortgagee. Lord Nottingham in 1676 was of the opinion that all mortgages, in form as well as in content, 'ought to be looked upon as part of the personal estate, unless the mortgagor in his own life time or by his last will do otherwise declare and dispose of the same.' Clayton's mortgage contracts avoided the problem of the claims of heirs, since the loan was only mentioned in the bond where the lender obligated his heirs or assignees to pay the debt in the event of his death. If the heir of the deceased borrower wished to repossess the secured lands he might do so, but he was still obliged to pay off by other means the debt in the bond. Clayton's mortgages conformed to the tenet of the Lord Chancellor's advice that the debt be personal and not real. In 1676 this principle was reinforced with the Lord Chancellor's clarification that 'leases are assets to pay debts,'[41] such as personal loans, of which mortgages now seemed to be one category. The fiction that the bond–lease mortgage contracts were not loans and hence not subject to the usury laws, as well as the dilemma which heirs might raise if the loan appeared as real security, perpetuated the bond–lease arrangements in the scriveners' dealings and worked against their combining the two parts of the loan into the single document Bridgeman recommended.

The bond contracts made little trouble for the scriveners. Credit lay in the leasing indentures, when they were subject to claims unknown at the time the loan was made. During the life of the mortgage the lender might buy in older incumbrances on his property.[42] Thus, there could be simultaneous claims upon the security other than the present loan, though to counteract the possibility of conflicting claims, the scriveners insisted that the rights to the fines be formally invested in the mortgages.[43] If there was later any question on the estate as to which tenancies the rent-collector

---

[40] *Freak* v. *Hearsey* (1664), in Keck, *Cases*, 51. See Anthony Keck's opinion in an executory case which he thought might be an exception to this: William Hunt's case (n.d.), MS Eng. Misc. E.372, Bod. Lib.

[41] *Thornborough* v. *Baker* (1676), in Keck, *Cases*, 286.

[42] *Elizabeth March, Richard Chawarth and Henry Malary Executors of Jane Duppa* v. *John Lee Senior and John Lee Junior* (1670), in Keck, *Cases*, 166. See also *ibid.*, 167.

[43] Ferdinando Davys to C., March 30, 1674, Box D, I.U.

controlled, he had a schedule of the fines to assert his jurisdiction. Apparently the fines to the mortgaged leases were not ordinarily written into the court rolls. When Gabriel Bedell was arranging to mortgage the manor of Carbrook, Norfolk, his counsel advised him that if one acre of his original purchase were included in the fines to Clayton, he might forfeit the whole.[44] Where there were unsettled or uncertain claims against the estate, a legal judgment was entered to secure the lender's investment. Thus, when Sir William Ayloffe mortgaged the estate of Great Braxted, Essex, in 1670, the scriveners secured a release written into the mortgage contract that a judgment of 1668 had already been settled.[45] In another instance, in Essex also, the estate of Cressing Temple was mortgaged in 1674 and they required that the judgments which had already been settled be assigned to the mortgagee.[46] Finally, the reversion was confirmed in this process of clearing the title, and if the descent of the property was uncertain, a will was made to direct the succession.[47]

Each of these various stages culminated in an indenture form, insuring that the scribal work was considerable in the process of copying out and then clearing and registering each title. For Sir Edward Smith's loan the scriveners' clerks prepared sixteen separate indentures, for Henry Slingsby, nineteen different conveyances, for Lord Packe, twenty-one scribal transactions and for Lord St John, twenty documents.[48]

When no copy of a conveyance was registered and there was no standard by which the other copies could be evaluated, fraud was possible. For seventeen years the scriveners were involved in one such case, and the experience shaped the procedures of their banking operations. The incident began in 1653 when the royalist squire Sir John Prettyman conveyed in fee part of his estate in Leicestershire to Clement Austen, who then leased the lands back to Prettyman for twenty-one years.[49] By transferring the use Prettyman avoided confiscation of these lands, while at the same time he enjoyed what was in effect a rent upon them. The immediate arrangement was not unusual; the snag lay in the reversion. The remainder

---

[44] James Porter to C., June 23, 1676, Box P, I.U.

[45] Ex. R.O., MS D/DAc(62).

[46] Ex. R.O., MS D/DAc(170).

[47] John Wildman to C., November 24, 1676, Box 5, L.S.E.

[48] 'Note of Writings made for Ld. Packe . . . ,' Box 10, L.S.E.; 'Sir Edward Smith's bill of writings, 1674,' Box 11, ibid.; 'Writings made for Henry Slingsby,' (n.d.), ibid.; 'Bill of writings made for Ld. St. John . . . ' (n.d.), ibid.

[49] The details of the case are summarized in Thomas Dove Esquire, Executor of John Dove Esquire, Defendant, to Mr. John Morris, and Mr. Robert Clayton's Petition of Appeal in Parliament (London, 1670); cf. L.R.O., MS 35'29/11A.

went into a triple succession: to such uses as Clement Austen should appoint for life, thereafter to his wife Anne during her lifetime, and upon her death to Clement's nephews, William and Thomas Austen for their lives. When Clement Austen died in 1657, Anne claimed her estate for life and thereafter married John Dove, to whom Prettyman now paid his rent. In January 1659 Prettyman bought William and Thomas Austen's share of the reversion for £1,200 in the name of Morris as trustee.

To the surprise of everyone concerned, Prettyman then produced another conveyance of the lands, with the same date as the first indenture made in 1653. In the newly found document Clement Austen conveyed the reversion to his two nephews, with no mention of a reversion to Anne. Prettyman refused to pay the Doves their rent. Dove then issued an ejectment against Prettyman, and for the next eleven years the matter went into the courts.

In 1660, when Prettyman got a verdict in his favor, Morris and Clayton sold their interest to Sir Thomas Cullum. But soon after, this judgment was reversed. The two scriveners were now more deeply implicated in the affair. 'If this practice be countenanced,' claimed counsel for the Doves, 'it will be in the power of any person that sells land, by making a new conveyance, and getting the same witnesses (who are often ignorant of the contents of deeds) to limit the estate to any other uses.' When the Lord Keeper decided in favor of the Doves, Clayton and Morris in 1670 appealed to the House of Lords, which refused to overturn the decision of the lower court.[50]

Which conveyance was the true one? Neither indenture had ever been registered. All the witnesses to both conveyances were now dead. There was no way that either conveyance could be certified. Concealed encumbrances, as this case demonstrated, could wreck the operation of a contract even after the loan had been sealed, and the fear that a similar claim would recur led the scriveners to adopt a more rigorous scrutiny to clear titles. In 1671 Clayton stopped all proceedings in one Mr Ashburnham's request for a loan and asked the man to return with interest the money he had been advanced. The scriveners' agent had uncovered in the records of the Court of Wards a settlement made many years before on his property.[51]

In another instance, from a series of letters which John Morris and Dymocke Walpole wrote each other from 1672 to 1678, the mark of the

---

[50]H.M.C. *8th Report*, Appendix, Part I (1881), 142. The scriveners' petition was dismissed by the Lords on November 22, 1670 (*L.J.*, xii, 370).

[51]John Palgrave to C., 1671, G.L., MS 10,049.

Prettyman affair was imprinted again in the scriveners' dealings. Walpole was acting for his cousin Charles Dymocke who wished to raise a mortgage to purchase an estate at Calkewell, Lincs., from John South. When Walpole came to London to search out the possibilities for the loan, Morris set two conditions. First, he wished to know the state of Lady South's jointure,[52] which, as it turned out, was an estate for life. Secondly, he wished to see the deed of mortgage which South's parents had signed in 1648. This deed was never found, and upon its absence the negotiations floundered. In the list of writings which Lady South gave Walpole this deed was not included. The guardian for Mr South's heir had sworn in Chancery that he had seen the missing deed, and that it had freed South's children from the obligations set in his contract. After much searching in the Chancery records Walpole found that the deed had been used as evidence in a case, dismissed in 1653 in the name of Clifton *et al.*, though he could find no other evidence of the missing conveyance.[53] In June 1673, six months after Walpole had first approached Morris, another lien was discovered on South's estate. Four months later Morris sent Charles Dymocke an abstract of title of South's estate, together with copies of all these conveyances as transcribed by clerks. He was afraid that this list did not include all the writings in connection with the property, and South then promised to search his own muniments.[54] There the matter rested for another four years.[55]

As long as the system of registering conveyances remained flawed, there was no way the scriveners could be absolutely certain all the claims against the estate had been settled, though once they established the practice of requiring that all the writings pertaining to the contract be placed with them during the life of the loan, the courts might find it plausible that stray conveyances later used as claims against the estate had been concealed for devious purposes. Nevertheless, a mortgagee was free to mortgage the same lands again, even if he gave no notice to his new lender that there was an intervening settlement. The junior (puisne) mortgage held against the older debt until both loans were satisfied.[56] If prior claims against the

---

[52]Keck's notes included changes in equity regarding jointures: see *Cases*, 272.

[53]Dymocke Walpole to John Morris, December 16, 1672, Hill MS 30.1A/2, Lincolnshire Archives Committee.

[54]Same to same, September 1673, Hill MS 30.1A/7, *ibid.*

[55]When Walpole attempted to renegotiate the matter with a brief particular of South's estate which he sent Morris. Same to same, April 26, 1678, Hill MS 30 1.A/16, *ibid.*

[56]*Goddard* v. *Complin* (1669), in Keck, *Cases*, 119, and *Sir Ralph Bovey* v. *Skipwith*, 23 Car. II (1671), *ibid.*, 201–2.

estate arose, the scriveners had, usually, ample leases from the borrower to insure their loan.

Attaching additional leases on to the original loan was a frequent method of increasing the principal or meeting loan payments in an emergency. For example, in 1666 the Earl of Banbury increased his loan of £6,000 by another £500 by adding additional leases to the original contract. When that loan expired in 1687, he borrowed another £3,100, over and above the original £6,000, by charging his estates again as security for repayment.[57] Similarly, when Thomas Stonor failed to meet his interest payments, he directed that additional rent charges he assigned to cover the amount due.[58] In another example, as soon as the entail on a portion of his inheritance had been docked, Sir Gabriel Lowe increased his mortgage with the scriveners by having the leases on this property attached to his original contract.[59] Likewise, when Luke Christie found he could not meet his interest payments, he proposed to sign over half of additional property worth between £1,000 and £2,000 per year upon a declaration of trust until this crisis had passed.[60]

The original loan was charged to specific rents surveyed and assessed during the negotiations. When the number of leases was finally trimmed to meet the principal, the records of neighboring properties not included in the loan were set aside in the scriveners' archives. It was these properties which were attached to the primary loan to make up an amended contract. Ordinarily these additional properties were not advertised in the lending market. As Gabriel Lowe saw his options in 1672:

I was in a fair way to have paid in the principal at that time by granting estates for life and by selling a smaller spot that I put to sale, but the uncertainty of the Dutch war has put all that to a stand at present.

He then asked for an extension on his mortgage.[61] Extension, or to use the contemporary word, 'continuance,'[62] was the alternative to attaching additional leases to the parental contract, though this option was dependent upon a willing mortgagee. Henry Rayson refused Sir William

[57] Northants. R.O., Clayton MS 9A–D.
[58] Thomas Stonor to M., July 7, 1671, Box 5, I.U.
[59] Christopher Cratford to M., August 21, 1671, Box 4, L.S.E.
[60] Thomas Christie to William Morris, March 13, 1672, Box 3, L.S.E. In another example George Pitt requested that in his mortgage of £1,000 a proviso be added that he might pay it in with a year's warning (George Pitt to M., September 10, 1673, Box P, I.U.).
[61] Gabriel Lowe to M., June 20, 1672, Box L, I.U.
[62] 'Forbearance' was the older word, then passing out of use. It was a sum paid to appease the lender to forbear putting into effect the punitive effects of the penal bond. See Robert Leigh's receipt for forbearance, June 28, 1659, Box L, I.U.

Hartopp's request for more time, as creditors of Rayson's father were pressing him for payment.[63] But all other things being equal, Clayton and Morris were usually sympathetic to lengthening the lives of loans.[64] Adding leases involved legal fees for the necessary conveyancing. The scriveners also had fees for extensions, reasonable compared with those in other lending markets. John Vernon cited extension rates in general use ranging from two per cent through five per cent per annum.[65] The scriveners' rates were one per cent per annum of the outstanding principal, over and above all other interest charges due on the loan.[66]

Alternative arrangements were simpler to compose if the two parts of the loan were kept separate, as, for example, when loans were assigned from one party to another. In 1664 Thomas Walpole wrote Morris for a loan of £100, to be secured by assigning a bond for £100 from a debtor. His lender would write a new bond to Morris, while Walpole would retain his 'counter bond' (defeazance), to be canceled when the contract expired.[67] In another example, Lady Ann Fanshawe in 1675 proposed to Morris that he lent her £2,500, whereupon she would transfer to him the mortgage she held on Sir William Ayloffe's estate.[68] Loans were assigned through bonds, but the property secured could remain in the hands of the first mortgagee if a warrant was signed to direct the rents into the hands of Clayton and Morris.

In these negotiations the scriveners assumed various functions, at times loan-broking, in other instances conveyancing, and otherwise, and most desirably, controlling the entire process. Since no loans were made in the name of the bank, the parties to the loan could control all stages of the negotiation, as well as the operation of the contract. At the same time, Clayton and Morris guarded their interests as brokers to the negotiation, though their only legal rights in these matters were brokerage fees.

Generally their clients seem to have respected the degree of effort the scriveners put into each negotiation. In 1673 Lord Belasyse wrote Clayton

[63] Henry Rayson to Sir William Hartopp, September 5, 1676, Box R, I.U.; see also Hugh Lawton to C. & M., December 23, 1664, Box L, I.U.

[64] Thomas Knyveton to C., March 15, 1665, Box B, I.U.; Gabriel Lowe to M., September 1, 1673, Box L, ibid.; same to C., February 13, 1675, ibid.; Benjamin Portlock to C., July 3, 1678, Box P, ibid.

[65] The Compleat Comptinghouse (London, 1678), 128–9.

[66] Cf. G.M.R., MS 84/1/3, fol. 96v (September 4, 1662); ibid., fol. 98v (February 12, 1663); G.L., MS 6428, i, fol. 111v (July 22, 1671); fol. 114v (February 13, 1672); fol. 113v (March 6, 1672).

[67] Thomas Walpole to M., December 10, 1664, Clayton MS A.1/1, Buc. R.O.

[68] Lady Ann Fanshawe to M., April 19, 1675, Clayton MS A.1/3, Buc. R.O.

about a friend who wished to lend £3,000 or £4,000 upon a good security of land, and as he saw it, he had two choices. If he knew his mortgagor very well – and he might just as well find his debtor as the scriveners – then he would use Clayton and Morris to act as conveyancers in the operation. On the other hand, if they offered him a particularly strong security, he would be thrown upon the special skills in land valuation which the scriveners had to offer and which raised their status above the ordinary role of conveyancer and broker.[69] In another instance, Lord William Cavendish did not recognize that he had incurred any obligation to the scriveners' expertise. In 1676 he threatened to give their own evaluation of one of his estates to another moneylender if they refused his demands.[70]

Once the papers to the negotiation were in the scriveners' hands, they asked the parties to the loan to submit their terms to the contract in writing. This was an informal statement from which proper conveyances were later drawn. Upon Clayton's direction Sir Francis Vincent in 1676 instructed his agent Samuel Wall to submit his brief for the loan he had requested. Clayton was asked to alter these proposals as he saw fit and return the amended letter to Wall, who would discuss the changes with Sir Francis.[71] Only then would this stage of bargaining end with the preparation of formal conveyances.

Occasionally the scriveners found at some stage in the negotiation that a client would ask his own lawyer to intercede in the drafting of the document, thereby challenging their own role as conveyancers. William Lee, to cite an example, wrote to Morris in 1673 that his lawyer Mr Thomas of the Temple would inspect a cache of writings in the scriveners' possession, with the prospect that he would draw up another set of covenants different from the scriveners' proposals.[72]

This stage in the brokerage process they did not relinquish willingly. Control of their clients' writings and their own extensive knowledge of conveyancing indentures was a powerful tool, as their interest in Sir Charles Wolseley's affairs proved. Sir Charles had been a client for some years when in 1675 he wrote them that his loan to Lord Aston would be due in a year. At that time he wished for them to find another borrower for

---

[69] Lord Belasyse to C., 1673, Clayton MS 8, Fairfax Collection.

[70] Lord William Cavendish's letter, February 23, 1676, Clayton MSS, Cardiff Public Library.

[71] Samuel Wall to C., June 16, 1676, Box W, I.U.

[72] William Lee to M., June 1673, Box L, I.U. See also W. Montague to M. & C., July 16, 1672, Box 9, L.S.E.; Christopher Cratford to Peter Clayton or Anthony Keck, May 30, 1678, Box L, L.S.E.

the money. 'I mean to be wholly ruled by your advice,' he wrote.[73] But by the following November his son Robert Wolseley had begun to take his father's financial affairs in hand. He had found another borrower himself, and he instructed the scriveners to make drafts of all the writings which he would collect with several of the indentures themselves.[74] In 1676, Wolseley wrote Clayton an indignant letter. The scriveners' clerks had given him a draft copy of a declaration of trust, which had been neither signed nor sealed. 'I dare not let my father know the truth of this matter until I have heard from you, and if I had not persons of known honour and worth to deal with, I dare never see him again after a carelessness that might be of such ill consequence to him . . . '[75] Peter Clayton denied the charge of trickery and wrote Wolseley that the original copy of the declaration was in the trunk of writings he had left in the Old Jewry.[76] The embarrassing fact was that the young man had only just realized his mistake, as his knowledge of legal documents was limited.

No clear line separated the role of the broker from his clients. The scriveners attempted to control the process of presenting to the lender the borrower of their own choosing. This they did by forbidding their clients to grant their own loans by writing checks for the contract and by requiring the lender to put up his writings as soon as the negotiation for the loan had opened.[77] But the lender also could search for his debtor at the same time as the scriveners. If he found his own debtor, the money was likely to be put out at interest sooner than if he waited for the scriveners to find a suitable borrower. In 1671 a Mr Heneage wrote Peter Clayton that his wool dealer wished to mortgage certain properties he had turned over to the scriveners to sell for security. Heneage then directed Clayton to conclude the deal with the man within the fortnight.[78]

After the loan was signed, mortgagor and mortgagee might correspond with each other until the debt was settled. Sir William Ayloffe wrote several angry letters to his delinquent borrower Henry Neville, who then asked Morris to tell the man that he would soon be paid.[79] The scriveners took two precautions to insure that the parties to a loan did not pay off the contract behind their backs. According to a phrase written into the bargain

---

[73] Sir Charles Wolseley to C., September 4, 1675, MS Eng. Lett. c.12, fol. 19, Bod. Lib.
[74] Same to same, November 20, 1675, ibid., fol. 23.
[75] Robert Wolseley to M. [1676], ibid., fol. 33.
[76] Same to C., November 18, 1676, ibid., fol. 35.
[77] See above, pp. 109, 117–19.
[78] Mr Heneage to Peter Clayton, Clayton MS A.1/2, Buc. R.O. See also Lord St John to C., December 1669, Box S, I.U.
[79] Henry Neville to M., January 3, 1675, Clayton MS A.1/3, Buc. R.O.

and registered in the Rolls, the loan was to be terminated at the scriveners' quarters and nowhere else. More important, the scriveners retained the defeazance which they handed over to the borrower when the final payment of the loan was settled. Only when he had this document in his own hands could he be absolutely certain that the punitive measures in the bond would not go into effect against him. To cite an example of this uncertain brokerage relationship, Sir Henry Hudson in 1676 found that he could not maintain the interest on his loan from Richard Pell, whereupon he wrote directly to his lender, offering to substitute a lease to honor his debt. Pell consented to these conditions, as well as to collect himself the rents due on the lease. Only at this stage were the scriveners notified of the arrangement, though Pell agreed to deposit the money with the scriveners until the loan was fulfilled according to the contract.[80]

On the other hand, it was possible for either party to reassign the loan through another broker if he found a better security. When Sir Robert Vyner's business faltered during the Exchequer crisis in 1672, his client Sir Thomas Foot transferred all the loans Vyner had negotiated on his behalf to the firm of Clayton and Morris.[81] The scriveners loaned his deposit in mortgages, but upon a query from Foot, the scriveners then reinvested his money in other collateral securities in Hertfordshire or places just as good.[82]

The scriveners often had some idea of what latitude would be theirs, even before the loan was negotiated. In 1676 Sir Patience Ward returned £600 to Clayton with the instructions that if an opportunity should arise of investing £500 of the deposit in a safe security, he was to take it, with complete freedom in the contract, using that letter as his authorization for the loan.[83] On the other hand, Richard Biddulph placed a note for £1,000 with Morris to be paid in four months toward a loan, though he withdrew the note after three months for a better investment elsewhere.[84] In another example, Morris promised to find a safe security for Daniel Moore's £300 on new buildings in the City. This investment proved to be unfeasible. To retain his deposit Morris promised him interest, and when the man demanded a better investment, Morris told him that he could not dispose of such a small sum on land.[85]

---

[80]Richard Pell to M., February 5, 1676, Box 10, L.S.E.
[81]Sir Thomas Foot to M., September 17, 1673, MS Eng. Lett. c. 201, Bod. Lib., fol. 34.
[82]Same to same, April 6, 1674, *ibid.*, fol. 47.
[83]Sir Patience Ward to C., 1676, Box W, I.U.
[84]Richard Biddulph to M., n.d., Box B, *ibid.*
[85]Daniel Moore to M., August 5, 1675, Box 9, L.S.E.

All loans between parties had to come in on deposit before the contract was concluded and the money was released to the debtor. The scriveners rarely seem to have consented to act merely as conveyancers, where they prepared the documents for the loan and then appeared at the transaction where the lender handed over the capital to his debtor.

On the other hand, Clayton was asked in 1673 to arbitrate in a heated dispute concerning a loan negotiation between James Hoste and Sir Samuel Barnardiston.[86] To insure that at some stage in the negotiation the lender did not withdraw his capital from their hands and then renegotiate the contract elsewhere, Clayton and Morris tried to preserve the anonymity of the parties as long as possible. If, however, all parties to the contract presented themselves, with their own conditions, the scriveners' role was circumscribed from the beginning of the process. For example, in 1671 Philip Styles wrote Clayton that if Sir Thomas Foot was willing to sell Captain Plant's land which was mortgaged to him, he had a client who would purchase the property. Clayton would negotiate an assignment of the mortgage and then prepare the articles for the purchase, if not also find the money for Styles's client to conclude the purchase.[87] In another instance, Edward Story wrote Morris in 1674 a letter introducing his kinsman who wished to mortgage a small reversion. If the scriveners could meet his needs, Story would stand surety for the title.[88]

Pawnbroking arose occasionally during the process of these negotiations. From 1660 until 1663 they loaned £535 on pawns. In the next ledger which has survived, covering the years 1669 until 1672, they made pawn loans amounting to £1,300. After that date no separate category was made for pawns, and there is no evidence that the scriveners allowed the same security registered under another category. In 1675 John Cressett asked Morris for a loan to bind his son as an apprentice. For security he proposed to sign a bond as well as a bill of sale to the scriveners of all his collection of pictures hanging in the Guildhall gallery.[89] A conditioned bill of sale, to take effect if the loan were unpaid, may have replaced pawns in the scriveners' affairs. Pawning valuables was often a desperate measure. In 1670 one of Clayton's clients was said to be 'so high nothing could scare him but . . . his money on the pictures,' which it was hoped Sir Robert Vyner would purchase.[90] For the pawnbrokers there was the prob-

---

[86]Peter Vandeput to C., July 7, 1673, Box V, I.U.
[87]Philip Styles to C., October 12, 1672, Box S, I.U.
[88]Edward Story to M., May 21, 1674, *ibid.*
[89]John Cressett to M., August 1, 1675, U.L. MS 553/7.
[90]Eng. MS 906, fol. 8, J.R.L.

lem of whether or not the goods presented to them for security had been stolen. Someone in the scriveners' shop in about 1661 drew up a list of the legislation by parliament and the Corporation of London to control pawn-brokers and their goods,[91] and in 1677 Clayton had a copy made from the records of the Court of Aldermen of a petition to parliament for another act regulating the brokers.[92] For moneylenders such as Clayton and Morris the problem of the claims of heirs to real security was by no means resolved by taking pawns. In Michaelmas Term 1679 Chancery declared that if a person who had pawned his goods should die, his title to the goods should pass to his estate, thus complicating his pawnbroker's claims to the security.[93] The sums of the loans accounted for with pawns were relatively insignificant. In 1671 Sir Robert Howard wrote Morris that Sir Thomas Englefield was pressing him for his rents on his mortgage and wished to pawn a jewel to tide him through this crisis. The gem was worth £300, he claimed, but upon possession the scriveners loaned him 150 guineas for six months.[94] Pawns were taken for other clients for the same reasons. Pawn-broking should be regarded as an adjunct to the large-scale loans of the scriveners' banking, rather than a separate side of their business.

Part of the same diversity was the custom of multiple securities to the same loan. In 1662 the scriveners loaned Sir John Prettyman £1,860, secured with rents in both Kent and Lincolnshire.[95] Likewise, from 1678 to 1680 Clayton and Morris assumed a part of Sir Robert Vyner's debts with a loan of £6,259 held with lands in Lincolnshire, his share of the Post Fines, stock in the Gambia company and other smaller securities.[96] In another example George Pitt asked Morris in 1673 for a loan of £10,000. Rather than make up one transaction for that amount he wanted the sum separated into ten different mortgages, so that he would have the liberty to pay each loan with a year's notice to each lender, while the scriveners would have the like privilege to recall each loan with a year's warning.[97] In the same year the scriveners loaned Sir Robert Howard £5,880 by refinancing an old mortgage on his estate of Wootton Bassett and by reassigning another debt contracted in 1668.[98]

[91]G.L., MS 5386.

[92]*Ibid.*

[93][William Brown,] *The Clerks Tutor in Chancery* . . . (1694), xxvi–xxvii.

[94]Sir Robert Howard to M., 1671, Clayton MS 1.A/2, Buc. R.O.

[95]G.M.R., MS 84/1/2, fol. 93v.

[96]'Account of Sir Robert Vyner 1678–80,' Sir Robert Vyner's Original Papers 1657–84, Fairfax Collection.

[97]George Pitt to M., September 10, 1673, Box P, I.U.

[98]G.L., MS 6428, ii, fol. 106v.

When the Stop of the Exchequer was announced, John Pennington wrote Morris that he was worried that his deposit with the scriveners would be arrested, as had been the case of the goldsmiths' clients.[99] In the Exchequer records of the crisis, the Audit for Tallies 1674–8 and the Goldsmiths' Accounts 1674–6, there was no reference to Clayton or Morris, for they had never placed their reserves in the hands of the government.[100] Moreover, the scriveners seem never to have accepted Exchequer receipts as security. Early in 1672 Richard Marriott wrote Clayton that the king's order to stop payments from the Exchequer had deprived him of £1,000 due upon a loan. He needed to borrow £600, and as security, he proposed his Exchequer receipt for his money, though he expected Clayton would not accept it.[101] Then, in 1678 William Gulston turned over one of the scriveners' client's tallies for £417 5s. 6d. to a friend who promised to find its worth. No information was forthcoming, and when the client pressed for payment, Gulston recommended that the receipt be discounted in the range of twelve to fourteen per cent, though this was merely a guess at its value. 'It's a hazardous thing,' he wrote, 'and I had rather let it alone . . . ,' which could as well describe the scriveners' attitude toward tally receipts accepted for deposits in their bank.[102]

Few forgot that the loan was a contract between gentlemen and that brokers were their servants. The requirement that oral pledges be written, the sealing of loans with formal indentures, and the entrepreneurialism which brought debtors to lenders unknown to each other previously introduced a distance between the parties in which honor and trust could be forgotten. Thomas Keyt complained to Morris and Clayton in 1674 of the impersonal forces that governed his loan. His attorney in Warwick had signed the papers for his mortgage, but no one had ever told him whose money he had loaned. His rents repaid the debt, which he would rather have cleared himself by his own hands. When his payment arrived late and he was threatened with a penalty, he complained he was being treated as an 'outlaw.' 'I take this to be uncivil,' he complained,[103] and the scriveners could well believe that a delicate balance between efficiency and respect

[99] John Pennington to M., *c.* 1672, Box P, I.U.

[100] P.R.O., E.403/2510; E.407/33; E.407/34.

[101] Richard Marriott to C., January 17, 1672, Box M, I.U.

[102] William Gulston to Peter Clayton, 1678, Box 7, L.S.E. On the other hand in 1674 Henry Avery loaned Sir Thomas Chicheley £3,000 on an Exchequer tally (G.L., MS 6428, ii, fols. 110v–113v). This was a client's decision about his own money rather than policy concerning loans in their own names.

[103] Thomas Keyt to M. & C., February 22, 1674, Box K, I.U.

had to be maintained with their clients, who for reasons other than finance might withdraw their business.

The role of the broker and the role of the moneylender were distinct, but the profits which accrued to the scriveners from their negotiations came from several sources that are not easily separated and are at times difficult to summarize. James Buck wrote the scriveners in 1671 on behalf of a Mr Clarke who wished to clarify the state of his loan. He had recently received £30 which he understood to be a part of the principal, but according to his calculations he was still due £60 for a year's interest, as well as the remainder of the principal.[104] Ordinarily no distinction was made between the principal, interest and other fees until all the parts of the loan had been paid in. Keck recorded a case in 1663 in which a mortgage had been assigned, though none of the three parties could agree what part of the loan already paid constituted principal and interest. The judge in the case decided that the money paid to the mortgagee should be considered for the moment to be principal paid by the assignee, and then he turned the matter over to the Master to examine the accounts.[105] That such a problem could come before Chancery for settlement is not surprising. It may be that the banking statements which the scriveners occasionally issued were made in part to separate principal and interest in order to prevent the matter coming to legal conclusions.[106]

There was a difference between the service of procuring the capital for a loan and the act of negotiating the transaction, both of which were within the realm of the broker. Brokerage fees regulated in the Usury Acts did not address themselves to these separate functions. In simple procuration a broker obtains capital from some source and then makes it available to the parties to the transaction. In the more general act of brokerage the loan procurer also arranges all the preliminary stages until the loan is passed from lender to debtor. He ascertains the security, which may involve considerable time and expense, especially in mortgage transactions. He decides upon the proper conveyances. If the broker does not consult a lawyer, he draws upon his own skills and experience, for which he is due compensation. He or his clerks then prepare the conveyances, which are passed to the parties for their approval and emendation. He arranges a time for the parties to sign the covenants, either in his shop or in lawyers' chambers. Once the papers have been signed and the money

[104] James Buck to C. & M., September 7, 1671, Box B, *ibid.*
[105] *Smith v. Pemberton* (1665), in Keck, *Cases*, 67–8.
[106] See above, pp. 115–17.

transferred, he or his clerks then take the indentures to be registered. Even then the broker's function might continue if the parties to the loan agree that he should be their intermediary until the debt is settled. According to Lord Nottingham's notes, neither mortgagees nor trustees were allowed by the law to take any consideration for their services,[107] yet loan-brokers might perform both these functions and at the same time be conveyancer, lawyer and scribe, if not surveyor and rent-collector. To this extent brokerage describes the entire scope of the moneylending role of the banker when lending out his clients' deposits at interest.

In 1660 the scriveners received a request for a loan from the landlord of Westhouse, near Billericay, who wrote down his own brokerage terms – £20 if the loan was £500, but £15 if the sum was only £300.[108] These were clearly procuration rates, set apart from any other fees the scriveners might charge. In the early years of their partnership Clayton and Morris assessed fees for obtaining capital at rates ranging from 0.5 per cent through five per cent. Who had been the active agent in procuring the loan and was due the fee, the lender by depositing his money with the scriveners or the scriveners who had solicited the lender's deposit? To avoid any conflict of interest over the ambiguous obligations of procuration, that word gradually disappeared from their ledgers and their clients' correspondence. In the loan which the scriveners were arranging for Henry Allnutt in 1671 he mentioned that he was willing to pay them for their efforts 'a gratuity to your satisfaction.'[109] In another example, in the following year, Richard Cowper wrote Clayton that if he found a mortgage for his estate, he would 'be grateful to you to the value of £400 in what specie you please to accept.'[110] Likewise, Henry Neville wrote Morris that when his loan was sealed, he would 'be able to give you a gratuity answerable to the civilities you have been pleased to show me.'[111] According to Richard Dafforne, the common accounting practice was to register gratuities in a special ledger for that purpose, then to transfer those fees to the ledgers to balance losses.[112]

No distinction appeared consistently in the ledgers between procuration and brokerage fees, nor did the scriveners register gratuities in a separate

---

[107] *Lord Nottingham's Chancery Cases*, ed. D. E. C. Yale, Vol. II, Publications of the Selden Society, LXXIX (1961), 55.
[108] Ex. R.O., MS D/DAc (23).
[109] Henry Allnutt to M., June 28, 1671, Box A, I.U.
[110] Richard Cowper to C., November 25, 1672, Box 4, L.S.E.
[111] Henry Neville to M., January 1675, Clayton MS A.1/3, Buc. R.O.
[112] *Apprentices Time-Entertainer*, 3rd edn (London, 1670), 41–2.

category. In no instance did the scriveners list a rate at which these payments were determined, and they seem not to have figured their brokerage
fees in terms of rates at all, but rather to have charged flat fees, varying
with each transaction. From a random sampling in the ledgers of brokerage fees written against the amount of the loan, the percentage rates range
from a minimum charge of 0.5 per cent to a maximum charge of six per
cent, keeping in mind that these were not calculations which the scriveners
made themselves. Moreover, several of these rates work out at odd
amounts – 1.08 per cent, 1.25 per cent, 1.66 per cent and 1.75 per cent –
and it is unlikely that Clayton or Morris ever demanded from their clients
fees with such uneven rates in mind.

The Usury Acts made a distinction between the fees a broker charged for
his services and the profit which accrued to the lender on the use of his
money. Once the loan began and the broker continued to perform services
with the operation of the loan, he claimed compensation for his pains. To
this extent brokerage assumed another dimension, closer to services on the
use of money – interest – than fees due on the obtaining of capital. When
the conditioned penal bond was the chief specialty of the scrivener-
brokers, their services ceased from the time the loan was negotiated until
the day the principal and interest were paid off. Once the technicalities of
mortgage finance made the broker a different sort of intermediary who
managed the loan during its life, his charges could not be accounted for
under the existing legislation. Garrett Moore complained that the legal
fees on his loan amounted to twice what a lawyer's fees would have been
had he pursued the case at trial.[113] The knowledge that Clayton and
Morris concealed charges under labels that do not bear a close affinity with
the services rendered and that they overcharged for some services because
there was not a proper category to list them under in their ledgers does not
mean that we must accuse them of behavior contrary to their labor.

There are significant distinctions between brokerage, procuration and
gratuity fees in the operations of this bank. When these labels appeared
insufficient for the services the scriveners had rendered with the operation
of the loan, their fees were then charged and listed as 'contingency' fees, the
greatest category of service fees they collected. Usually the scriveners
recorded these charges in their journals with no other explanation, or
merely with the scales at which the fees were figured. In 1663 they
mentioned a fee due for the charge on returning money from the country

---

[113] Garrett Moore to Thomas Leman & C., June 27, 1675, Box 9, L.S.E.

to London.[114] Contingency fees cover the realm of the rent-collector and the bailiffs who managed mortgaged estates on behalf of their clients. Each expense was itemized in the clients' accounts and then transferred under the general heading 'contingency' in the scriveners' credits. With the exception of Garrett Moore's letter, there is no other suggestion in their clients' correspondence that these charges were assessed out of proportion to the services rendered. Only in two accounting periods, 1658 through 1660 and 1673 through 1675, did the scriveners make a distinction between brokerage fees and contingency fees. In all other periods they assessed either brokerage or contingency fees but not both. The tendency was for a single label which would include the entire range of their professional activities.

During the first two years of their partnership, 1658 to 1660, they recorded a total of £1,505 in interest fees, while during the same period they collected £2,592 in those irregular collections written in their ledgers as contingency fees. Because these incidental credits are greater than their profits on the use of money, one first suspects that this label is a disguise for concealed charges, tantamount to hidden interest fees. Contingency costs (debits) reappeared in the ledgers only during the accounting period 1675 through 1677. Other costs paid out as a consequence of managing loans appear under the label 'miscellaneous' and are distinct from the expenses of operating the household–shop, as well as legal and notarial fees, which are listed separately.

In 1680 these two categories of miscellaneous operating expenses appeared for the last time in their ledgers. In the final journal which has survived, covering the years 1682 through 1685, only one category appeared for their contingency costs, as a corollary to the single category covering the range of their service fees. Between 1682 and 1685 the totals balanced each other almost exactly: £5,748 was taken in as contingency credits in managing their loans, while simultaneously they paid out £5,749 as a consequence of managing their loans.

The label 'contingency' in their ledgers was not a false category to disguise hidden interest charges, and there is no other category in their ledgers which could have concealed similar illegal profits. Just as there were opportunities to realize profits unforeseen at the time the loan was negotiated, so also there were irregular, incidental expenses in connection with the loan that had to be paid from some source during the life of the loan. Except for the last accounting period, these profits and charges do

[114]G.M.R., MS 84/1/3, fol. 99r (March 31, 1663).

not balance each other. Between 1669 and 1673 they paid out the large sum of £11,424 in costs, while in the same period they registered no contingency credits. In the following period, 1672 through 1675, they took in £11,387 in profits – a comparable sum to the preceding debits, though, again, they had to pay out in the same period more than half of what they had taken in in costs. But over the entire range of periods that can be accounted for between 1658 and 1685 (the ledgers from 1664 to 1669 and 1681 to 1682 are missing), the scriveners lost in the balance £5,906.

Each of the scriveners' debtors was free to inspect these ledgers and to query each contingency profit and loss assigned to his accounts. The debtors were unlikely to approve any expense which had been assigned in a dubious way, for example, in a manner which implied that the debit had never actually left the scriveners' bank. At the same time, Clayton and Morris were unlikely to register in their books profits which could not be justified to the authorities suspecting that they had only to open these ledgers to find an array of illegal charges easily detectable. Their elaborate mortgage operations brought managerial expenses which the laws had not foreseen, and it also brought profit opportunities unknown to the men who had framed the usury laws.

When the king stopped payments out of the Exchequer in 1671, he did so realizing that the bankers most likely to complain could be silenced with his threat to apply the usury laws against them. Soon they were pardoned, but in such a threatening atmosphere even figures like Sir John Banks, who was not a banker, was compelled to seek a royal pardon for his own moneylending activities.[115] In January 1672 Clayton and Morris preempted the possibility that they would be charged with usury by requesting a royal pardon, 'though not conscious of any ground of offence,' their plea read. A warrant for the royal pardon was written the same day as their request.[116] Whether they felt themselves vulnerable to the charge because of the way their service fees were figured in relationship to the loan, or whether they felt that the charge could be substantiated on the question of the use of money by itself, is unclear. Thomas Doleman accused Clayton of taking £2,500 out of a loan of £15,200, a charge which the scriveners did not completely deny.[117] If the sum was interest, their rate had been 16.4 per cent, but it was difficult to prove in this case and others where the line was drawn at which service fees ended and interest on the use of money began.

[115]D. C. Coleman, *Sir John Banks, Baronet and Businessman* (New York, 1963), 67.
[116]*C.S.P. Dom., 1671–72* (London, 1897), 98.
[117]Eng. MS 959, fol. 30 (n.d.), J.R.L.

Usury is a legal and moral concept applied to charges on the use of money once the loan has begun. Before the contracts were signed, Clayton and Morris would deliberately undervalue the property to be mortgaged.[118] The discrepancy between the appraised value and the actual income, minus costs, from the loan was a source of their contingent profits. When there were no charges against these credits, the scriveners were free to use the money for their own purposes, mainly for loans put out in their own names, in a way difficult to challenge. Their clients were entitled only to the interest set in the contract and had no claim against any other profit which the loan brought. These charges could be defended with the argument that contingent debits were likely to consume these credits. No one outside the bank had any way of knowing that before one charge was made upon another the credit had been put out to loan, as this would only have been recorded in the secret journals.

Manipulating their clients' deposits for their own lending capital came under the same rubric, that as long as the money was exploited outside the definitions of a formal contract, no abrogation had been made upon the use of money defined in the usury laws. At the opposite end of the process − the termination of the loan − the scriveners and their clients realized another type of profit when the loan was extended. Extensions were registered in their ledgers as 'continuance,' in theory the fee paid upon that part of the loan unpaid at the termination date set in the contract. There is one documented instance of how the continuance process worked. In 1671 Gabriel Lowe borrowed £1,000 from the scriveners for one year. Apparently it was agreed at the time the loan was sealed that the repayment of the loan would be delayed beyond the date set in the contract, for after eighteen months Lowe sent Morris his continuance fee, with a note reminding the scriveners that it was the first money due on the account.[119] Sir Robert Clayton wrote the man in the last part of 1674, asking for another payment for continuance, but saying that at that time he did not need to recall the money, even though the payment of the principal was due soon, on March 1, 1675. At that time both parties agreed that the time for repayment of the principal would be postponed again, with Lowe continuing to pay fees until Morris had need to recall the money.[120]

The scriveners' policy of giving to the lender the opportunity to extend his investment obviated the long period between the paying off of one loan

---

[118] See below, pp. 173–4.
[119] Gabriel Lowe to William Mouris [sic], September 1, 1673, Box L, I.U.
[120] Same to C., February 13, 1675, Box L, I.U.

and the reinvestment of capital in another. Men like Sir Charles Wolseley, whose livelihood depended upon the interest derived from their loans, wanted no interruption between the loans the scriveners arranged for them.[121] Their clients must weigh up two considerations of this practice, which in effect was the making of two loans. First, even though they must pay one per cent per annum of the unpaid principal for the privilege of continuance, they forewent the legal charges and brokerage costs of two separate loans with all the proper contracts, assessments and registrations. Secondly, upon these conditions they might have their loans sooner than if they were to wait for other terms. Extensions strengthened the term of mortgages beyond the life of the leasing arrangements to enrich its definition as a long-term security.

Continuance fees were clearly usury when new interest was charged upon outstanding loans already bearing interest at the maximum rate. After 1675 the scriveners registered no extension fees as continuance in their ledgers, but the practice persisted, for in 1678 their agent Portlock mentioned the moderate terms of continuance which Clayton and Morris gave.[122] Over the thirteen years documented in the ledgers which survive from 1658 through 1675 Clayton and Morris realized a total of £14,963 in continuance fees charged on loans put out in their own names, thirty-eight per cent of the amount they accumulated over the same period as interest fees.

The character of the mortgage was a longer-term loan than the penal bond. It was also larger-scaled, though the evidence in the Clayton papers does not permit precise knowledge of how long or how great were the mortgages which the scriveners granted. No clear distinction appears in the ledgers between loans granted upon mortgage and loans unsecured with land. In Abbott's ledger kept from 1646 to 1652 only two loans, one for £235 and the other for £100, are described as mortgages. More commonly, it appears, the bond counterpart of a mortgage was registered in their ledgers as a bond.[123] When the leasing covenants were completed to provide the security, no notice was made of the fact in the ledgers, for this final transaction was a practical and legal arrangement rather than a financial transaction. What appear to be bond–loans in the ledgers are

<hr />

[121] Sir Charles Wolseley to C., November 20, 1675, MS Eng. Lett. c.12, fol. 23, Bod. Lib.
[122] Benjamin Portlock to C., July 3, 1678, Box P, I.U.
[123] See n. 38. But see the particular of the manor of Chadshunt, Warwickshire (n.d.), which stated that a bond would be written in the town to assure that both parts of the covenant would be honored (MS DR 76/2/2, Shakespeare Birthplace Trust). Later, in London, a money bond and the leasing counterparts would be drawn up as the mortgage contract.

undoubtedly in many instances mortgages. Taking the scriveners' own words that it was difficult to find a mortgage security for less than £100,[124] the loans they negotiated in excess of that amount were, on average, considerably larger. In the first two years after Abbott's death, when the future of the business was uncertain and the two young men had little capital of their own to lend, they negotiated four separate transactions above £100 for their clients, at an average of £1,578 for each loan. Then, in the following four years, 1660–3 inclusive, they completed twenty-one separate loan negotiations above £100, including loans in their own names as well as those on behalf of their clients. The average loan amounted to £1,308. The record is broken during the next four years, but from 1669 until 1672 Clayton and Morris negotiated for themselves and their clients seventy-eight loans larger than £100, and the average amount was £2,022. During the next accounting period, 1672–5, when the agricultural recession was severe and the demand for mortgages was great, they completed 136 large-scale loans, altogether amounting to £296,878, or an average of £2,183 for each loan. In the next two years the demand for large loans became even more intense, and the scriveners were able to place £403,059 with debtors in 118 separate transactions, the average loan being £3,416.

The years 1672 through 1677 were the scriveners' most prosperous, as these figures indicate. The 254 loans registered in the ledgers during the period are not all, for in addition to these transactions they were making, covertly, other loans accounted for in the journals now lost. One must make some allowance for those negotiations which faltered during the process, either through reasons of credit or reluctant lenders. Land assessments most certainly were completed but failed to culminate in loans, so that the number of surveys made was greater than the number of mortgages granted. During the same period Manley published the first edition of his essay on 'court keeping,' and the scriveners established residential agents in several counties to assess land and to manage mortgaged estates. A majority of the particulars and parts of surveys survive from this period, when the clerks in the bank were burdened with copying out conveyances of the sort associated with mortgage loans. Altogether this activity strongly suggests that a great percentage of those 254 loans over £100 granted during the period were secured with land.

The discrepancy between the law and application of the banking mortgage in the scriveners' operation was not a subterfuge whereby they adopted particular covenants to avoid the usury laws. There was a gradual

---

[124]Thomas Elmes to C., August 1675, Box E, I.U.

evolution in contract forms, from informal proto-contracts, taken to be mortgage loans only between the scriveners and their clients, to formal, registered indentures. As long as the security was kept separate from the bond, the contract fell under a different legal rubric than if the same contract were ostensibly a mortgage. Within Chancery law itself the jurisdictions of mortgaged and unmortgaged lands were not always precise, and the scriveners' conveyancing followed, often, this lack of distinctions. Lawyers and bankers might regard the problem of conveyancing differently, but the practice the scriveners adopted was not illegal and their conveyances were drawn to protect their clients. Clayton and Morris were distinguished in the banking world for offering safe mortgages, and if this usually referred to the credit of their securities, it also implied that their legal expertise was likewise reliable.

CHAPTER 6

THE NEW LAND ASSESSMENT: FROM THE TERRIER TO THE ESTATE PARTICULAR

———————— • ————————

The unique achievement of Clayton and Morris in banking history was
their innovation in credit: to be precise, that they devised a reliable method
of valuing land put up as security in mortgage contracts. When land
changed hands in the process of banking, lender and borrower faced each
other in an impersonal relationship; this was unlike a local transaction, in
which a man went to his neighbor's farm to inspect his investment at the
site. When the negotiations occurred in the scriveners' bank, these two
brokers in the contract asked men to put their money down on property
they had never seen and whose value otherwise they could not predict
during a period of falling rents. The scriveners resolved this contradiction
by convincing many men of Restoration England that their own valuations
of property were more reliable than any other. However expert they might
have been in drawing up airtight conveyances, however amenable they
might have been in allowing their clients to use paper instruments in their
credit negotiations, it was the accurate determination of the value of real
security, valid over a number of years, that distinguished these scriveners
from other bankers of Restoration England. This achievement was recognized as crucially significant in the history of credit, when another banker
of the day, Francis Child, wrote in 1671 to a client explaining why the
goldsmiths had failed to gain control of private credit. Although they had
the capital to lend and could hire lawyers to perform their conveyancing,
he noted, Clayton was able to monopolize the large-scale loan market
because he held the key to accurate land assessment.[1]

[1] Francis Child to Henry Marten, May 9, 1671, Box 4, L.S.E.

The scriveners' role as brokers in lending contracts rose once they held the key to land valuation. In a simple brokerage operation the intermediary to the contract put lender and debtor in touch with each other, prepared the contracts and registered the deeds. He acted as servant to the parties concerned. Under the scriveners' management credit was now transferred from the borrower's word and records into their own hands. Whatever protestations the borrower might have, however much the lender might complain, the reliability of credit lay with the scriveners. For their assessments of land rested upon the work of surveyors, lawyers, and, later, their own agents with similar training, and it was this research behind the transfer of credit which made their word indisputable. Skills, more than services, characterized this change and gave to their role as brokers a professional quality.

The form of assessment which evolved under Clayton's direction was the estate particular, an estimation of land based on professional evaluation and advertised as the security for mortgage loans. Until Clayton could be satisfied that none of the rents had been concealed, so that he might attach the best leases as security, he was not fully master of a negotiation. Where lands were unsurveyed and boundaries in dispute, the same problem of reliability arose. Because the estate particular gave both an accurate and complete estimate of the worth of an estate, it quickly acquired validity in the mortgage market, eventually replacing those land estimates which vendors themselves had been accustomed to submit in the negotiations for loans. Soon the Court of Chancery granted Clayton's particular legal status. After Manley's method of assessment was published in three editions (1674, 1679 and 1720) the estate particular acquired an importance unknown previously.

In the first half of the seventeenth century there were two great sales of lands in Ireland in which many Englishmen bought property on the strength of abstracts describing the estates. Undoubtedly the ancestors of the estate particular are the briefs of these lands in the Londonderry Plantation and later those estates which Oliver Cromwell confiscated and for which Sir William Petty prepared the 'Down Survey.' There is also a direct connection between the estate particular as it emerged in the scriveners' hands and the sale of estates confiscated in England from the Crown, the church and royalists during the Puritan Revolution.[2] Reference has

---

[2]T. Phillips, *Londonderry and the London Companies, 1609–1629* (London, 1928); T. W. Moody, *The Londonderry Plantation* (London, 1929); Sir William Petty, *The History of the Survey of Ireland, commonly called the Down Survey . . . A.D. 1655–56*, ed. T. A. Larcom (Irish Archaeological Society, Dublin, 1851); S. J. Madge, *The Domesday of Crown*

already been made to the particular Robert Abbott made in 1656 for John Lewys from the records of the parliamentary commissioners for an estate in Yorkshire.[3] These surveys were sometimes retained with the estate muniments. When Clayton later received the papers of the manor of Eller-becke in Yorkshire, he found there a survey made and signed by the four commissioners who circumspected the estate in 1651.[4] But even after 1652 Abbott had no clear idea of how to advertise property. As late as 1656 in another sector of the financial world of London, the lack of any recognized way to describe property for sale hampered the individual trying to sell land in an ordinary manner. When Henry Oxinden of Barham decided to sell some of the properties in 1656 to a merchant in London, his cousin Henry Oxinden of Deene, an East India merchant, advised him to revise the description he had sent to London:

Whatever you have an intention to sell I advise to put in your particular, for the merchant examined strictly what other things you own in the parish. I believe your red house must go in too. Make your particular distinct, everything by itself, for he liked not your putting so many little houses together.[5]

In its fully evolved form the scriveners' particular included three sections. The first part was an enumeration of the legal rights and franchises belonging to the property. The second was a topographical survey of the land. Lastly, the capital value of the property was described, including the rents and at times the timber estimates. Even though this part of the particular had the appearance of a rent roll, the rents were market rates rather than the actual rents, and in this respect the banking particular is markedly different from its analogues in the earlier part of the century. Only those leases were included which were negotiated for security; the remaining leases did not appear in the particular. Many particulars included other information as well, such as the distance of the property from local markets, roads and waterways,[6] but these were ephemeral comments, designed to enhance the attraction of property whose value was already reflected in the rents. With the exception of those properties in and near London, where the residences were the chief attractions in land sales,

---

Lands: A Study of the Legislation, Survey, and Sales of Royal Estates under the Commonwealth (London, 1938).

   [3] See above, pp. 54–5.
   [4] Manor of Ellerbecke, 1651, Yorkshire Deeds, Brotherton Collection.
   [5] The Oxinden and Peyton Letters 1642–1650, ed. Dorothy Gardiner (London, 1937), 221.
   [6] See, for Kent, D. C. Coleman, 'London Scriveners and the Estate Market in the Later Seventeenth Century,' Economic History Review, second series, IV (No. 2, 1951), 223–8.

tenants' rents were the most valuable parts of the estimate, though the most volatile. The three-part particular eclipsed the terriers and vendors' rent rolls when rents began to level off after the mid-century. The comprehensive particular of Clayton and Morris was designed to offset the expectation that the value of rents during the survey would continue to fall during the life of the loan, and these buffers in the banking particulars were absent from the abstracts of sales advertised earlier in Ireland and in England, where the lands were sold absolutely rather than offered as real security.

In its mature state the estate particular was a business form with a precise meaning. But the word 'particular' – meaning no more than details of a description of land – was used in different contexts before and after the scriveners' advertisement had emerged. When Mr Goodman in 1655 sent Abbott his 'particulars of my grounds at Gadsby [Leics.] as they are newly let,'[7] he used the term as a vendor's estimate, the type of survey which ultimately Clayton's estate particular superseded. Rent rolls, court rolls, surveyors' field notes and estimations in the form of correspondence might all be referred to as 'particulars' when they were sent to Clayton and Morris in London. Various stages and drafts of what became the final document were reworked in their quarters and were never circulated in that state as bargaining instruments, even though they were called 'particulars.' Likewise, there are forms labelled 'rent rolls' in these papers which are not a complete list of the rents of an estate, as the term ordinarily means, but rather selected tenures which were offered in the first stages of the negotiations.

Five separate stages are traceable in the transition from the terriers and rent rolls prepared by landowners to the estate particular as it emerged under the direction of Clayton and Morris. One stage did not necessarily outmode previous forms of assessment, however. Where Clayton's agents resided to cover estimations in certain locales, the system of assessment was reliable. Daniel Sharpe, who worked for Clayton and Morris in Norfolk from 1670 to 1676, executed commissions more precise and comprehensive than the assessments which survive for any other county. Where a great estate was to be mortgaged, and a surveyor and lawyer were sent out for that purpose, that commission was likely to be even more exact. The best documented examples are Sir Robert Clayton's purchase of

---

[7] L.R.O., MS 35'29/292. In 1673 Daniel Sharpe sent Clayton a 'more exact particular' of the lands in Carbrooke, Norfolk, mentioning that the former estimate was only a 'particular of the rents as the lands are now let . . .' (Daniel Sharpe to C., August 1, 1673, Box 11, L.S.E.). Thus among Clayton's agents the word was acquiring a specialized meaning.

Marden Park in Surrey and Peter Clayton's purchase of the manor of Burton Lazars in Leicestershire.[8] But throughout the 1670s, when the method of assessment was worked out along the most exacting principles, the scriveners began to mortgage estates as far north as Yorkshire, when they were often forced to rely almost entirely upon the rough assessments of country lawyers.

The first valuations were descriptions which landowners presented at the inception of the loan negotiations, and there are numerous examples of these in the Clayton papers.[9] There is no reason to assume that these were necessarily inaccurate. When Clayton sent Mr Hungate's list of his rents in Norfolk to Daniel Sharpe, he returned the list unchanged: 'Upon view and the best account and a diligent enquiry I could get of the said estate there appears no cause of making any alteration . . . it being exactly what the last tenants to the . . . estate paid.' He found no discrepancies 'which I should have made if I had found just cause and good reason for it.'[10] But a process whereby a borrower valued the security was inherently weak, as one land-owner in Norfolk recognized in 1666, when he had a local lawyer notarize his rent roll before he sent it to Clayton.[11] Perhaps most of these vendors' estimates should not be judged as to whether or not they were true or false but rather as the first step in what was expected to become an attempt at rigorously accurate assessment. A Mr Temple in Warwickshire sent the scriveners a list of his rents with this notice: 'Wherever it is conceived by a purchaser that [I have] over valued the land, let the place where be set down, and if he cannot make it out, [I] will abate, but [I am] uncertain of the exact number of acres of some of the grounds therefore it may be sur-veyed as a purchaser pleases and valued by a surveyor.'[12] In 1664 Lord Sandys sent Clayton an estimate of the lands he offered for security, 'which shall be made good in every point both to the measures and the values,' but he anticipated that someone from London would come down to check his proposals.[13] The negotiations had to begin at some point, and it was natural that the man who wanted a mortgage would first write to Clayton

[8]See a copy (1838) of the survey of the manor of Bletchingley, taken in 1677 and 1680 (Durham County Record Office, MS D/BR F22). The survey of Burton Lazars made for Peter Clayton by Thomas Crodwin is in L.R.O., MS 35′29/103.
[9]See, for example, 'The Lands for securing £5000: Mr Clayton' (c. 1660s), N.R.O., MS 3384.
[10]Daniel Sharpe's letter, February 12, 1675, Box 11, L.S.E.
[11]N.R.O., MS 3286. See also ibid., MS 3292; L.R.O., MS 35′29/271, 35′29/414.
[12]Shakespeare Birthplace Trust, MS DR 76/2/9 (n.d., but after 1669).
[13]Lord Sandys to C., August 20, 1664, Box 11, L.S.E. See also N.R.O., MS 3405.

the amount he wished to borrow with a list of his rents to support his application.

In the course of the seventeenth century the legal profession expanded its scope of operations to include the management of estates.[14] As the numbers of lawyers increased, they took on commissions which previously had not been the exclusive domain of lawyers. As a part of this change, lawyers entered the land market as entrepreneurs in estate matters. After 1650 the management of a number of large estates changed, as the lords' stewards left or died, and no one arose from the ranks to fill their positions.[15] Gradually manorial courts became less important to the day-to-day operation of estates. Into this vacuum lawyers became involved through the practice of 'court keeping.' Young lawyers who had finished their legal training but had not yet been called to the Bar often supported themselves temporarily by handling the affairs of the lords' courts. This gave them a direct relationship with the tenants, leases and the land, and often one lawyer handled several courts in his locale.[16] Because of the access these men had to manorial records, they took temporary commissions from Clayton and Morris to search through the court records of other landowners. In 1666, for example, Clayton asked a lawyer who kept the court at Woodbastwick in Norfolk for his judgment of that estate. This man sent back a list of the rents, with no acreage listed, apologizing that 'this is as exact a particular as I can make at present without my notes and books,'[17] for the request was answered before he returned to the estate. Likewise, in 1667 Sir Thomas Neville made for the scriveners a rent roll of the Duke of Buckingham's manor of Kirkby Moorside in Yorkshire.[18] This was not 'court keeping,' but it arose from that practice, and was the first source of impartial judgments of the value of land which superseded valuations prepared by landowners.

[14] B. L. Anderson, 'The Attorney and the Early Capital Market in Lancashire,' in *Liverpool and Merseyside: Essays in the Economic and Social History of the Port and the Hinterland*, ed. J. R. Harris (New York, 1969), 50–77.

[15] E. Hughes, 'The Eighteenth Century Estate Agent,' in *Essays in British and Irish History in Honour of James Eadie Todd*, ed. H. A. Cronne, T. W. Moody, and D. B. Quinn (London, 1949), 187–8; P. Roebuck, 'Absentee Landownership in the Late Seventeenth and Early Eighteenth Centuries: A Neglected Factor in English Agrarian History,' *Agricultural History Review*, XX (March 1973), 1–17; J. V. Beckett, *Coal and Tobacco* (Cambridge, 1981), 26–34; and see J. R. Wordie, *Estate Management in 18th Century England: The Building of the Leveson-Gower Fortune*, Royal Historical Society Studies 30 (London, 1982).

[16] Roger North, *The Life of the Right Honourable Francis North, Baron of Guildford* (London, 1724), 22–3, 33–5. See L.R.O., MS 35′29/293, as well as the extracts from the court baron of the major of Garveston, Norfolk, 1657–8 (N.R.O., MS 3279).

[17] N.R.O., MS 3429.

[18] Manor of Kirkby Moorside, 1667, Yorkshire Deeds, Brotherton Collection.

This second stage in the Clayton papers is demonstrated by revised rent rolls, that is, landowners' own original valuations submitted to other persons for a second analysis or for additional information. In 1657 Abbott verified his valuation accordingly, when he arranged the sale of certain of Sir John Prettyman's lands in Leicestershire. From the leases and indentures put at his disposal he compiled a schedule of all the lands, with the number of acres per farm as well as the common annual rental value per acre. This brief was then taken to the estate by someone else who wrote his findings in the margin beside Abbott's figures. The new calculations were seventy acres short of Abbott's estimate. Where Prettyman's acreage corresponded with the new survey, there was a discrepancy of £2 in the prevailing annual rents, to the disadvantage of the new purchaser.[19]

Other examples appear in the Clayton papers of two separate estimates written upon the same document. From a rent roll which the scriveners received from the manor of Loddington, Leics., c. 1671, they made another list of the tenancies, rearranged by individual farms.[20] Both documents were then taken or sent to the site, and the actual rents noted in the margin, with an estimate of rents anticipated after the current leases expired.[21] In another instance, someone in the bank wrote upon a vendor's list of properties at the docks at Rotherhithe, 'memorandum: to go on Tuesday next in the afternoon,' for verification.[22] In another example, Thomas Clayton took with him a rental of one of Lord Spencer's estates in Northamptonshire, where he checked the rents with the tenants and drew a map of the plots.[23] Similarly, when a survey was taken of the farms in Raunds and Hargrave in Northamptonshire in 1674, the original estimate was ten acres short.[24]

The scriveners made other variations upon vendors' rent rolls. When a rental of 1663 of the manor of Carbrooke, Norfolk, was taken to the site, two other farms were listed increasing the annual rents by £60.[25] In another instance, a rent roll of Huntingdon, Warwickshire, was taken to the manorial court to find the charges upon the estate; they were then written alongside the rents and returned to London.[26] For the manor of

[19]L.R.O., MS 35'29/21. The lawyer John Palgrave composed the rent roll by each farm in Felmingham and Northrupp, Norfolk, some time before 1671 (N.R.O., MS 3341).

[20]L.R.O., MS 35'29/355B. See also L.R.O., MS 35'29/59, with the memo 'You are desired to give a particular of what other lands are in Blaston aforesaid & the value of them belonging to Mr. Goodman, that are not mentioned in the above particular . . .' and compare with L.R.O., MS 35'29/64.

[21]L.R.O., MS 35'29/355F.   [22]S.R.O., MS 61/5/6.

[23]Northants. R.O., Clayton MS 708.

[24]Northants. R.O., Clayton MS 155 (cf. ibid., 154).

[25]N.R.O., MS 3250.   [26]Shakespeare Birthplace Trust, MS DR 76/2/13 (n.d.).

Weethley, Warwickshire, there survives a long list of the incumbrances upon the estate taken in 1667 from the court there to supplement other parts of the valuation.[27] In another example, from the early 1670s, Daniel Sharpe received an acreage of the lands of the major of Sharnbourne in Norfolk. He appended a list of the grazing and gleaning rights of the manor, and when this was returned to London, it was assembled with the rental which had already been verified.[28] An estimate of the manor of Weybourne, Norfolk (1669), was compiled on legal foolscap by a lawyer.[29]

However, not all the information Clayton needed in valuations required legal expertise: that is, when the estate was not a manor or where there were no legal records to search. In 1668 the scriveners received an assessment of twenty-seven separate farms in Chart Langley and Sutton Valence, Kent, whereupon they ordered an inspection at the farms, and the tenants produced their own copies of their leases.[30] This was information taken in the fields. In another example, the lands of a farmer near Dover were 'very much under measured,' and the farmer who had requested the mortgage had neglected to mention in his letter the timber, which the scriveners' agent appraised at £50.[31] On the Duke of Richmond's lands near Sittingbourne there was a 'great deal' of timber, unmentioned and unvalued in the rental which the duke had sent to Clayton and Morris. Likewise, on another farm in Kent Clayton's agent found thirty-five acres of cherry and forty-four acres of woodland unlisted in the landowner's statement.[32]

Gradually after 1660 Clayton and Morris began to train their own personnel to carry out land valuations. These men were sent with specific instructions to compile an original valuation deriving entirely from their own research, unlike other calculations which were revisions or extensions of information begun by landlords or their servants. Richard Gulston's assessment of Lady Fanshawe's farm at Brickenden in Herefordshire (undated but probably taken in the 1660s) is an example of this type of agent's estimation.[33] It takes the form not of an abstract but of a letter, and after describing the farm, turns to other matters of business for the

[27] Shakespeare Birthplace Trust, MS DR 76/2/26.
[28] N.R.O., MS 3365.   [29] N.R.O., MS 3416.
[30] K.A.O., MS U214 E7/7.
[31] K.A.O., MS U214 E7/36. See also the particulars of the manor of New Port Pond, Essex (1662), Ex.R.O., MS D/DAc 81.
[32] K.A.O., MS U214 E7/57. See also the assessment of six farms in Wasperton, Warwickshire (1667) in Shakespeare Birthplace Trust, MS DR 76/2/24.
[33] 'Lady Fanshawe's farm at Brickenden,' Box 7, L.S.E.

scriveners. Another example of an informal agent's valuation is Simon Neale's letter concerning Lutterworth, Leics., in 1664.[34]

As long as 'court keeping' demanded special legal training, Clayton's agents were limited in the range of estates they could handle. To break this dependence upon lawyers, Thomas Manley wrote an essay entitled 'The Legal Part of Surveying,' which described the work that lawyers did when they kept manorial courts.[35] This was first published in 1674, as an appendix to William Leybourne's guide for surveyors, but the divisions and terminology he set appear in agents' reports as early as 1670, suggesting the essay must either have been circulated among them in manuscript or been relayed by a set of oral instructions.

For his description of the composition and procedure of the court baron, as well as for the glossary which he compiled of the antiquated legal terms used in the seigneurial courts, Manley undoubtedly consulted William Sheppard's The Court-Keepers Guide . . . , which had been published in its fifth and final edition in 1662. Unlike Sheppard, who outlined a general method of administering estates, Manley was concerned only with the way in which the courts could be directed toward manorial evaluations. His procedure appeared in three parts. With a letter of warrant from the lord the agent summoned a court baron and impanneled a jury among the tenants, while the steward was instructed to turn over all the terriers, court rolls, rentals and records of the customs of the estate. The agent then proceeded to conduct his Observations, a process one of Clayton's clients called taking 'the particulars of the law.'[36] Using the older rentals he wrote down in his book how the rents had risen or fallen in the past. Daniel Sharpe in 1673 conducted the Observations on the manor of Carbrooke, Norfolk, following express instructions from Clayton.[37]

The next stage was the Valuation,[38] undertaken after the surveyor had made his measurements of the land and given his notes to the agent. The latter now went into the fields and farms themselves with the notes he had

[34]L.R.O., MS 35'29/382.

[35]Published as Part VII (pp. 401–20) of the third edition of William Leybourne's The Compleat Surveyor (London, 1674).

[36]Ibid., 409–10. Cf. the Observations and Valuations taken in the Manors of Hockwold and Wilton, Norfolk (n.d.) in N.R.O., MS 3294; ibid., MS 3405.

[37]Daniel Sharpe to C., August 1, 1673, Box 11, L.S.E.

[38]Manley, 'The Legal Part of Surveying,' in Leybourne, The Compleat Surveyor, 410–11. Cf. a description of seven outlying tenures in the manor of Hockwold, Norfolk, discovered during the valuation taken there in 1673 and attached to the Observations and Valuation (N.R.O., MS 3294); 'A Rental of part of Eltington,' Northants., Northants. R.O., Clayton MSS 70A; a rent roll and survey of the manor of Brancaster, Norfolk, made in 1670, with the valuation taken by Daniel Sharpe (N.R.O., MS 3240).

taken in the court. His purpose was to notice any piece of land occupied or otherwise in use which was unlisted in the rental, as well as all pieces of land that could be profitably exploited but at present were not utilized.[39] For example, in 1673 Daniel Sharpe took a Valuation of Babingley, Norfolk, and listed all the closes, heaths, marshes and warrens that he found, just the sort of obscure outlying parts of estates that Manley had in mind in his essay.[40] But mineral mines, quarries, fishing, fowling, and hawking profits, peat, turf and the profits of fairs and markets were also included in his list of possibilities. As the agent registered these lands in his book, Manley suggested that he estimated their potential value.

Assisted by the jury he had selected at the beginning of the assessment, the agent then proceeded to the final part of his work, which consisted of a Charge of forty-one questions put to them in what was called the Court of Survey, or, simply, the Charge.[41] The articles of this query were taken almost word-for-word from John Norden's *The Surveiors Dialogue* . . . , last published long before in a 1618 edition. The jury was asked to supplement the evidence taken during the Valuation with the village lore and gossip: was any bastard heir to the land? Was any freeholder guilty of a felony or treason and had the lord not yet received his forfeiture? Had the lord stinted the tenants by taking part of the common lands, and, conversely, how much of the lord's demesne had the tenants themselves taken without leases? What buildings had been erected without the lord's licence? Did the tenants know of any mines, quarries or mosses of peat that the agent did not find during his valuation? These were the sorts of prickly questions the jury pondered. The agent was likely to receive answers such as this, regarding the rights of the commons in the manor of Sherborn, Norfolk:

the lord can put a beast during the time of summer. The townsmen only have a liberty to fell turves for their necessary fuel and from the time of Shackbee until St. Andrew to feed with their great cattle and not other wise at any time of the year.[42]

All this had a logic and unity in the abstract. There was a great difference, however, between the theory of how 'court keeping' should work and the realities of the practice, as Clayton discovered the same year Manley's essay was published. When Lord Colchester asked for a

[39] Frederick Hastings to C., 21 March, 1668, Box H, I.U.
[40] 'The Valuation of Collonell Cobbs Estate – Babingly . . . ,' N.R.O., MS 3214 4 B.1.
[41] Cf. Manley, 'The Legal Part of Surveying,' in Leybourne, *The Compleat Surveyor*, 411–18, and Norden, *Surveiors Dialogue* . . . (London, 1607), 49–122.
[42] N.R.O., MS 3365.

mortgage on his estate at St Osith, Essex, the scrivener sent the lawyer Robert Hyde to examine the estate. 'I observe the method you gave me,' he wrote back to Clayton, 'and set down an individual answer to each branch of the charge,' which refers directly to the procedure of assessment in Manley's essay. But the bailiff Whitgrave obstructed Hyde's investigation at every turn, from the moment he arrived on the estate. When Hyde read his letter of authority from Clayton, 'not only to state and examine but to determine and allow his accounts,' Whitgrave demanded to see the warrants. Hyde refused. 'I told him I judged it at present . . . unnecessary in regard he might be satisfied with your letters and with his owners view of the authority.' The bailiff refused to cooperate until he received a legal warrant superseding his authority. Finally Whitgrave produced two rent rolls, but each time Hyde transcribed any of the information in his notes, it was subjected to the approval of the bailiff, his wife and several witnesses.[43]

Whitgrave feared that his long term of corrupt management would be exposed, as indeed it was. But the incident, exaggerated by the special circumstances, typifies the opposition which Clayton's agents were likely to meet when these Londoners who had never before been on the estate arrived without warning and demanded to know the innermost secrets of the village economy.

When Manley published the second edition of his essay on 'court keeping' in 1679, he gave closer attention to the legal structure of the investigation, assuming that only a greater show of authority, redolent of the seigneurial courts of the Middle Ages, would produce the results he desired. From the lord of the manor the agent was to procure a legal warrant – preferably written in Latin and signed and sealed by him, delegating the office of steward to himself for the period of the assessment.[44] A copy of such a warrant (in English) survived in the Clayton papers:

We do desire that you will show unto this bearer Sir William Gulston all our majors, lands and hereditaments which we have purchased of and from Sir William Hartopp and Thomas Hartopp his son, and that you do acquaint him what every individual's rent is, and not only so but also that you do give him the best satisfac-

[43] Robert Hyde's letter, August 1674, Box 8, L.S.E.
[44] [Manley,] 'Legal Part of Surveying,' in Leybourne, *The Compleat Surveyor*, 4th edn, 426.

tion you can in everything he shall desire you to inform him of, according to your knowledge . . . [45]

When the Court of Survey assembled, it must have had all the trappings of the shire court, with cries of 'Oyez, Oyez,' oaths sworn on the Bible, and the agent presiding as judge, while the bailiff executed the proceedings. Not only was the jury sworn in, but each tenant also took an oath before he presented his leases and answered the questions in the Charge. All the while the agent was jotting down notes and listing diagrams, which the tenants never saw. Next day they were told that they might change the answers given the previous day, as if they were automatically suspect and the evidence were going to be used against them.[46] It presents an awesome picture.

Surveying was the second element in the estate particular. Manley's essay on 'court keeping' was published as an appendix to a manual on scientific surveying, and he assumed that the legal review could just as well be executed by a professional surveyor as by an agent who had no training as a lawyer. None of the court reviews surviving are as exhaustive as the procedure Manley outlined and only a few of the surveys were completed as thoroughly as Leybourne recommended. Both works should be regarded as frames of reference, from which Clayton's agents and surveyors might take what they needed to clarify the peculiarities of each mensuration and the specific instructions they had been given about the security.

By the middle of the seventeenth century surveying had become a highly sophisticated occupation. The plane table, the circumferentor and the theodolite were all in use then, and men trained in mathematics and in the use of these instruments had acquired techniques which set them apart from amateurs.[47] In 1671 William Watts wrote Clayton for his assistance in securing a '*Fide* Surveyor's' position or, alternatively, a 'land watch' position in London. If these positions were already disposed, he would settle for tide surveyor's place in Yarmouth.[48] Bona fide surveying had

[45] Warrant to Sir William Gulston (copy; n.d., 1670s), Box 7, L.S.E. In 1681 William Hardy advised the scriveners to ask the lord of the manor, Lord Sherrard, if they could attend the court along with himself, to support the ticklish business of dividing the farms (William Hardy's letter, March 15, 1681, Foster Library, Lincolnshire Archives Committee).

[46] [Manley,] 'Legal Part of Surveying,' in Leybourne, *Compleat Surveyor*, 4th edn, 426.

[47] G. R. Crone, *Maps and Their Makers*, 5th edn (London, 1978), 93–111; E. Lynam, 'English Maps and Map Makers of the Sixteenth Century,' *Geographical Journal*, CXVI (1950), 7; A. W. Richeson, *English Land Measuring to 1800; Instruments and Practices* (Cambridge, Mass. and London, 1966), chs. 1–5; E. G. R. Taylor, *The Mathematical Practitioners of Tudor and Stuart England* (Cambridge, 1954), 220.

[48] William Watts to C., July 1671, Box W, I.U.

come into its own, and Watts recognized that it conferred higher status than the other two positions.

Clayton used surveyors to measure his own estates, testifying to the importance of accurate mensuration. In 1662 he hired a surveyor to measure his land in Bardney, Lincs.[49] His seat at Marden Park was surveyed during the early 1670s, and in June 1674 he paid William Marr to calculate the boundaries of the neighboring manor of Westhall, 'as it is distributed in the map of Marden.'[50] In 1677 and 1678 Clayton paid Marr for circumscribing the manor of Bletchingley, Surrey. In another instance, two men, Elhannon and Samuel Tucker, surveyed Clayton's manor of Ebony in Kent, in 1685.[51] Peter Clayton followed his brother's example in 1682, when he used Richard Bradley and Richard Saunders to measure the lands he acquired in Burton Lazars and Great Dalby, Leics.[52]

Apparently Clayton was especially careful when purchasing lands for his own acquisition: there is less evidence that the lands which he negotiated as security for his clients were measured by men who were surveyors by profession. Norden recognized that the techniques of simple land measurement could be levied by laymen.[53] Clayton's surveyor measured Bardney with a chain pole,[54] and when Richard Saunders took the measurements of Great Dalby, he used a ground measurement also, for his notes record that a sudden discharge of water interrupted his progress.[55] Since measurements could be taken without the use of elaborate instruments (with the possible exception of the plane table), there was no reason why Clayton's agents could not perform simple mensuration, with Leybourne's treatise as a guide for any unusual situations which might arise.

Landowners' estimates of their own acreage were often guesswork, 'the reputed acreage by which it is taxed,' as one client wrote in the rental he sent to Clayton.[56] The terriers which Clayton and Morris received and their agents examined were based usually upon testimony taken from the tenants about property boundaries. In his notes made in the fields of Elkington, Northants., without the aid of a terrier, Clayton's agent described divisions apparent only to the tenants. One of the sections was

---

[49]S.R.O., MS 61/5/65.

[50]G.M.R., MS 3/4/39.

[51]G.L., MS 6428, iv, fol. 176v (November 16, 1677 and June 3, 1678); fol. 158v (April 6, 1680).

[52]L.R.O., MS 35′29/107/244, MS 35′29/107/245A, MS 35′29/107/245B.

[53]John Norden, *The Surveiors Dialogue* ... (London, 1618), 38–9.

[54]S.R.O., MS 61/5/65.

[55]L.R.O., MS 35′29/254A. [56]L.R.O., MS 35′29/355A.

'a ground Richard Line called Cockshill,' and the same man Line then took the agent over to three grounds which he leased called 'Blake lands.'[57] When Peter Clayton acquired his freeholds and leaseholds in Burton Lazars, there was no clear distinction between where the boundaries of his lands ended and where the Bishop of Ely's lands began, and much wrangling followed over these disputes.[58]

Customary measures of land in use in the seventeenth century might differ considerably, for local variations of the standard mile were still in use, as were the ancient labels of division, such as fardindeals, obolates, denariates, solidates and librates. Older surveys had taken the lord's demesne lands with a different measure (*mensura major*) than the pole used to circumscribe the customary lands (*mensura minor*). Manley recommended that all lands be circumscribed with the standard mile,[59] and this had been Clayton's practice long before Manley's essay was first published. In 1662 his surveyor at Bardney wrote down in his notes that he had used the statute measure of 16½ ft to the pole (Gunter's chain) and 18½ ft woodland measure.[60] Thomas Crodwin surveyed the freehold and leasehold lands in Burton Lazars, according to the statute measure of the early 1580s.[61] If we can assume that Manley's instructions on 'court keeping' influenced the legal research in the evolution of the particular, his instructions for a similar standardization – the use of statutory definitions in superficial land measure – must also have influenced boundary measurements as they were detailed in the particulars. Many of the landowners' estimates of their acreage were described to the scriveners only by the units of acres, though when the same lands were measured at Clayton's instructions, the survey was often given in acres, roods and perches. It may be that no more actual land was discovered or lost in the survey but rather that the discrepancy can be accounted for by the use of different measures.

Accurate surveying was essential to real security in several respects. If the entire estate was being secured, a circumscription of the borders of the property was taken to distinguish it from the neighboring lands. Usually, however, the amount of the loan was so closely tied to the rents that only selected tenures were attached. Within the perimeters of many estates there

[57]Northants. R.O., Clayton MS 70B.
[58]L.R.O., MS 35'29/123, 128, 129, 137, 188, 189, 190, 191, 192, 193, 208, 211, 215, 216, 217, 219, 220, 225.
[59]Manley, 'The Legal Part of Surveying,' in Leybourne, *Compleat Surveyor*, 3rd edn (1674), 418–19.
[60]S.R.O., MS 61/5/65.
[61]L.R.O., MS 35'29/103.

were freeholds and lands of inheritance, and the borders of the secured copyholds had to be carefully determined and delineated from these others and the demesne to prevent boundary disputes once the loan was sealed. For instance, after a survey was taken of North Creake, Norfolk, the lands of the bishop in the manor were found to lie compactly within a fold course and not to be contiguous to the lands to be mortgaged.[62] On the other hand, Sir Christopher Wray had managed to conceal from the scriveners that he had mortgaged secondary lands remote from the center of his estate, and it was this kind of deception that Clayton hoped would turn up in a proper mensuration, if not during the Valuation.[63]

From the fields and the halls these notes were assembled in the counting-house in London and revised to become the advertisement of the security. In the summary of the topographical survey and the legal assessment the complex procedures of 'court keeping' and mensuration were often hidden by the simple breviate of the terms of sale. What was omitted from the estate particular was less significant than whether the facts of the research were distorted, most notably through the valuation set on current rents. The third source of the estate particular was the market value of the prevailing rents, figured in London by the scriveners. This rate was based upon an estimate of the annual value per acre of land to be mortgaged, calculated by the scriveners in the bank, if their agents had not already made those determinations in the margins beside the rentals they sent to London. The scriveners assumed that the lowest ratio of rents to acres represented the poor land, while the highest ratio reflected the best. The first evidence that the relationship of rents to acres disclosed the quality of land appears in 1657, when Robert Abbott figured in the margin of the schedule he made for Sir John Prettyman the annual value per acre of each lease.[64] In another example, probably compiled some time between 1658 and 1660, the field notes made of several tenures of Eltington, Northants., gave the value per acre of each farm.[65] Similarly, in 1661 Clayton asked Thomas Barker to inspect the lands in Northamptonshire which a Mr Stafford had offered to Sir John Cutler for security. Barker confirmed the rents without surveying the lands.[66] With only the landowner's general estimate of the acreage, Clayton could then make the same calculation to find out which lands were the most and the least valuable.

[62] N.R.O., MS 3340.
[63] Before his negotiations began for a loan from Clayton (Lincolnshire Archives Committee, Hill MS 30 1.A/12).
[64] L.R.O., MS 35'29/21.
[65] Northants. R.O., Clayton MS 70B.   [66] Ibid., MS 16.

Once the relationship of rents to acres had been determined, the scriveners assigned market rates for each acre of land. A letter survives about these rates, implying that they were a customary appraisal which the scriveners gave. Ellis Goodwin in 1659 wrote the scriveners for a mortgage on what he promised was a good security, and he hoped to obtain the lending rate of either 13s. 4d. per acre or 10s. per acre; 'But if you should value them but at 6/8 an acre . . . ,' he concluded, as if this was known to himself and others as a bottom price the scriveners offered.[67] In 1683 Peter Clayton offered the same rates for the lands which he purchased from the Bishop of Ely: one noble (6s. 8d.) per acre for the poor land, one mark (13s. 4d.) per acre for the good land.[68] In 1671 and 1673 the scriveners tentatively considered a mortgage rate for two estates, both at a compromised rate of 10s. per acre, before the lands in question were surveyed.[69] The rates themselves do not appear in any other instance, as one would expect, being guarded information which the bankers were unlikely to let slip.

Allowance had to be made for the type of lease in question. Walter Long wrote Clayton in 1663 that in many counties a fee farm rent was worth more than land held by years' purchase,[70] and other exceptions had to be made for the variations in the types of leases considered for the security, apart from the quality of the land. It seems safe to say that the amount advertised in the estate particulars as the current annual rents was in fact a devalued estimate of the actual income. When Morris reduced the assessment made on Sir Thomas Englefield's estate he wrote to London:

I perceive there has been either a mistake in Mr. Morris's delivery of my proposition, or a misunderstanding on your side, since I find your offer is but eleven hundred pounds, whereby you exclude me Midsummer quarterage, which I never mentioned to Mr. Morris or even thought on . . . My demands are now twelve hundred pounds if I sell my life in Wootton Bassett estate; for that I would have you imagine that I am sensible if I part with it upon your terms . . . [71]

In 1686 the Bishop of Ely remarked to Sir Robert Clayton about the rates which Peter Clayton had obtained from him with his lands in Burton Lazars:

As for the value I send you the very papers wherein the particulars were computed and agreed between Mr. Peter Clayton and myself, though as Mr. Thirsby and others that were present do very well remember (and as yours is a memorandum in

[67] Ellis Goodwin's letter, February 18, 1659, Box 7, L.S.E.
[68] L.R.O., MS 35'29/107.
[69] Bod. Lib., MS Eng. Lett. c.16, fol. 16; N.R.O., MS 3214.
[70] Walter Long to C., January 12, 1663, Rylands Ch. 2775, J.R.L.
[71] Sir Thomas Englefield to [C.], August 10, 1676, Box E, I.U.

one of these accounts) everything was under-rated and set to your brother's advantage since which I am well-informed that the real yearly income is far more improveable and considerable than it was at that time acknowledged to be.[72]

The scriveners' procedure in lending money precluded such complaints. The particulars went only to prospective mortgagors at their request. Once a suitable lender had been found, the erstwhile mortgagors were then notified of their devalued assessments, usually after they had waited for a long period for their deposits to be put out to loan. Up to the moment of contract, both parties could remain unknown to each other, so there was little chance that the mortgagors would confront their mortgagees with the current income of the property listed in their rent rolls. In 1674 Mr Clitherow's bailiff came upon a discrepancy of £63 between the scriveners' assessment of his master's estate and what he knew to be the actual income, though he did not attribute the variance to miscalculation or fraud.[73] Who was he and a host of other bailiffs and landowners to quarrel with these London professionals, who had searched through the court records, who had queried the tenants, and who had finally left their estates with notations unseen by the men who farmed and ran the estate? With so few options, they had little recourse other than to accept the scriveners' terms, which, after all, could be defended with the likelihood that the current rents would fall to the level of the lending rate during the life of the mortgage.

Timber valuations appeared frequently in the particulars, as a *douceur* to the rents which remained the supreme and constant factor in the particulars. Almost all estates had tenants, while the woods had been cleared on many properties. It was so difficult to control illegal felling in the woods that the timber described in the particulars might be drastically cut by the time the mortgage was concluded and the lender came into his investment. If the plantations were too small to cut for the market, the wood might nevertheless be used for fuel and to repair the buildings on the estate. To this extent each purchaser was likely to be interested in even a general description of the wood. On other estates, where plantations were protected from predators, trees of sizeable growth could be felled and sold, and this commercial attraction was emphasized in the particulars. There are a few clues in the Clayton papers to indicate how the value of timber was determined. In the parks of two Surrey estates, the trees were counted and valued by type. At Durdens, twenty large elms were reckoned to be

---

[72]Bishop of Ely to C., May 18, 1686, Box T, I.U.
[73]Richard Stevens's letter, December 20, 1674, Box S, I.U.

worth 40s. each, but oak, elm, ash and beech trees in smaller plantations were worth 30s. each.[74] At Witley Park the age of the oaks was calculated as part of their value. The finest specimens, of 100 years' growth, were worth £1 each, whereas less good specimens of the same age were worth only 10s. each. The remaining trees fell in a declining ratio according to age: for 50 years' growth, 5s.; 40–50 years' growth, 3s.; 30–40 years' growth, 1s.[75] Both these estimates were almost certainly based upon the supply of timber masts to the navy. During the second Dutch War Clayton hoarded timber felled from the Forest of Dean. After the naval commissioners had refused to meet his extortionate demands, parliament seized his supply.[76] In 1669 he resumed his supply to the navy. In that year or thereafter the parkland estimates in Surrey were probably made, though it is impossible to be certain, for both estimates are undated.[77]

Another method of valuing timber was based upon a general estimate of the acreage of the plantations. The surveyor who made the assessment in 1672 of Sir Robert Clayton's estate at Bardney, Lincolnshire, using the woodland measure of 18 ft to the chain pole for his measurement, estimated that each acre was worth £3, to be felled by twenty acres per annum over a seventeen-year period. The brushwood, he estimated, was worth £12 10s. 0d. per acre, to be cut all at once.[78] Only if the wood in East Bradenham, Norfolk, were managed well and brought into a course of felling of seven acres each year would it bring £3 an acre, Sir Thomas Percival estimated.[79] Likewise, in 1678 Sir John Bramston complained to Morris that the £3 per acre valuation of the timber on his estate would have held in his father's time at eighteen to twenty years' growth. In the previous winter, however, his wood had been worth only £2 10s. 0d. per acre.[80] Was the scriveners' rate an over-valuation designed to protect a portion of their investment over a number of years, when the wood would be sold at fluctuating rates in local markets? This £3 per acre estimate applied to woods which were well-stocked. In 1678 Clayton's agent used a rate of 4s. per acre in his valuation of the woods at Sandon and Jepcracks, Essex, for the brush had been severely overcut there.[81] Long-range projections of

[74]S.R.O., MS 61/5/14.
[75]Ibid., MS 61/5/19.
[76]C.T.B. 1667–1668 (London, 1905), Vol. II, 260, 268–70, 284.
[77]C.S.P. Dom., 1668–69 (London, 1894), 173.
[78]S.R.O., MS 61/5/65.   [79]N.R.O., MS 3226.
[80]Bod. Lib., MS Eng. Lett. c.14, fol. 35.
[81]'I am bidden £3000 to leave wood for all the tenants and the hall for firing and repairs which is of no small value . . . ,' William Wollaston to M., July 14, 1674, Box 6, L.S.E.; Ex. R.O., MS D/DAc 120.

timber values appear occasionally in the particulars, but these considerations lay outside their mortgage calculations, largely because the woods
were more likely to diminish in size than the rents were apt to fall in value.
Some allowance had to be made for repairs to the manor house and other
parts of the estate, which the woods supplied.[82] But the critical factor was
the illegal depletion of the timber resources. In the assessments of Mr
Hungate's estate in Norfolk in 1673 and 1674 the woods of about 120
acres were judged to be worth £40 yearly; when the mortgage negotiations
were in process in January 1675, Daniel Sharpe visited the estate and
found that all the timber had been cut.[83] The tenants who preyed upon the
woods of mortgaged estates were responsible for the fact that timber valuations were not included as a matter of course in the final calculations
made for mortgage loans. Shrewd landowners like Sir Charles Harbord
were doubtful that the timber evaluations in the particulars they received
were a realistic guide for their investment.[84]

In the estate particulars timber estimates never became an essential component. Timber was ordinarily advertised to enhance the value of rents,
and in this sense it bore the same weight in the particular as the descriptions of the topographical features of the estate, as well as its geographical
location in the neighborhood. These features were reflected in the rents,
whereas timber retained a value all of its own. Many mortgagors, and
Clayton and Morris as their brokers, must have realized sizeable profits
from the sale of timber on mortgaged estates, but the sale prices were not
credited to their accounts as a separate or even recognizable category, and
thus it is uncertain what the actual profit was.

By the time the mortgage was sealed, the loan and the security might
have been adjusted to fit the precise requirements of the contract and could
be quite different from the terms of security which had appeared in the
estate particular. In 1659 Ellis Goodwin sent the scriveners a rental of his
lands with this note: 'I shall not tie you to the precise sum of £800 but will
be content to take £1000, that possibly being a sum more ready and
possible.'[85] Thomas Stanley wrote Morris in 1671 that he desired to
borrow £600 'upon the land particularized in that lease . . . which you
have, unless it might be upon so much land as you will take out of it, proportionable to the sum borrowed . . .'[86] Similarly, in 1673 Richard Parker

[82]See below, p. 205.
[83]Cf. William Ruding's estimate, 1673; another rental with the estimated acreage,
October 1674, and Daniel Sharpe's assessment, January 1675 (N.R.O., MS 3226).
[84]Daniel Sharpe's letter, 27 August, 1673, Box 11, L.S.E.
[85]Ellis Goodwin's letter, February 18, 1658, Box 7, L.S.E.
[86]Bod. Lib., MS Eng. Lett. c.16, fol. 16.

wrote Morris that if the lands he had offered for a loan of £1,000 were insufficient security, he would give more,[87] and, conversely, in the same year George Pitt directed Clayton to reduce his negotiations with Sir William Russell by excluding the saltworks calculated in the particular.[88] In 1673 Gabriell Bedell agreed to include in his mortgage twenty-four acres of marsh lands not offered originally as security.[89]

Clayton and Morris often retained leases unlisted in the advertisement to offer to the lender if the original bargain was unsatisfactory. If there were no other lands, there were ways in which the loan could be adjusted without adding or subtracting lands. In 1677 Morris sent his agent Peter Woodcock a rental of Blaston, Leics., with these instructions: 'You are desired to give a particular of what other lands are in Blaston . . . that are not mentioned in the above particular.'[90] Based on the rental of the land-owner, Mr Goodman, the scrivener had already rejected most of the leases – all the farm houses and cottages and pasture lands unlikely to hold their rents during the depressed agriculture of that time. Only the mansion house, the arable closes and nine cottages in the town were left in the land-owner's proposal, though Clayton added 'Cobley's Close,' which had somehow turned up in other records. The rent from the parsonage was held in abeyance, in case a suitable purchaser could be found.[91]

The revised rental was sent first to Leonard Bradshaw in Keythorpe who already held a charge on the estate and seemed interested in taking up a new mortgage. In the appraisal he sent to Clayton on October 21, 1677, he complained that the mansion house was over-valued, the other leases only slightly so, but it is clear that the attraction which the house commanded made other information less relevant.[92] Peter Woodcock confirmed his estimation of the rent of the mansion house. One of the tenants told him that the current rents in Goodman's list were accurate, though he doubted that in twelve months they would hold. Nevertheless, he had found another prospect, a Mr Atkyns, whom he thought would take the terms in the particular, but later it seemed that his interest, like Bradshaw's, was in the mansion without the other leases. Woodcock could find no other lands to add to the proposal.[93]

These negotiations lay with Goodman's neighbors, who were more

[87] Richard Parker to M., June 23, 1673, Box 10, L.S.E.
[88] George Pitt to C., December 1673, Box P, I.U.
[89] Daniel Sharpe's letter, May 2, 1673, Box 11, L.S.E.; John Palgrave to C., July 1672, G.L., MS 10,049.
[90] L.R.O., MS 35'29/59.
[91] Cf. *ibid.*, L.R.O., MS 35'29/64.
[92] L.R.O., MS 35'29/61A.
[93] L.R.O., MSS 35'29/62, 35'29/63.

likely to know how the rents would hold than a lender farther away who was unfamiliar with the region. No assessment was made of the royalties of the manor and, indeed, the estimation fell below the standard outlined in Manley's essay, because of the attraction which the house commanded. Moreover, no final particular was made of the transaction. It would be wrong to suggest a monolithic pattern or standard, as local variations often introduced contradictions.

Since the articles of the particular were evidence for legal contracts, the estate particular was inherently juristic. Advertised as a synthesis of facts and frequently attached to the conveyance itself, by default of any other contemporary document the particular was the most reliable estimate of the value of property at the time of the sale. In 1675–6 the legal nature of the particular came before the courts. On the basis of an estimate of lands listed in a particular Twiford mortgaged his lands to Warcup, who took possession and discovered that the lands fell short of the acres listed in the particular. He sued for recovery. The court declared that the particular described the lands only by estimation; because there was only a matter of four or five acres in question, the plaintiff could have no redress. The particular itself was not at fault, only a part of it. By implication, if the circular advertised the land measured by a survey, this document was to have legal validity: in its own way it was as binding as the deed.[94] A scientific circumscription of the land became almost mandatory as one of the essential components of the particular. The banker who sold security in this manner was indissolubly wedded to the surveyor.

Even before the particular acquired its legal character Clayton's enterprise brought him a larger audience than his clients. During the winter of 1669–70 the House of Lords appointed a committee which heard evidence concerning the poor state of the economy. One of the proposals was to reduce the rate of interest, and because the question was controversial, other witnesses were called in to testify to the likely effects. Speaking in favor of the lower rate were a group representing merchants' interests. Clayton and Captain Titus spoke against reduction. If the interest rate were lowered, they argued, clients would call in their mortgages and refinance at the lower figure.[95]

Self-interested as it was, this was as close as Clayton ever came to public

---

[94] *Twiford* v. *Warcup* (1675–6) [L.R. Ch. xi (1668–93), p. 630]. At the same time the court held that the principle could not be applied to land sold by absolute conveyance. See also *The Case of Thomas Rowney Gent. Executor of Edward Twyford Gent. in Trust for the said Twyford's Children* (n.d.).

[95] H.M.S., *Eighth Report*, Appendix Part 1 (London, 1881), 133–6.

association with a formal economic principle. But the arguments expounded evidently interested him. As the pamphlet war followed the parliamentary debates Clayton's expertise in land values attracted him to the propagandist Thomas Manley. The rate of interest and its relationship to the price of land seemed sufficiently important to his own interests to permit his curiosity to pursue the question further.[96]

To support reduction in the interest rate Culpeper published in 1669 a new edition of his father's attack upon usury, written in 1621. The elder Culpeper had assembled information about the price of land before parliament reduced the legal maximum of interest from ten per cent to eight per cent in 1625. Using his father's figures the younger Culpeper then analyzed the effects upon land prices since 1625, and concluded that the price of land had risen since then. If parliament were to reduce the rate even further, land prices would not fall as a consequence of cheaper money.[97]

Rents had dropped in the course of the century as the price of grain had fallen. To answer the Culpepers Thomas Manley addressed himself to another aspect of the problem, namely, how the yield from land might be increased through proper use. Manley's essay *Usury at Six per Cent. Examined...* (1669) defended the prevailing rate, though his reasons were different from Clayton's. In about 1670 he drew up his essay on 'court keeping' for Clayton, and though the precise date is somewhat conjectural, more solid evidence associates Clayton with Manley in 1670. In that year Culpeper published a retort to Manley[98] who then took up his pen again to write a reply. In 1672 he sent Clayton a long letter outlining the points of his argument. He mentioned Clayton's 'former promises to cubb with me' in publishing the rejoinder, which must have been given sometime in 1670 after Culpeper's second tract appeared and before Manley's essay was written.[99] From the notes he sent Clayton Manley seems to have enlarged his focus to assess the effect of the reduced interest rate on trade and commerce. With his other tract this would comprise a more general

[96] In a more wide-ranging context the pamphlet debates on this question lasted from the publication of Josiah Child's *Brief Observations Concerning Trade and Interest of Money* (London, 1668) to Locke's *Some Considerations of the Consequences of the Lowering of Interest, and Raising the Value of Money* (London, 1692). See H. J. Habbakuk, 'The Long-Term Rate of Interest and the Price of Land in the Seventeenth Century,' *Economic History Review*, second series, V (1952), 26–45.

[97] Sir Thomas Culpeper the elder published *A Tract against Usurie...* in 1621. His son's edition was published as *A Tract Against the High Rate of Usury... To which is added a preface...* (London, 1668), which went into several printings in the same year.

[98] *The Necessity of abating Usury re-asserted...* (London, 167).

[99] Thomas Manley to C., February 13, 1673, Clayton MS 53, Fairfax Collection.

treatment on economics, and Clayton may have expressed his interest in the second essay to deflect criticism that his opinions to the Lords Committee were his own narrow concerns.

Manley's essay was never published. By 1672 parliament's concerns over the interest rate had cooled. If he had submitted his essay to Clayton in 1670, it might have been published with the scrivener's assistance. But there is no reason to assume that Clayton's ideas on economics had taken the rather firm form which Manley advocated. The price of land which Culpeper and Manley discussed was the rack rents of land rather than the market value which was the critical factor in Clayton's negotiations. Manley was perhaps flattering Clayton in asking for his assistance when he offered him the economic responsibility of his association in a tract, certainly a new twist in the career of this mortgage tycoon.

In summary, land assessment is a feature represented by a type of document unique in the records of early English banking, the estate particular. In the archives of seventeenth- and early-eighteenth-century banks particulars or documents similar to them have survived only among the Clayton papers. There the particulars stand alongside checks and notes, signifying their importance in banking history. The particulars were as integral to the process of moneylending as penal bonds and the leasing counterparts of mortgage contracts and should not be confused with property sale, as if in another context Clayton sold land as a land agent. Even more important than the particulars themselves is the complex process of valuation which they betray. The first and briefest lawyers' notes, the full reports which agents composed along the lines Manley suggested, the revisions made by the scriveners before the market document was completed – these stages evolved in a manner that gave the scriveners control of mortgage credit. Someone considered that the pattern established by Clayton a half-century before was sufficiently relevant in 1720 to warrant publishing Manley's essay on 'court keeping' for a third time, in another edition of Leybourne's surveyor's guide.

CHAPTER 7

THE MANAGEMENT
OF MORTGAGED ESTATES

———————— • ————————

This chapter describes the final stage in the process in the scriveners' mortgage banking – the service offered to their clients whereby the bank managed the lands recently mortgaged. For those clients who had no other means of managing distant properties, Clayton and Morris filled the gap between their mortgagees' lands and the control temporarily relinquished by their mortgagors with men who acted as their own bailiffs and estate agents. Thus, a man in Sussex might take the mortgage on a property in Leicestershire, while neither he nor his servants actually visited that county during the life of the loan. Clayton's men collected the tenants' rents, farmed the demesne lands and returned this money to London, where it was credited to the lender's account as principal and interest repaid on the loan. If he so desired, the lender could then send his servant to withdraw his money in London with a check. Moreover, if he had arranged to transfer the loan and sign the covenants at his own house at the start, it was possible that his investment from beginning to end never compelled him to leave his own estate in Sussex. Attractive as this service was, it was a voluntary arrangement. Many lenders seem themselves to have managed the properties mortgaged to them. Where the scriveners provided this service they completed a process whereby the entire lending procedure was controlled by themselves. In the transition through which brokers intervened more completely between the parties to the loan, the methods they achieved in land management became the last, vital step.

At the same time, the responsibility of directing estates from London faced Clayton and Morris with the challenge of agriculture itself. During the assessment their agents briefly visited properties, made their inspec-

181

tions and then departed. At the next stage an agent returned to the same estate to assume control of the lands attached in the mortgage contract, collecting tenants' rents and farming the lord's lands. As each estate was diverted from a landowner's direction, it then became a satellite economy controlled from a bank in London. Changing control from the countryside to London gave the problem of estate management an urban and business-like character. Clayton and Morris had little direct experience with farm-ing themselves until Clayton purchased an estate at Marden Park in Surrey and Morris acquired Greenlands in Buckinghamshire. By trial and error learnt through their agents and through the correspondence of their clients, they soon devised a method of managing estates. What they actually perceived to be the basic problem of agriculture in this period, in its dislocation and recession, is a part of the problem, as is the system they perfected to achieve this outreach into the manorial economy.

The clients of the bank were men struggling to survive in a new, often unsuccessful agronomy, and the correspondence between the countryside and the bank reflects this dilemma.[1] The change from pasture to tillage in many areas was certainly known to the scriveners. In 1664 their agent Simon Neale sent Clayton an assessment of a property in Leicestershire which reads as a summary of the general predicament of agriculture as it had changed in the course of the century. The current rents of the property – Sir Henry Pickering's land outside the market town of Lutterworth – were set long before on grazing leases, though half the fields had been plowed up after the leases were granted. From his inspection of the accounts of Pickering's father Neale concluded that the transition from an entirely pastoral situation to one where tillage had become increasingly common had begun about 1639. Stock prices at that time were so low that the tenants could not have paid their rents without converting some of the land to farming and selling the produce in the local market, as well as in Coventry and Leicester, both towns ten miles distant. As late as 1660 one of the tenants, a Mr News, had resisted these changes, 'his profession being a grazier and not a farmer,' but the way of the future seemed clear to him and to his neighbors who wanted farming leases alongside their pasture lands.[2]

Those tenants at Lutterworth and other farming communities in transition tied to rents fixed long ago at brisk woolen prices and unable to change to mixed agriculture often had no choice but to desert their copy-

---

[1] See above, pp. 12–14.   [2] L.R.O., MS 35′29/382.

holds. If there were no tenants to take up the leaseholds, the lands in the demesne increased, to be farmed by the scriveners' agents as they saw fit. From this transition from pasturage to tillage evolved much of the background which the scriveners knew to be the structure of agriculture.

From these secondhand sources the scriveners learnt another aspect of absentee management, that what passed itself off as the common dilemma of farmers was at times no more than inefficiency and corruption. Clayton's suspicious gaze saw through this disguise. He had a Janus-like vision, with one eye in the City toward the records of the assessment and the other eye in the country toward the complaints and excuses of his agents and tenants. Good banker that he was, Clayton never lost sight of the part which proper reckoning should play in reconciling the problem of appearance versus reality in estate management. From the Valuation he had a clear idea of what was due to him, and to this standard the management of estates must adhere. Testament to Clayton's role in the process came from Stephen Monteage's *Instructions for Rent-Gatherers Accompts*. Primarily this work is a treatise on accounting. The tenants' names and their rents due were to be compiled from records in the City and listed in a small ledger. This was the standard to which the rents in the country must be justified. From the demesne lands, which were farmed, the variety of entries is diverse, though Clayton and Monteage suggested which items they expected to find in the account, to restrict the possibility that fraudulent entries could conceal the corruption of their agents.

The system which Clayton devised to manage estates distant from London was an absentee arrangement whereby their agents traveled between a network of estates, dealing with tenants and farming matters. A new employee, the rent-collector, became the key figure in expropriated control and another rung on the hierarchy of the bank's personnel. On large estates the rent-collector was a new and temporary official sent out to audit the accounts of bailiffs and stewards at the same time as collecting their revenues twice yearly. Though his authority superseded that of the bailiffs, each official had his own sphere of responsibility. In one instance Monteage describes the rent-collector as managing stock of cattle and sheep on the lands in hand.[3] In another example the rent-collector only received rents from the bailiff. On smaller estates, where there was no bailiff, the rent-collector received the rent roll and list of arrears from the lord and collected the customary rents himself.[4]

---

[3] Stephen Monteage, *Instructions for Rent-Gatherers Accompts* (London, 1683), 10.
[4] *Ibid.*, 21–2.

Monteage's model, oddly termed 'the manor of Grub Street,' is depicted through a series of hypothetical debit and credit accounting entries. Here are both grazing and farming tenants. Recently the number of leaseholds has increased, as tenants have vacated their leaseholds, 'a thing which happens upon most estates since the fall of land in every country.' In the example of Grub Street the demesne lands have turned to pasture, but Monteage established this situation in his example to illustrate how stock-raising was to be registered in accounts. Clever readers would easily make the corresponding entries for corn-farming, if the lands in hand had been turned to that purpose. Development of the demesne lands forms the emphasis of Monteage's idea of management in pastoral agriculture by increasing the sale of sheep, cattle, pigs, butter and cheese. He cites expenses for hedging and ditching – for enclosure of the vacated leaseholds. No drovers' wages appear among the debits. Charges for an inland bill of exchange are listed in these entries, implying that the rents were remitted to the lord by someone other than drovers or the rent-collector. This suggests that the flocks were sold locally by the bailiffs, in the market or through brokers. A minimum outlay of investment and the least amount of overseeing – no more than twice yearly – are the priorities of the system.[5]

This treatise on rent-collecting is comparable to the two essays which Thomas Manley published on 'court keeping.' Both sets of instructions were directed to men who were neither the lord nor his servants but new entrepreneurs in manorial affairs. These men visited estates only long enough to do their work, then moved on to other properties for the same purpose. Both agents arrived with precise instructions, but whereas the 'court keeper' was to gather information for his assessment through the manorial court, the rent-collector had no such base in the manor from which to do his work. The records of the assessment were the first part of a series of calculations culminating in the terms of a loan, but Monteage's essay has a more general appeal. Someone who was unfamiliar with the estate, such as a lawyer or newly appointed bailiff, and who had just been given a rent roll of tenants he had never met to begin at once his connection with the estate would find Monteage's work useful.

Monteage did not explain how the rent-collectors arose in the bank. That part of the mortgage process involving land assessment came from commissions originally given to lawyers. The work of rent-collectors was too closely allied to the soil and the tenants for lawyers to feel comfortable

---

[5] *Ibid.*, 10, 17, 19, 21, 25.

with work they felt belonged to bailiffs. The lawyer Robert Hyde wrote Clayton that his best services lay in arbitrating matters of equity between gentlemen, rather than in resolving the 'twisted, knotty fetters' of corruption that he found in the manor of St Osith, Essex.[6] During the 1670s Thomas Clayton, William Hardy and Daniel Sharpe took assessments and managed estates,[7] and it may be that Clayton found in these men a combination of factors rare in lawyers. Most of the information which survives about management comes from their letters to London. Clerks in Clayton's household rode out to properties without an agent nearby to handle these affairs. In one instance in Leicestershire, Clayton appointed one of his mortgagors, a Mr Houghton, to collect the rents on one of the estates of Sir John Prettyman, also one of Clayton's debtors. After suffering for five or six years the humiliation of seeing his rents diverted into his neighbor's hands, Prettyman complained to Clayton, who replied that he had the same tie upon Houghton's estate, to insure his honesty. If he discovered otherwise, that Houghton was holding back some of the money due to him in London, Prettyman would then have his revenge by collecting the rents on Houghton's estate.[8]

The scriveners watched their rent-collectors closely, scrutinizing the accounts they sent to London for any omissions at variance with the surveys made previously. Temptations arose when these agents realized that they could dun the tenants or exploit the possibilities of the demesne lands in ways concealed from their accounts to the scriveners. One way of curbing corruption was to put in writing the precise duties of these agents. When such orders were presented, a proper reckoning could be made later if the rent-collectors violated their duties. When Daniel Sharpe, for example, was sent to Norfolk in 1671 to the recently mortgaged estate of Carbrooke, he carried with him a set of instructions from London outlining his work on the manor. This charge does not survive. Quite likely the substance of his first orders resembled the bookkeeping part of a rent-collector's task which Stephen Monteage later published. Upon Sharpe's arrival on the manor, he received a letter from William Clayton referring to his previous orders, as well as to a warrant he had made delegating his authority on the manor. Another set of instructions was enclosed, limiting further the agent's discretionary powers. If anything extraordinary happened, they read, he was to consult the scriveners' lawyer William

[6] Robert Hyde's letter, August 1674, Box 8, L.S.E.
[7] *Ibid.*
[8] Sir John Prettyman to C., 1675, Box P, I.U.

Gulston, who was then in Norfolk. Otherwise, no decision not delegated in his instructions could be made without consulting first Morris and Sir Robert Clayton. All rents received were to be sent to London as soon as they were collected, and for this money the scrivener would send him receipts to be credited against his Michaelmas and Lady Day accounts. On the manor itself Sharpe was to repair the houses of four tenants, but only if their rents were not in arrears. Take special care, Clayton urged, to see that no timber was felled except for repairs. Sherring, the woodman, was to be discharged and replaced by another tenant. Any deserted tenancy was to be occupied immediately by the bailiff, who would be given a lease dated from the time of his occupation as soon as the rent-collector made his next return.[9]

The scriveners' rent-collectors upset too many vested interests in the manor for their instructions to work as easily as the scriveners hoped. The Duke of Richmond's tenants refused to pay their rents to the scriveners' agent in 1671 when he first appeared on the estates.[10] In another example, in Norfolk in 1674, the tenants at Threxton, Larlingford and Whimburgh balked at paying their rents to Daniel Sharpe, claiming that the former bailiff had taken their rents before he departed.[11] Old relationships between the landlord's bailiff and his tenant were ruptured when the rent-collector arrived. Even if he brought with him a legal warrant from the landlord to support his authority, the rent-collector sometimes found the bailiff so entrenched that the new rent-collector was ignored. When Robert Hyde returned to manage the estate in Essex which he had previously assessed, the same contretemps presented itself as before, in the figure of the bailiff, 'whose actings have been and are wrapt under such obscurity that there's nothing but time and a very diligent scrutiny can bring things to light.' His patience was repaid. All the problems which he encountered on the estate he traced to the corruption of the bailiff Whitgreave. His cousin, who collected the quit rents of several outfarms and the tithes on the manor and handled the sale of the timber, refused to make any account to anyone but the bailiff. None of the tenants would even confront Hyde until they had first consulted Whitgreave. For years he had permitted paper arrears to grow in the accounts he presented to the landlord, while at the same time, and surreptitiously, he had made private compacts with

---

[9] William Clayton to Daniel Sharpe, n.d. [1671–2?], Box 11, L.S.E. Sharpe's authority had been delegated in a letter of attorney with, apparently, instructions along the lines of Monteage's advice: N.R.O., MS 3264.
[10] B.L., Add. MS 21948, fol. 66.
[11] Daniel Sharpe's letter, April 30, 1674, Box 11, L.S.E.

the tenants to line his own pockets with their rents.[12] Upon his appointment in 1668 Whitgreave had put up a bond to deliver to his landlord a reckoning, which, if fraudulent, could be charged to his security. Clayton discontinued this system of bonded accountability by putting his agent on a salary of £60 yearly. By requiring that all the rents and most of the remaining income be sent immediately to London, where the expenses would be paid and accounts tallied against the rent roll compiled during the assessment, he ensured that the agent's range of action was considerably narrower than Whitgreave's had been.[13]

Clayton knew other instances in which what appeared at first to be poor agriculture was in fact no more than corruption. In 1674 Humphrey Tompkins took over the running of the scriveners' property at Down Rossall, but not before the former bailiff, one Griffith, had submitted a long list of padded expenses to be paid off before he left. Then, in collusion with one of the tenants, the displaced bailiff stole the corn from Tompkins's granary and sold it in Shrewsbury.[14]

More spectacular corruption presented itself when the scriveners, acting for trustees, took over the management of the Duke of Buckingham's estates in 1671. From the duke's vast estates, the manorial accounts were sparse, most having disappeared during the Puritan Revolution.[15] Consequently, regular and exact collections of rents and fines had ceased during the early 1650s.[16] Not until after the Restoration, in 1661, did the duke appoint a deputy to survey the yearly value of his manor and lordship of Villiers in Ireland, but he made no effort to have a comprehensive survey made of his English estates until 1668, when he appointed Edward Christian steward of his estates. In May 1671 Buckingham ordered Christian to render an account.[17]

So few accurate records of the duke's finances came into the scriveners' hands in 1671 that they had no choice but to retain Edward Christian in his position for two more years. Since he knew the estates, the bailiffs and the tenants, he was the only person capable of recording the income from each property along the strict lines which Monteage defined. The survey made of the duke's properties in 1668 was of little use to the scriveners,

---

[12] Robert Hyde's letter, August 1674, Box 8, L.S.E.
[13] Ex. R.O., MS 68 D/DAc 244–5.
[14] Bod. Lib., MS Eng. Lett. c.201, fols. 92–3.
[15] L.J., IX, 467, 528.
[16] Calendar of the Committee for the Advance of Money, 1642–56 (London, 1888), 533.
[17] 'A View of Mr. Christian's Accompts . . . [1668],' Clayton papers, Osborn, Yale MS 202/23.

who made no mention of it. Since the source of corruption was Edward Christian, who had helped to make the survey, the scriveners could expect that his current accounts were falsified. In 1671 the duke's steward saw that his own position would soon be eliminated, and during the time left to him, he stole £352 from the duke's own money and embezzled other large sums written off as law charges, riding charges, coach hire and other miscellaneous expenses. From the bailiffs he extorted £213 in blackmail, threatening to reveal their theft from the estates to the trustees, long before Clayton and Morris had begun to inspect the system of management.[18] Nothing so displayed the power and wealth of this impudent steward's machinations as his challenge before the Lord Chancellor himself of the legality of the warrant issued to depose him.[19]

Once the scriveners' rent-collectors had established their authority on each estate, they proceeded to control the tenants with instructions received from the scriveners. If the bailiff had been discharged, the scriveners often found it necessary to have one of the tenants serve as their representative or to act as assistant to the receiver between the visits he made to the estate. At the lowest level of the scriveners' hierarchy of personnel were these deputies, rewarded for their services more often with favors than with salaries. Forcing tenants to pay their rents and arrears meant invariably that some tenants would have to vacate their leaseholds. At the same time, however, certain other peasants were willing to take up the vacated leaseholds. Through this type of enterprising person the scriveners and their agents forged weak compacts to prevent the private agreements with the other tenants which had been the source of corruption of the bailiffs. In 1671 on the manor of Loddington, Leics., Peter Woodcock, the rent-collector, deputized a tenant, one Verney, as his assistant to help him arrange new leases and to handle affairs during his absence.[20] In another example, on the manor of Whimburgh, Norfolk, in 1672–3, William Canham threatened to leave his farm unless his lease were set upon a new rent, which he submitted directly to the scriveners. They agreed to his terms, for which he was required to act as their agent there.[21] Likewise, on

[18] 'Accompt of the Duke of Buckingham's First Trustees, Michaelmas and Christmas, 1673,' ibid.

[19] Bod. Lib., MS Eng. Lett. c.201, fol. 114.

[20] L.R.O., MS 35'29/357 A & B; ibid., 35'29/258.

[21] Daniel Sharpe to Thomas Leman, March 31, 1672, Box 5, I.U.; William Canham to C., 1671, Box 3, L.S.E.; same to same, March 10, 1673, Box 4, ibid.; Daniel Sharpe's letter, May 2, 1673, Box 11, ibid.

another estate in Norfolk Clayton appointed as wood-collector Sir Philip Tyrwhitt, who then recommended a Mr Fanning to receive the rents on Clayton's estate at Bardney, Lincs. In the following year Fanning was rack-renting the leases and securing the deserted farms in his own name, pre-sumably the favor he received for his pains in the scriveners' plans.[22] Another tenant who rose to the lowest ranks in the scriveners' service was John Freeman, in the manor of Burton Lazars, Leics. In 1682 he began col-lecting the rents for the leases Peter Clayton had taken, and for his efforts he was given £5. Acting upon new instructions, Freeman in the next month began an unofficial survey of the Bishop of Ely's lands in the manor. He sent Peter Clayton a list of the outlying tenures which he claimed by right belonged to Peter Clayton but which over the years had fallen into the bishop's hands. He then made a deposition that these lands were lands of inheritance of Sir William Hartopp, from whom Peter Clayton had bought his leases. When they reverted into Clayton's hands, the tenants' rents were raised.[23] In another example, a tenant betrayed the interests of his fellows on the manor of Kirkby Moorside, Yorks., during the 1680s and Clayton's tenant-cum-rent-collector got affidavits from the tenants about their destroying the woods, 'when he has given them their bellies full of drink that they do not know very well what they do . . .'[24]

Rent-collection was necessarily tied to the setting of leases, though upon what lines these judgments were made and where lay this responsibility in the scriveners' hierarchy is unclear. There was a general banking policy in lease-setting, apart from any considerations of estate management. Because many lenders tended to extend their debts beyond the amount set in the original contract, uncertainty of when the mortgage would finally be settled made the scriveners reluctant to give leases beyond the original life of the loan. For this reason, as well as for the credit-worthiness of the estate as it was assigned or discharged, short-term parole leases were the rule, at least until 1677, when the Statute of Frauds and Perjuries required that all leases be written.[25]

In one unusual instance the matter of lease-setting was referred by the rent-collector to Clayton, who then made a decision which went beyond the customary procedures of leasing. All the tenures in the estate, in Leicestershire, fell due at the same time, whereupon the scrivener ordered

[22] Sir Philip Tyrwhitt to C., August 23, 1673, Box 4, L.S.E.; John Rea to Thomas Leman, August 25, 1674, Box R, I.U.
[23] L.R.O., MS 35'29/188; ibid., 198, 202, 224.
[24] Langley Gace to C. [1680], Langley Gace Letters 1674–98, Fairfax Collection.
[25] Statute of Frauds, 1677 (29 Car. II, c. 3).

that an auction be held in the estate at which the new leases would go to the highest bidder. When the day arrived, the furious tenants had no choice but to concede, though they agreed among themselves beforehand that no man would take a lease for more than a year.[26] On most estates the leases did not fall due simultaneously, and in this instance, presumably, the demand for land by the tenants was greater than in other situations in which vacated leaseholds were common. Nevertheless, the example is a window on Clayton's own idea that land was a commodity subject to the forces of competition.

At the same time that the scriveners had their own ideas about the setting of leases, each estate presented its own problems with the tenants' leases. Monteage is silent upon the question of how rents were determined, though two examples in the Clayton papers show that rents were expected to conform to what prices would bring. In 1673 Daniel Sharpe summoned one of the scriveners' tenants in Norfolk, a Mr Apsley, to set his rents for the following year. The man showed him his accounts of lamb sales, amounting to his rent at Lady Day. In the next week Sharpe planned to inspect his waste book, receipts and the condition of his farm.[27] In another example, in 1674, Robert Hyde sent Clayton a 'calcularoid' of a farm he let in Essex:

a good pennyworth at the rate I let it all, for fifty cows and 160 ewes raises £160 of the rent [£180] which he keeps upon part of his marsh land. [The tenant] has at least 100 acres of wheat and other corn besides keeping of ten or twelve cows for himself, horses, young cattle, 200 sheep, etc.[28]

There was no question of forcing the tenants to honor the terms of leases, if no record survived of the leases or the rents. This was the problem the scriveners faced when they assumed management of the Duke of Buckingham's estates. They had no choice but to make new contracts with the tenants who were held to the rents they were paying from 1671 to 1673 when Edward Christian took this information for Clayton and Morris.[29]

Aside from the question of what the rental payments should be, the scriveners were concerned that the leases should reflect the agriculture of the tenants. Most likely significant leasing transformation would occur in a changing agricultural pattern such as Simon Neale described at Lutterworth in 1664, and this offered one way of offsetting the depressed circum-

---

[26] L.R.O., MS 35'29/357A.
[27] Daniel Sharpe to Thomas Leman, March 5, 1673, Box 5, I.U.
[28] Robert Hyde's letter, 1674, Box 8, L.S.E.
[29] 'Accompt of the Duke of Buckingham's Trustees at the Time of the Transfer to the Second [Trustees],' fols. 3–5. Clayton papers, Osborn, Yale MS 202/23.

stances. Conversion from pasture to arable presented new problems at the same time that it offered relief. When the fields were plowed, boundary stones were knocked down and hedges disappeared, confusing property definitions.[30] Even structures were destroyed in the sake of the plow, as Clayton discovered in 1666, when a farmer destroyed a small shepherd's croft.[31] The scriveners' policy was not to halt this process of agricultural change, but rather to control it for their own profit by giving, generally, short-term tenures at new rents. Otherwise, the tenants might make these changes at will, as had happened at Lutterworth. In 1674, from one of the Duke of Buckingham's estates in Yorkshire, the rent-collector wrote Clayton that the tenants planned in the spring to plow the demesne lands for their own fodder, a desperate step taken by poor men without corn or sheep, recently dead of the rot. Their plans were ill-informed, the rent-collector thought, for every year the mown hay on the demesne was unsold, as hay prices generally were so low.[32]

In another example, the scriveners controlled the process to better advantage. The graziers at Down Rossall, Salop, were in desperation, sowing grain on the heath: 'many poor people and they fear the worst, they are at your mercy . . . ' By 1673 this situation had changed, for the scriveners' rent-collector was letting some lands for pasture, others for hay, and even other land on leases for weeks and months.[33] In the following year Morris instructed him to allow no more farming leases.[34]

Similarly, in Norfolk Daniel Sharpe followed the suit of his tenant who asked for a three-year lease accommodating his arable lease with some pasture grounds for his sheep at spring-time.[35] As tenancies fell vacant Daniel Sharpe stocked them. 'I made £43 clear of the grounds unlet at Whimburgh which I could not let for £35.' Bad though the grazing trade had been for the past three years it could not get much worse, he thought.[36]

In dealing directly with the tenants, without the advice of their agent, the scriveners were reluctant to give new leases unless they knew how the lands were to be used. William Hall, a tenant at Higham, Northants., wrote Morris in 1676 for an abatement of his rent. From London came the brief rebuff that it was in the nature of tenants to complain. Hall then changed

[30] Manley, 'Legal Aspects of Surveying,' 414.
[31] Thomas Clayton to C., February 2, 1666, MS D/CE/23, Buc. R.O.
[32] Christopher Hawley to C., March 4, 1674, Box H, I.U.
[33] Bod. Lib., MS Eng. Lett. c.201, fol. 90.
[34] Ibid., fol. 95.
[35] Daniel Sharpe to C., 1671, Box 5, I.U.
[36] Daniel Sharpe to C., September 18, 1671, ibid.

his tactics, to ask for a new lease. Wool and corn prices had been low for some time, he wrote, but the past summer dairying had fallen also. This was the cause of his predicament. But next to his house was a piece of land, fit neither for mowing nor grazing, situated high above the other lands. This land he wished to plow for hay. To support his request for a three-year arable lease of the close, the man added a deposition from his neighbors testifying, first, that his present rent was set out of proportion to the productivity of his land and, secondly, that the high ground, unused in its present state, deserved a low rent.[37] Support of the rent-collectors encouraged similar requests which the scriveners in London could not verify from the records taken during assessments.

Tenants found often that the only way of surviving in the depressed market was to secure an abatement of their rent. In 1671 one man in Norfolk threatened to leave his farm unless he received a reduction of ten shillings on his rent.[38] In another example, on a Mr Crouch's estate near Henley, a tenant without a lease planned to leave his farm, even if an abatement was given 'in respect of the hardness of the times . . . '[39] When such threats meant that there were no other tenants nearby to take up deserted leaseholds, Clayton and Morris were generally open to granting rental abatements, especially if they received concessions in return. When Sir Thomas Foot reassigned his mortgaged estate in Oxfordshire to the scriveners' management, a tenant, Mr Howtyn, did them a small legal favor and asked for a rental abatement of £10.[40] Similarly, in 1679 the scriveners agreed to abate Stephen Springate's rent in Kent, as well as to pay all taxes and those repairs which did not exceed £20 yearly.[41] In another example, Katherine Squire, a tenant on one of the Duke of Buckingham's Yorkshire estates in 1684, asked Clayton for £15 abatement on the 'new close.' At the same time she offered more than the prevailing rents for other farms. As for 'the [neathern] Salterford I will give £10 to come in to that and pay the old rent.'[42] Ordinarily rental reductions for repairs were approved by the scriveners only when this had been agreed beforehand. Abatements were not rights to be assumed by tenants like Richard Wood who in 1674 asked

[37] Northants. R.O., MS 100A; *ibid.*, 100B.

[38] Daniel Sharpe's letter, September 18, 1671, Box 5, I.U. With the same resourcefulness characteristic of his work for the scriveners, Sharpe then amended the land valuations which he sent to London, describing the tenures as upland, arable, pasture, meadow and marsh (N.R.O., MSS 3229 A & B, 3240, 3365).

[39] Richard Stevens to C. & M., June 5, 1672, Box 5, I.U.

[40] Philip Style to M., February 28, 1672, *ibid.*

[41] C. and M. to John Palgrave, June 7, 1679, G.L., MS 10,049.

[42] Katherine Squire to C., December 20, 1684, Box 5, I.U.

Morris what allowance he would give for the repairs he had made.[43] New tenants, however, might bargain with the scriveners over the question of rents and repairs before the leases were signed. In 1673 Humphrey Tompkins reported that no tenant would take the home farm at Down Rossall until repairs were made.[44] In another use of abatements, William Hardy reported to Morris from Alford in 1687 that he had set the alienation fines of widow Fowler and Mr Dayes at the highest rates, though each tenant expected some relief when his rent was abated.[45] The tone of the letter is that the rent-collector was following a directive from London whereby reductions were granted during hard times with the hope that when things improved, this concession would be discontinued.

Closely associated with rental abatements were arrears of rent. Deferred rents were integral to the system of rural credit, enabling tenants to ride the crises besetting them. When things were better, they could resume their rents according to their leases and make up the rents postponed. Abatements seem usually to have been a condition of the tenure, made at the time of the lease, whereas arrears arose unexpectedly. Arrears were debts, and as such, subject to legal pressure; if these obligations accrued upon mortgaged lands, a debt had arisen upon another debt, thus complicating the question of who owed whom what. Anthony Keck recorded for Clayton a case in Chancery in 1675 in which the court decided that the arrears must be paid off before the collateral security could be collected.[46] In many instances this was clearly impossible, if the tenants were unable to pay. Arrears were not advertised in the particulars as assets of estates, for they were of questionable validity to the lender. Nevertheless, arrears became potent legal tools in the hands of the scriveners. In 1685 Clayton issued a declaration of ejectment against a tenant in Holbeach, claiming that the rent on his lease for Michaelmas 1633 had never been paid.[47] This extraordinary incident no doubt had punitive motives, a sort of legal control the scriveners could wield with arrears.

Arrears were of several kinds, which the scriveners treated with corresponding seriousness. Short-term arrears were often paid between terms. In 1681 William Hardy repeated to Morris what Dymocke Walpole had

---

[43] Daniel Sharpe's letter, April 30, 1674, Box 11, L.S.E.

[44] Bod. Lib., MS Eng. Lett. c.201, fol. 90.

[45] William Hardy to M., December 14, 1681, Foster Library, Lincolnshire Archives Committee.

[46] (Anonymous,) in Keck, *Cases Argued and Decreed in the High Court of Chancery from the 12th year of King Charles II to the 31st* (London, 1697), 261.

[47] J. Stukley's letter, May 12, 1685, Box 5, I.U.

written the scrivener in 1673, that tenants in Lincolnshire delinquent with
their Michaelmas rents made up their arrears with the goods they made
and sold at the Plow Monday markets.[48] Over the ten years 1671–80
William Hardy mentioned arrears as an ordinary expectation of agriculture, often with the implication that there was little cause for alarm. In
1671 the tenants at Orby had a poor harvest, he wrote, but if some failed
to pay their rents, there were other tenants who would take up the leases.[49]
When the drains failed at Ingoldmells and Halberstoft in 1673 and 1674,
the tenants there did not take arrears; instead, they asked for abatements,
which was the lesser course.[50] Then, in 1677 Hardy reported that most of
his tenants would pay their rents slowly that year, though there was little
danger of long-term loss.[51] In 1681 Hardy reported a comparably optimis-
tic situation to London. The scriveners' tenants were the best of any in the
county; there was no danger of losing any rents, even though these tenants
paid slowly.[52]

In other regions arrears became a more serious problem. From Norfolk
Daniel Sharpe's reports on arrears during the hard times of the 1670s were
increasingly pessimistic. In 1671 he was 'forced to deal gently' with the
tenants, who 'desired me to apologize for them' with their arrears.[53] When
this tactic failed, he took a hard line. By 1673 he 'often told [the tenants]
they should be severely dealt with' for not paying their rents, and he sought
the advice of a local lawyer to take legal action against them.[54] In the
Midlands Thomas Clayton had similar troubles. In 1673 he could collect
no rents at Raunds, and the tenants at Pickworth were similarly
negligent.[55]

Beyond a certain point the scriveners were forced to take recourse
against recalcitrant tenants. In 1676 William Hardy was planning a trip to
London to discuss the matter of the ejection of an obstreperous tenant. It
was the first such action he had contemplated, and no instructions about
ejection had been given to him when he had first become the scriveners'

---

[48]William Hardy to M., December 14, 1681, Foster Library, Lincolnshire Archives
Committee.
  [49]Same to same, November 17, 1671, *ibid.*
  [50]Same to same, June 28, 1673; same to same, February 3, 1674; same to same, December
6, 1674, *ibid.*
  [51]Same to same, January 16, 1677, *ibid.*
  [52]Same to same, December 14, 1681, *ibid.*
  [53]Daniel Sharpe to C., July 7, 1671, Box 5, I.U.
  [54]Daniel Sharpe's letter, August 1, 1673, Box 11, L.S.E.
  [55]Thomas Clayton to C., October 12, 1673, MS D/CE, Buc. R.O.

agent. Clearly his letter reveals that such a matter was highly unusual.[56] From another county, Norfolk, Daniel Sharpe was exasperated in 1673 with the common retort he heard from the tenants, that they had already paid their arrears to the stewards preceding him on the estates. From the stewards came the counter-reply that the tenants were lying; none had paid them a penny of their back-rents. Refusing to be outwitted any longer, Sharpe took one of the tenants, Arthur Parker, to court. Parker's neighbors swore under oath that he had duly paid his rent to the steward, but Sharpe proved that the steward in question had died a fortnight before the alleged payments were in his hand. With this victory Sharpe then turned to the steward at Whimburgh who was given a list of the tenants in arrears with quit rents. The tenants would see whether or not Ives had reported their arrears, and Sharpe would be present to witness the accusations likely to be hurled on both sides in this confrontation.[57] Sharpe's tactics were unusual. Lond-standing arrears were difficult to substantiate in court when the bailiffs' records had disappeared and when the other tenants were willing to testify that their neighbors had never been behind with their rents.[58]

Taking legal action against tenants challenged the influence which the scriveners could command in local politics. Clayton was not above asking the Lord-Lieutenant of Norfolk to reduce the assessments on lighthouses charged upon his clients' estates.[59] In another instance, he bribed the J.P.s in Purfleet, Essex, to deny alehouse licenses to all but his own enterprises in the region.[60] In a more important context he and Morris never gained influence among the county benches to assist them in their management of mortgaged property.[61] The law did not recognize the scriveners' policy forbidding tenants to reinvest their arrears without their consent, as the justices at the Norfolk assizes declared in 1674.[62] The matter arose again in 1684, when Clayton brought suit for the arrears of George Green, who pleaded that he had already paid as much in repairs ordered by the rent-collector.[63]

[56]William Hardy's letter, November 15, 1676, Foster Library, Lincolnshire Archives Committee.
[57]Daniel Sharpe's letters, August 1, 1673, August 27, 1673, April 30, 1674, Box 11, L.S.E.
[58]Robert Hyde's letter, August 1674, Box 8, L.S.E.
[59]Daniel Sharpe to C., July 7, 1671, Box 5, I.U.
[60]J.R.L., MS Eng. 959, fol. 191.
[61]They tried, however, in 1673 to persuade one of the Buckinghamshire justices to act as steward of the Villiers's estates there, but he refused because of conflict of interests. Robert Chapman to Thomas Leman, December 15, 1673, Spec. MS Coll. Buckingham, C.U.
[62]Daniel Sharpe's letter, April 30, 1674, Box 11, L.S.E.
[63]George Green to C., January 17, 1684, Box 7, L.S.E.

When the scriveners decided they had no recourse but to evict a tenant, they had to issue a declaration of ejectment, served by the sheriff and his bailiffs. This was a drastic procedure, which in 1673 reached a violent conclusion. At Down Rossall Thomas Kniveton's house was:

beset round with eleven or twelve resolute bailiffs, and as soon as they had secured every door, they forced and broke the outer door, and after that they did likewise broke some more doors, I being in the house and hearing them so resolute . . . I did not believe that any persons upon above action and the first writ would do any such thing.

This fracas was not finished until the frightened man had been shot in the leg and then arrested.[64] In another instance, Clayton's counsel in Norfolk recommended in 1674 a similar extreme recourse, but only if it were done cautiously, concealed from public scrutiny.[65] Why would the scriveners have used such desperate measures to pursue debts which were ordinarily a part of the credit process? If arrears were incurred before the scriveners' clients came into the estate, they were debts marginal to the terms of the contract. There was the alternative method of assessing penalty fines (*nomine poenas*) upon arrears.[66] Perhaps the drastic measure of ejection was used by the scriveners to resolve more the problem of the debtor than the debt, and the compelling reasons behind these few cases of ejection lay in the struggles between the rent-collectors and tenants determined to resist their authority, a theme previously demonstrated in these operations.[67]

On the other hand, speculating in the depressed markets of the 1670s could be a reason for taking short-term arrears, profitable both for the tenants and the scriveners. As the price of beef declined, some farmers changed or expanded their pasturage from dry to milch and were as able to sell their products in the dairy markets as they were to sell their cattle. Sir John Bramston pointed out these alternatives early in 1672, in a letter of apology he wrote to Morris, explaining why he had not made his Michaelmas mortgage payment. At the time of slaughter he had fat oxen:

but beef is so cheap & so has been that every men advised the keeping them for a

---

[64] Thomas Kniveton to C., June 1673, Box B, I.U.

[65] Daniel Sharpe's letter, April 30, 1674, Box 11, L.S.E.

[66] *C.T.B.*, Vol. VIII (London, 1924), 1157. Before the sale of the Duke of Buckingham's estate at Uffington his trustees considered serving warrants upon tenants delinquent in their rents (Leeds, Sheepscar Library MS Acc. 1202/102[41]). Apparently the trustees did not employ overt legal action against any of the duke's tenants, but the threat of court procedure might well have been a reason for their regular resumption of rents.

[67] See above, pp. 167–8, 186–8.

butter market. I did not think [his lender] had need for his interest . . . it shall not displease him . . .

When he found a market for his butter, he wrote, he would send the money on to London.[68] In the Midlands during the 1670s butter- and cheese-brokers arranged with farmers to buy their dairy products before the time of the markets.

Clayton's rent-collectors were also aware of the possibilities of alternating agricultural markets for their products cultivated on the demesne lands. In 1674 William Hardy wrote the scriveners that the hay was so poor that it was not worth giving to cattle. In Orby, however, he had twenty acres of good hay which he would sell if the price was right. If not, he would buy cattle to feed on it, then sell the cattle.[69] Later he wrote Clayton that the price of hay was so low that he could not sell it, and he asked his permission to buy six or eight bullocks to graze there.[70] Since he had first reported this possibility, Clayton had apparently required his own authorization for this decision. The tenants had followed Hardy's example by 1681, for he wrote the scriveners in December that the beef markets in London had been so poor that few farmers would send their cattle to market, hoping to reserve them for other purposes. As a consequence, tenants' rents that season would only trickle to London.[71]

In Norfolk Daniel Sharpe in 1674 fattened his cattle on the hay growing on lands which tenants had deserted.[72] Then he arranged to sell his stock to brokers in the neighborhood representing butchers in London, though they later reneged on their contracts when the price of beef dropped even further. In the previous year he had enclosed a bill of exchange to the scriveners drawn on a horse-broker in London,[73] suggesting that his hay was used to feed horses. In another instance, horses and cattle were both eating the hay at Bampton, Oxfordshire, so Richard Coxeter reported to Morris in May 1676. Corn, hay and wool were worth little. Throughout the summer he planned to sell the dung until the beasts were slaughtered.[74] All these examples of intelligent options in demesne farming formed the

[68]Bod. Lib., MS Eng. Lett. c.14, fol. 16.
[69]William Hardy's letter, December 6, 1674, Foster Library, Lincolnshire Archives Committee.
[70]Same to C., March 8, 1676, ibid.
[71]William Hardy's letter, December 14, 1681, ibid.
[72]Daniel Sharpe's letter, November 1674, Box 5, I.U.
[73]Daniel Sharpe to Thomas Leman, June 18, 1673, ibid. See also same to same, December 22, 1675, ibid.
[74]Richard Coxeter to M., May 1, 1676, Spec. MS Coll. Buckingham, C.U.

gist of Stephen Monteage's advice to the rent-collectors, working on widely scattered estates.

The land would seem to govern the loan entirely, as these examples illustrate, so that once the loan had been signed the scriveners passed the fate of the contract to their agents in the country who managed the mortgaged property. The demands of mortgage banking were more intricate than this dependence indicates, for the success of the loan did not rest entirely upon the ideals of high farming. At the same time, there was a reverse policy in which the loan dictated how the land was managed, toward a policy set in the bank's headquarters in the City, subject to change throughout the life of the loan. Clayton's policies were not fixed necessarily toward the greatest yield the land could bear, and to that extent banking and land use illustrate a principle different from that argued by Manley and Culpeper on the relationship between the price of land and the rate of interest.

This interplay of banking policy in the City and land management is best illustrated in a particular series of records in the Clayton papers, the accounts of the trustees of the second Duke of Buckingham, kept from 1671 until after the duke's death in 1687. The Buckingham trust became the greatest single financial operation the scriveners handled, to the extent that the duke's affairs became in effect a separate department of the bank, administering states scattered from London into Yorkshire through its own self-contained and residential rent-collectors. This special commission had a unique relationship to the bank's London center, parallel to rather than integrated with the scriveners' other affairs. A group of trustees, including Clayton and Morris, directed policy governing the duke's finances. The scriveners executed the trustees' decisions through an apparatus similar to the bank's other operations in the country.

This arrangement was unusual, but Buckingham's finances acquired a notoriety of their own. By tradition the Duke of Buckingham has become the Restoration rake *par excellence* whose excesses brought him financial collapse.[75] For his pains in the duke's affairs Clayton was later singled out from the other trustees, to be accused of mishandling the duke's inheritance and thereby contributing to his ruin.[76] From the evidence presented to the trustees – now a part of the Clayton papers – the reputation of both

[75]Buckingham's biographers all support the duke's financial ruin after 1671. Lady Burghclere, *George Villiers Second Duke of Buckingham 1628–1687* (London, 1903); H. W. Chapman, *Great Villiers* (London, 1949); J. H. Wilson, *A Rake and His Times* (New York, 1954).

[76]See above, p. 6.

men must be revised, for Buckingham died a rich man. The legend of his poverty and ruin is false. The duke has another place in history, apart from his finances, but this slur upon the reputation of Clayton embraces his competence as well as his integrity. Far from exhausting the duke's fortune, Clayton and Morris at the behest of his trustees terminated Buckingham's most pressing debts and brought to date the operation of his estates to conform to a style fitting a great Restoration courtier. To exonerate Clayton from the charges that he misappropriated the duke's fortune draws one back to the theme of this chapter, for no other single case study of estate management is so richly documented in the Clayton papers.

To overhaul the duke's fortune his trustees were given the greatest latitude, free from his own advice and intervention. His only stipulation was that they should remit to him an annual allowance of £5,000 from the lands ceded to them.[77] For the first two years of their control the trustees had no precise idea of the duke's income and debts, misled as they were by the falsified accounts which his steward Christian rendered for his service in the duke's affairs from 1668 until the beginning of the trust. With virtually no record of the duke's debts and no estate records, the trustees were not able until 1673 to calculate the duke's debts, which they estimated to be £135,308. As he failed to meet his interest payments some of the duke's mortgagors entered his property and directed this income from Christian's control, a fact the steward failed to report at first to the trustees. If all the alienated mortgaged lands were resumed, the trustees estimated, and if all the lands in hand were let, the duke would receive from his lands a gross annual yield of £18,951 14s. 9d. from the following sources:

London
    York House
    Wallingford House
    Strand tenements
                         £2,079 0s. 0d.

[77] In addition to the scriveners, the first trust (1671–3) included Sir Thomas Osborne, John Tillotson, Sir Charles Harbord, Ranald Grahame and John Wildman: B.L., Add. MS 5821, fol. 222v. There were two successive trusts, the second from 1673 to 1675 and the third from 1675 until the duke's death in 1687: Folger Shakespeare Library, MS X.d. 492.

Rutland
    Burleigh
    Egleton
    Greetham
    Okeham
    Leighfield Forest
    Hambleton

                               £3,681 15s. 9d.

Buckinghamshire
    Winslow
    Eaton
    Bletchley
    Fenny Stratford
    Whaddon
    Nash
    Biddlesden

                               £2,293 18s. 0d.

Yorkshire
    Helmesley
    Kirkby Moorside

                               £5,060 19s. 4d.

Lincolnshire
    Uffington
    Tallington
    Wragby

                               £2,535 6s. 8d.

Leicestershire
    Shepshed
    Garrenden
    Daulby
    Broughton

                               £3,300 15s. 0d.
                                ————————
Total   £18,951 14s. 9d.[78]

[78]'A View of Mr. Christian's Accompts Given to His Grace the Duke of Buckingham ending 26 August 1671,' Clayton papers, Osborn, Yale, MS 202/23.

Once the trustees had established the yield of the duke's income, with a schedule for the gradual repayment of his debts, they planned for his future with another consideration in mind: how the duke wished to live. Two opposing forces had pulled at his finances before Clayton and Morris began to revamp his fortune. On the credit side, his estates were run on an antiquated system of household management, like that of a medieval lord who traveled around his estates, living off the food stored at the previous harvest. Buckingham was not among the number of peers who returned to his estates after the Restoration, to repair the damage done during years of exile. The second duke was as much a 'court' peer as his father had been, though the first duke had spent much time hunting on his estates in Rutland, near his duchess's relations at Belvoir. Rustic pursuits seem to have bored his son, who never even bothered to repair his houses in Rutland which Cromwell's soldiers had looted beyond habitation. As so little of his time was spent on his estates, where otherwise he and his retinue could have lived off the home farms, the duke's living expenses were probably proportionally greater than his father's.

At the same time, his altered life-style dictated more contemporary debit finances. For even though he might not wish to travel extensively in the country, a great peer like the duke needed a splendid country house and estate befitting his rank, preferably at a location near the court. As none of the properties he had inherited and retained suited this purpose, the duke and his trustees looked elsewhere. At Cliveden they found the spot, a short distance by river to Windsor and along the artery to London. To pay for the project the trustees agreed to sell York House and his other properties in the Strand. York House was sold first, and a few years later, the construction of Cliveden began. Buckingham's critics did not regard these sales as a trade-off. York House was sold as a desperate measure to satisfy the duke's creditors, so the legend runs, and then later, in an act of wilful extravagance, he engineered the final act of his ruin with the purchase of Cliveden.[79] Buckingham's enemies ignored the fact that all the other baronial mansions in the Strand, with the exception of Northumberland House, were pulled down by 1700 by owners who, like the Duke of Buckingham, no longer wished to live in such uncomfortable palaces.[80] For his base in London the duke rented a house in the West End, which

[79]Buckingham's biographers perpetuate the tradition of the duke's financial ruin through his own reckless designs. Lady Burghclere, *George Villiers Second Duke of Buckingham 1628–1687* (London, 1903); H. W. Chapman, *Great Villiers* (London, 1949); J. H. Wilson, *A Rake and His Times* (New York, 1954).

[80]*Survey of London*, XVIII (London, 1937), 93, 123, 125.

with his country place and primary residence in Berkshire was to be a combination in form strikingly similar to the living arrangements of peers with bases in southern England during the eighteenth and nineteenth centuries.

Over the same period when these financial transactions were made, the trustees brought a new administration to the estates. They dismissed Edward Christian and abolished the system by which he had controlled the duke's estates. This had been the old household system of management, in which each estate was controlled by a bailiff responsible to the steward, a figure in the duke's household. After receiving income from the bailiffs, the steward paid off the duke's personal debts. What weakened the steward's position was that each bailiff was virtually autonomous on his estate, meeting all expenses locally before he then remitted a net sum to the steward, either with no accounts at all or with records so vague that no bailiff could be held responsible for his finances. Edward Christian had been hired to coordinate the duke's bailiffs, but at the same time he had no power to displace them or in any other way to alter this arrangement which made himself susceptible to charges of corruption. When the duke fell into straits, his estates were mortgaged, placing his mortgagees in the same position as Christian, with no clear idea of the value of each of the estates, which were entrenched with corruption making good management difficult. Under the chamberlain system the estates were the pivot, the steward no more than a receiver of rents, and mortgages a last-ditch attempt to prevent disaster. The way to master the system was to build up the largest possible aggregation of estates, with the hope that the net return remitted to the household would meet expenses.

When the trustees took over the estates, they replaced the chamberlain system with new priorities. Their first decision was to reduce the interest on outstanding loans. With the exception of two loans taken at five and six per cent, the other mortgage rates varied from nine to eighteen per cent. If the interest payments could be reduced, the duke's projected income could meet all his expenses, including his allowance, with a comfortable margin to meet extraordinary expenses and reinvestment. With this plan the trustees arranged with Colonel Titus on May 2, 1671 that the interest accruing on his mortgage of Garrenden after that time would amount to no more than six per cent, and this practice held until the loan was paid off in 1675. Those loans at six per cent were carried to the end of the contract, such as Lady Sheffield's mortgage of £9,500. For the remaining mortgages, the trustees either paid off the loan altogether or refinanced the commitment at six per cent.[81]

[81]G.L., MS 6428, III, fols. 250v, 334v.

As it happened, this policy of reducing all mortgage commitments to six per cent proved to be a temporary measure. Soon after Clayton's men took over the management of the duke's lands, it was clear that the Helmesley estate was undervalued and could produce a greater income from its rents than the estimate of 1673. At the same time, on other properties, the fall of rents was so acute that the long-term net return promised to be less than the mortgage commitment. Apparently Clayton and other trustees did not believe that instituting long-range agricultural improvements was worth the effort. With the duke's residence in the South, it mattered little if the focus of his income shifted elsewhere, in this case to the North. In the wake of household management the trustees abandoned their original plan that solvency lay in the exploitation of the duke's patrimony. From 1674 to 1678 the trustees sold estates. In Lincolnshire, Wragby, Uffington and Tallington were sold, as were Daulby and Broughton in Leicestershire and Bletchley, Whaddon, Nash, Eaton and Fenny Stratford in Buckinghamshire, which together with the London properties amounted to £101,238.[82] The new owners of Daulby and Broughton and the Buckinghamshire lands all sold their purchases within the next few years, a comment on Clayton's assurance that those lands were not good long-term investments.[83]

With the sale money the trustees made several adjustments to Buckingham's fortune, as well as purchasing Cliveden. The Helmesley mortgage was redeemed, with the rental income reverting to the trustees. Clayton's prophecy was fulfilled: even with the sale of the other estates, redeeming the Helmesley mortgage kept the duke's annual rent roll at £17,127 6s. 4d., only £25 7s. 8d. less than his rents before the land sales.[84] Cliveden house made no immediate drain on the duke's capital, for it was financed on the long-term credit which artisans customarily gave.[85] Buckingham's outstanding debts were gradually reduced by 1676 so that his income exceeded his liabilities, including his allowance. From 1676 through 1679 the average yearly net credit balance in his account was £8,459.[86]

The accounts for the last two years of the duke's life are missing, though

---

[82] J.R.L., Charters 2742, 2745, 2746, 2748, 2750, 2751 and 2799; G.L., MS 6428, ii, fols. 249–51; iv, fol. 12.
[83] B.L., Add. MS 5821, fols. 225–6; E. F. Ward, *Christopher Monck, Duke of Albermarle* (London, 1915), 270–1.
[84] 'The Baylifs Accompts . . . 1675,' fol. 50, C.U.
[85] B.L., Add. MS 5821, fols. 225–6; Ward, *Albermarle*, 270–1.
[86] G.L., MS 6428, II, fol. 300v *et seq.*; *ibid.*, III, fol. 303v *et seq.*; *ibid.*, IV, fol. 9v *et seq.*

his trustees controlled his estates until his death.[87] No other fragmentary evidence suggests that the pattern of solvency established after 1676 was interrupted.

Once the household system was abolished, Clayton replaced those positions with other men in a new arrangement. No figure was appointed to replace Christian, as Clayton and Morris themselves assumed the duties of chamberlain. They now received the rents from the bailiffs and paid off all the charges upon the properties except the minor expenses. Each bailiff was made directly responsible to the scriveners, who trained each man in his duties and in precise record-keeping. One of their new agents was Richard Boddily, a shepherd on the duke's Buckinghamshire estates before the bulk of his land was sold in that county. In 1671 Boddily was ordered to collect the remaining rents and to keep exact accounts of all the income on the farms, along the lines laid down by Stephen Monteage.[88] At Helmesley Harry Crosland was given favors to break up the former bailiff's influence there, whereupon a tenant, Christopher Hawley, was by 1674 appointed as rent-receiver. His own holdings in the manor were worth between £300 and £400 per year, and he was given abatements of his rents as perquisites upon his appointment as rent-collector.[89] The loyalty of the bailiffs in Yorkshire and Rutland was tested in 1685 when the duke tried to circumvent the income from his manors there from the trustees into his own hands. He appointed another set of rent-collectors, and although the trustees' agents won the struggle for control, Langley Gace was almost killed by the tenants.[90]

The new bailiffs upheld the priority of rents over any considerations of direct farming. On the Yorkshire properties there was little turnover of leases. In 1677 Langley Gace received only £15 12s. 0d. in fines, on the few leases changing hands, and few tenants there deserted their farms, as the rents paid to the trustees increased.[91] On all the estates from 1674 until 1682 the bailiffs collected arrears of rent amounting to £2,908 11s. 7d., more than half of which were owed to the duke during the last years of

---

[87]The duke died intestate, without legitimate issue in 1687, whereupon his executors began to settle the Villiers' patrimony. The long period of executorship, when the estates were dispersed, contributed to the popular misapprehension that the estates were sold to pay the duke's debts.

[88]G.L., MS 6428, iii, fol. 160r; G.M.R. MS 84/1/3, fol. 292v; Clayton papers, Osborn, Yale MS 202/23, fol. 50.

[89]Christopher Hawley to C., March 4, 1674, Box H, I.U.

[90]Langley Gace to C., 1687, Langley Gace Letters 1674–98, Fairfax Collection.

[91]Spec. MS Coll. Buckingham, fol. 13, C.U.

Christian's tenure, 1671 to 1674.[92] With rising receipts of rent and arrears, together with the stability of tenures, the strict exaction of rents established in 1673 overcame the long period of bailiffs' corruption and tenants' evasions. On the duke's properties in the Hatfield Chase, which was not under the control of the trustees, large arrears of penalties arose for delinquent rent (*nomine poenas*).[93] Similar fines do not appear in the trustees' accounts, suggesting that they were willing to strike a compromise with the tenants – ordinary resumption of rents and eventual repayment of arrears in return for the cancellation of penalty fines.

From the duke's demesne lands the largest source of profits came from the sale of timber, particularly from the extensive logging on his estates in Buckinghamshire.[94] Richard Boddily repaired the hedges of Whaddon and enclosed fifty-one ewes and a ram, thus renewing pastoral farming[95] on one of the few estates in the county kept by the duke. At Kirkby Moorside from 1673 to 1675 in the first two years after the scriveners took control from Christian's bailiffs, and before any long-term improvements were made, the sale of sheep, cattle and wool brought £1,226 6s. 5d.[96] This suggests that pastoral farming was already well advanced there and that prices had not suffered adversely in the recent years, a conjecture supported by the healthy rents paid by the tenants there and at Helmesley. There is little evidence that direct arable farming was ever carried out by the trustees to any significant extent. The possibility that Buckingham could suddenly have broken his trustees' control mitigated any considerable expense for long-term improvements, though in a wider context tillage was not a feature which the scriveners promoted in any of the home farms of the estates they managed for their clients.

Tenants' rents assumed the highest priority in the scriveners' policy of absentee land management. To that extent land use in the context of mortgage banking operated differently from situations where landlords controlled their estates directly, free from lending commitments. Mortgage loans were attached specifically to rents given precise calculations at the time of assessment. Liabilities of properties were not ordinarily their reinvestments but rather their arrears and abatements, now a

[92]'Accompt of the Second Trustees,' Clayton papers, Osborn, Yale MS 202/23, fol. 17.
[93]*C.T.B.*, Vol. VIII, 1157.
[94]'Accompt of the Second Trustees,' Clayton papers, Osborn, Yale, MS 202/23, fols. 13, 31, 41.
[95]Spec. MS Coll. Buckingham, fol. 1, C.U.
[96]*Ibid.*, fol. 12.

part of the lending debt. The long-term mortgages granted by Clayton and Morris were unspecified in duration at the beginning of the contracts, which made the scriveners reluctant to institute long-term improvements in their clients' mortgaged properties. When the rents were sent to London to repay mortgages, these assets were isolated from a series of coordinated arrangements in the local economy. Old relationships between landlords and their tenants were broken during the tenure of the loan. If this was only a temporary interruption, often the tenants and their lands became parts of an impersonal process rationalizing their worth in a lending contract controlled at a distance, in the City of London.

CHAPTER 8

THE AFTERMATH
OF RESTORATION BANKING

———————— • ————————

During the 1680s certain changes occurred in the Old Jewry organization suggesting that the bank was never the same again. The first blow was Morris's death in 1682, when Clayton lost his partner and closest friend. In his will Morris provided for his nieces and nephews and made smaller bequests to his servants. All his remaining capital and interest in his investments made with Clayton went to his surviving partner.[1] Morris's death by itself left little impact on the capital of the bank, for all the loans which the two men had placed jointly in their own names – a great part of the lending fund of the bank – were now the property of Clayton. But following his partner's death, Clayton lost the men who had advised him and who had managed the affairs of his operation. Anthony Keck left the household in the Old Jewry about the time of Morris's death, as did Stephen Monteage, and no persons of comparable skills replaced these two men who had contributed so much to the legal and accounting development of the bank. In 1685 Peter Clayton died, removing the scrivener's most trusted assistant from the center of his operations. For almost twenty years he had overseen the clerical side of the business, and his position was not filled by Thomas Leman, Peter Clayton's deputy. These vacancies in the leadership of the firm made the bank's future uncertain.[2]

At the time of Peter Clayton's death in 1685 Sir Robert Clayton was fifty-five years old, with no children of his own to succeed him in the

[1] P.R.O., Prob. 11/37.
[2] See above, pp. 71–5. In 1695 Stephen Monteage became a staff member of the Bank of England (Bank of England, Staff Book B98).

business. His health gradually deteriorated. Throughout the 1690s he suffered from a chronic kidney infection, and in 1700 he wrote Sir Francis Child that he had lost his voice.[3] At the same time he devoted more of his attention to his estate in Sussex and reduced the staff in his London household accordingly. Seventeen people were living in the Old Jewry mansion in 1678.[4] By 1694 these numbers had dwindled to three maids and six men, besides Clayton and his wife. One of these men was a grocer and another a butler, leaving only four men to execute the functions of the bank in London.[5]

Clayton made his intentions clear in 1698 – that he was holding the business until his nephew and namesake, the eldest son of his brother William Clayton, was groomed to assist him. In 1698 he wrote to the young Robert Clayton, who was traveling in Italy, 'I grow old and cannot bear the fatigue of business as formerly and expect some relief from you after you have gratified your curiosity and that you apply yourself to business of another nature . . .'[6] This younger Robert Clayton had a careful education and exposure to the world denied to his father and uncle. In 1694 he was being tutored at All Souls, Oxford by Matthew Tindal and a Frenchman, a M. de la Roche, who reported to his uncle that he was especially adept in mathematics.[7] The Grand Tour was to be the culmination of his preparation. But when Sir Robert Clayton received from the citadel of popery itself the young man's comment that St Peter's Basilica was 'better than our own little crooked Kit Wren could do,'[8] he terminated the trip and ordered his nephew home. 'Few of the travelled Monsieurs' wished to be bankers, he had observed.[9] His doubts came suddenly to a tragic conclusion several months later when the young man died of smallpox in Lyons on his return to England.[10]

Sixteen years after the death of John Morris, Clayton had to find a new heir for his fortune, at a time when his own health had worsened. No evidence in the Clayton papers tells of any training given to William Clayton, the late Robert Clayton's brother, and the man who was to inherit his

---

[3] C. to Sir Francis Child, 1699, Clayton MS A.4/1, Buc. R.O.
[4] C.L.R.O., Assessment Box 11, MS 7 (Poll Tax Assessment, May 5, 1678).
[5] *Ibid.*, Assessment Box 113, MS 1.
[6] C.'s letter, December 8, 1698, Clayton MS D/CE, Buc. R.O.
[7] Matthew Tindall to C., September 25, 1694, *ibid.*, M. de la Roche to same, October 23, 1694, *ibid.*
[8] Robert Clayton to C., Clayton papers, July 7, 1698, 1698 May–July, Osborn, Yale.
[9] C. to Robert Clayton, June 18, 1698, Clayton MS D/CE, Buc. R.O.
[10] [The late Robert Clayton's tutor] to C., November 12, 1698, Clayton MS D/CE, Buc. R.O.

uncle's fortune upon the scrivener's death in 1707. In 1733 William Clayton was created Sir William Clayton, Bt., of Marden Park, by which time the banking operations in London had certainly ceased, though it may well have been long before then that the bank had come to an end. Thus, the death of Morris, followed by a subsequent period of uncertainty as to the bank's future, together with the death of Sir Robert Clayton's first heir, who might have perpetuated the firm, followed by the succession of Sir William Clayton, Bt. – these events, spanning nearly fifty years, promoted the demise of the bank opened in Cornhill in 1638.

This gloomy prospect was unknown when Morris died. As a greater share of the management of the firm became Clayton's responsibility, he turned more of his attention to investments in foreign trade. In itself this was not a radical departure from the past, for before Morris died, the two scriveners had turned to trading circles in the City in need of their capital and financial advice. This seemed a viable way of scattering their risks, as good investments in land became harder to find. Between 1673 and 1675 the two scriveners loaned the East India Company £30,156 19s., secured under the company's Great Seal.[11] On February 11, 1674 the Court of Committees ordered £19 3s. 4d. to be paid to Clayton for his advisory services,[12] though this was as close as he ever came to the inner councils of the well-established corporation.

With the new, inexperienced Hudson's Bay Company the scriveners found easier prey for their ambitions. In 1675 Clayton and Morris became cashiers to the company, receiving the money from fur sales in London and making its disbursements. Then, as the gentry and court stockholders of the company began to sell their shares, Clayton persuaded a group of City financiers to join him in lending money to the company and introducing principles of good business to an organization formerly slack in these matters. Feeling his way as treasurer and moneylender to the company, Clayton asked what the company could put up as security for his loans. In an interesting confusion between the trading community and this mortgage banker, the scrivener took their charter, which by the directors' understanding was a pledge of their good intentions, while the scrivener apparently took this to mean that the company's lands in the New World were his security.[13]

[11] This information, taken from the General Ledgers of the East India Company, was conveyed to me by Miss S. R. Johnson of the India Office Library.

[12] E. B. Sainsbury, ed., *A Calendar of the Court Minutes of the East India Company 1674–76* (Oxford, 1935), 15.

[13] E. E. Rich, *History of the Hudson's Bay Company*, Hudson's Bay Company Record Society (Toronto, 1942–6), Vol. I, 88–9, 94, 96, 152.

Soon his bullying tactics, together with his demands for eight per cent interest on his loans, lost Clayton his position in the company's affairs. In 1682 the company made its banker Sir Stephen Evance, who was never allowed to occupy the position of treasurer which Clayton had formerly held.[14] The leadership in the organization had matured under Clayton's tutelage to the point that it no longer required or trusted alien interference to the same degree.

After he severed his connection with the Hudson's Bay Company in 1682, Clayton found it difficult to regain a similar footing among other commercial groups in the City. As the trading companies acquired political affiliations, it became risky to attach oneself to a commercial enterprise. In the parliament of 1681 Clayton had moved to introduce an Exclusion bill, leaving no doubt as to his radical Whig sympathies. When the City of London's charter was withdrawn in 1683, Clayton lost his political base in City politics when he was deprived of his representation to the Court of Aldermen from Cheap Ward.[15] To the Whig business interests who might have wanted his money, Clayton must have seemed a liability. Not until the Revolution of 1688–9 was this disadvantage removed, though by that time his connection with investments in trade had ended, probably because his particular banking specialty was incompatible with trading credit.

At the same time the Whig Revolution brought him closer to the councils of government. Clayton became one of the first contributors to the capital of the bank in 1694 by his subscription of £2,000. Although this amount qualified him to be elected to the court, he did not become a director until 1702. At his death the bank transferred £3,995 of his stock to his executors. Thus, over thirteen years Clayton's stock in the bank barely doubled. Whatever Clayton might have had in mind for the future of his own banking operations when he wrote his nephew Robert Clayton in 1698, he had not established a tradition of moneylending to the trading companies, nor was his role in state finance anything more than lukewarm.[16]

---

[14] *Ibid.*, 170. See also *Minutes of the Hudson's Bay Company, 1679–82*, ed. E. E. Rich (Toronto, 1942), 34, 36, 334–5, Appendix B; *Minutes of the Hudson's Bay Company, 1682–84*, ed. Rich, 136–7, 219.

[15] T. B. Macaulay, *History of England from the Accession of James II*, ed. C. H. Firth (Oxford, 1913–15), Vol. III, 1270.

[16] Information concerning Clayton's investment in the Bank of England was conveyed to me by G. C. Gough, Deputy Governor of the Bank. Clayton's putative loan of £30,000 to William III in 1697 to pay off the troops is not substantiated in the *Calendar of Treasury Books*. The rumor derives from N. Luttrell, *A Brief Historical Relation of State Affairs from September 1678 to April 1714* (Oxford, 1857), Vol. IV, 293, but Clapham found no evidence

During the period of the bank's maturity, from 1660 to 1685, Clayton and Morris occupied a unique place in the private banking market. Today the scriveners' bank might appear to be an interesting artifact outside the mainstream of early banking development, its contours fashioned largely by goldsmiths. The powerful claim to prominence assigned to the goldsmith-banking tradition is its record of continuous survival. Hoare's, Child's, Martin's and Coutts's banks survive today in an unbroken tradition originating with goldsmiths' shops in the seventeenth century. Was there by 1700 a distinct form of finance characteristic of a sector of goldsmith-banking, enabling it to triumph over its rivals? The evidence is otherwise, for the great majority of the Stuart goldsmith-banks perished. If the rise of deposit banking is due more to accident and exception, in a pattern exclusive neither to the money-scriveners nor to the goldsmith-bankers, as both groups lost their hybrid relationships to their crafts, the innovations of Clayton and Morris in banking history assume a different importance, as does the record of the handful of goldsmith-bankers who managed to survive the century.

Three distinct groups are recognizable among goldsmiths who also offered banking services. The first group was distinguished as money-lenders to the Crown, though these bankers commonly made loans to citizens and accepted deposits from private clients. In the *London Directory* of 1677 the 'king's bankers,' among them Isaac Meynell, Edward Backwell, Sir Robert Vyner and Gilbert Whitehall,[17] are described as keeping 'running cashes,' indistinct from other bankers who had never acquired special privileges of lending to the Crown. After the Exchequer crisis of 1672 the 'king's bankers' declined gradually. One by one the royal moneylenders closed their doors, leaving a second cluster of goldsmith-bankers directing their attentions to private clients. From these men there arose by the 1690s a small, advanced elite whose banks survived into the first decades of the eighteenth century, in several instances much longer. From this third group and the practices they instituted, English private banking assumed the ability to survive from generation to generation. The majority of the goldsmith-bankers were not a part of the same pattern.

The first general description of the banking community in London after

---

to confirm the diarist's suggestion that a group of private bankers aimed through their own subscriptions to undermine the bank (Sir J. Clapham, *The Bank of England: A History* (Cambridge and New York, 1945), Vol. I, 58).

[17] See Appendix 3.

the failure of the 'king's bankers' in 1672 is the account given by the author of *The Mystery of the New Fashioned Goldsmiths*, who related that while their role as cashiers was well established by 1676, the goldsmith-bankers during the same period had not emerged with any sophistication as loan-brokers outside royal circles. From this pamphlet comes the venerated explanation of the origins of private banking in England, though that part of the tract was only incidental to the author's intention. *The Mystery of the New Fashioned Goldsmiths* is a diatribe written to expose the irregular ways in which the goldsmith-bankers speculated with their clients' deposits. By about 1676 the goldsmith-bankers had disoriented their reserves from trade and received deposits from the rents which landowners directed to their coffers. As they began to take in interest-bearing deposits, they turned to speculative investments to repay their clients' interest. With the prospect of making interest quickly on their deposits, clients were likely to recall their deposits without notice, with the result that their banks were forced to invest these reserves in risky, short-term investments. With this premium on liquidity now controlling their deposits, no banker could afford to tie up his capital in real security. As the numbers of private bankers increased rapidly after 1660, they turned increasingly to a great variety of high-yield, wildcat speculations: pawns, bottomry, 'notorious, usurious contracts,' discounts, even loans granted upon securities which heirs expected to receive at some indefinite time in the future. This was the 'mystery,' or concealed scandal, which the author exposed.[18]

Two contemporary accounts survive describing private banking in the early eighteenth century. This new evidence comes directly from two bankers, Thomas Snow and Thomas Martin, who summarized their profession in legal depositions in 1722, claiming to describe private banking as they had known it to be the practice since about 1700. The time-range of their observations might even precede the eighteenth century, since the banks of both men derive from the 1670s. Brief as both statements are, these sources are the only general descriptions of the period, inviting a comparison with the account given in 1676 in *The Mystery of the New Fashioned Goldsmiths* and the ways in which the banking profession had changed during the interval. Along with the sparse records of a few private banks, this is the only direct evidence of the history of the goldsmith-bankers in the late seventeenth and early eighteenth centuries.

Thomas Snow came from a family of bankers in operation at least by

---

[18]See pp. 18, 20, 32–3. 'Mystery' also connotes a gild, in this instance a perverse practice within a respectable company.

1670. Jeremiah Snow had a bank in Lombard Street at that time, but it was the establishment of Snow and Walton at the Golden Anchor in the Strand from which Thomas Snow emerged. By 1700 the original founders were dead, and Thomas Snow took over the business.[19]

The other deponent, Thomas Martin, was the founder of a more famous bank bearing his name. Martin in about 1700 absorbed a bank tracing its origins to Charles Duncombe, who was distantly related to one of the 'king's bankers,' Sir John Duncombe. Charles Duncombe was apprenticed to another royal moneylender, Edward Backwell. After completing his training Duncombe formed a partnership with Richard Kent, and upon Kent's death (before 1687) Valentine Duncombe joined the partnership. In the early days of his association with Kent, Charles Duncombe became Receiver of the Customs, fulfilling a type of collection service which the goldsmiths rendered before him. This service, like his business in exchange, recalls the activities of Vyner and Backwell. Only gradually did Duncombe begin to take in the deposits of private clients. By the time that Thomas Martin made his deposition the transition from receiver of state revenues and moneychanging was complete: private deposits now formed the bulk of the bank's reserves.[20]

Thomas Snow and Thomas Martin defined banking in similar terms – that it consisted chiefly in the receiving and paying of money on deposit, according to their clients' instructions.[21] The cash-keeping role of bankers is more detailed than the account of banking given in 1676. 'Banker,' 'Goldsmith' and 'Cashier' were terms they used interchangeably, with no indication that any label represented a function more specialized than any other. Both men spoke of their own special interests. Cause for the depositions arose when Martin was sued by a deceased client's executors for a deposit he had held for twenty years without paying interest. According to Snow, depositors left their money with bankers for safekeeping and for the convenience of having in London a cashier to pay their debts. To both men banking was a set of simple cash-keeping services, so valuable to clients that only uncommonly were depositors paid interest on their accounts. 'On the contrary,' said Snow, 'for some persons having deposited money in bankers' hands have made them allowances for their

[19] F. G. Hilton Price, *Handbook of London Bankers* (London, 1890–1), 128–9.

[20] J. B. Martin, *'The Grasshopper' in Lombard Street* (London, 1892; reprint edn, New York, 1968), 30–47; G. Chandler, *Four Centuries of Banking* (London, 1964), Vol. I, 100–10.

[21] Both depositions are in P.R.O., E.133.145/65 (7710). I am indebted to Mr Andrew Federer for this reference.

care, trouble and pains in receiving and paying such moneys and for their keeping an account. 'The rare instances in which bankers paid interest on deposits were by private agreement, and Snow believed that if such practice became public knowledge, the bankers' credit and reputation would be ruined. If their clients were occasionally to regard the practice as unjust, it was in keeping with the general practice of the London banking community of the time.

Both Snow and Martin remarked upon the widespread use of negotiable instruments at this time; the practice was now supported with legal sanctions. According to Martin bankers customarily gave notes for deposits received, promising to repay the sums at par. Snow described three different types of note in use. The bankers' note, drawn in the name of the bank, was for a timed deposit. 'Cash notes' were more commonly given to clients for their deposits, payable to the clients themselves or to bearers on demand. Still in use at this time were simple receipts for deposits. Snow did not comment as to whether or not this obligation to repay was actually written into the receipt, thereby giving it the character of a promissory note, or whether or not the terms of repayment were parole contracts, similar to Clayton's notes long before. But in another example altogether there is evidence that oral contracts were still used with negotiable instruments. In 1706 William Sheppard of St George's Parish, Southwark was sued over the question of whether or not a note he issued had been supported at the time it was given with the unwritten promise to repay interest on the money.[22]

The practice of withdrawals from accounts was in line with the motives of their depositors, Snow alleged. Those clients wanting to transfer their capital fairly soon after it was deposited ordinarily took bankers' notes. They then assigned these instruments to other parties who presented these negotiated notes at the bank for collection. Other clients put their money on deposit primarily for safekeeping. These long-term depositors ordinarily took receipts, but rather than negotiating these instruments to third parties, they made withdrawals by writing 'bills' on account.

Neither banker made reference to his loans, which in the instance of Martin's Bank were mortgage securities. When John Biddulph Martin prepared his history of Martin's during the nineteenth century, he found a list of conveyancing charges compiled c. 1704. The bank at that time used mortgages in fee in its contracts. Copies of indentures of lease and release

---

[22] P.R.O., C.110, Box 11, Bundle for 1706.

and bargain and sale were still in the archives.[23] As a bank lending money upon land Martin's Bank bore an affinity to the land banks of the late seventeenth century. The first land bank was founded by John Asgill and Nicholas Barbon in 1695, while in the same year John Briscoe founded the National Land Bank. The two establishments were merged in 1696 as the National Land Bank of England. These banks aimed to attract landowners by allowing credit upon their estates. By 1696 the land bank projects were moribund, their appeal lessened, perhaps, by the focus which private banking took during the 1690s, with its landowning depositors and invest-ments in mortgage loans.[24]

In 1722 Snow and Martin were careful to avoid any insinuation that their banks were similar to the joint-stock land banks of the recent past. Martin's Bank was particularly vulnerable to this association. One of Thomas Martin's clerks, Robert Surnam, left his bank in 1718 to become deputy cashier of the South Sea Company, and in 1721 he was arrested when the Bubble burst.[25] Bad investments brought the South Sea Company to ruin. Did Surnam's connection with both the company and Martin's Bank imply the bank's loans were likewise unsound? Better in 1722 for Thomas Martin to emphasize the cash-keeping nature of his business and omit any reference to his loans.

Martin's Bank developed in two stages, first establishing its role as cashier and somewhat later acquiring the skills permitting it to offer mortgage loans. Some banks, presumably, never made this transition, never resolved the problem of sound investments for their deposits. But where the records survive for banks managing to survive for more than a few years, the pattern of Martin's Bank reappears: a period of expertise in the paying and receiving of money, followed by more specialized techniques in loan-brokerage involving mortgage securities. This had been the way the bank of Robert Abbott and his successors had attained its specialized role as a moneylending facility. Only after Abbott's death, in what became the second generation of the bank, were Clayton and Morris able to integrate mortgage credit within their operations.

Hoare's Bank had a foundation and early history transcending the 'old-fashioned' goldsmith dealing in precious metal to the 'new-fashioned' cashier who later began to offer banking services to its clients. In 1673

---

[23] Martin, 'The Grasshopper' in Lombard Street, 195.
[24] W. R. Scott, The Constitution and Finance of English, Scottish and Irish Joint-Stock Companies to 1720 (Cambridge, 1910–12), Vol. III, 246–52.
[25] Chandler, Four Centuries of Banking, 106.

Richard Hoare established the bank at the Golden Bottle in Cheapside, with his cousin James Hoare. James Hoare was Comptroller of the Mint, where previously he had been Surveyor of the Meltings and Clerk of the Irons. In the early days of their bank this connection with the Mint continued, as James Hoare's appointment to the office of the Mint for the coinage of farthings, begun in 1672, lasted until 1676.[26] The bank's tradition as a goldsmith's shop declined only slowly, as these banking functions began to supersede the craft of working in precious metals and jewels. As late as 1735 Hoare's Bank was described as an 'open shop,' selling jewels and carrying on pawnbroking alongside its business in mortgage loans.

In 1690 Hoare's Bank moved from Cheapside to Fleet Street and after its relocation stopped paying interest on clients' accounts. By this time the bank's range of services had expanded. Throughout the 1690s much of the bank's work lay in investing its clients' deposits in mortgages and small-scale governmental loans. In the records of these early banks Hoare's is unique for the evidence that the bank employed a number of journeymen. The work of these agents is uncertain, though by implication they traveled outside London into the country. Richard Hoare established an arrangement by which his customers could cash their checks in the country drawn on their accounts in London, and his letters of credit supported that process. In one recorded instance the Hoares acted as receivers of public subscription money. When the town of Warwick was leveled by fire in 1694, contributions were collected from churches throughout the realm and sent to these men who were acting as receivers, like Clayton and Morris in 1675, when fire destroyed Northampton.[27]

In another instance the same focus on public and private collections of money, as well as mortgage investment, appears in the records of the goldsmith-banking firm of Fowles and Wotton during the 1690s. Sir Thomas Fowles was doing business as a banker at the time of Backwell, when he put large sums of money on deposit with him. In the *Little London Directory* of 1677 his name appears as one of the bankers maintaining running cashes. At some later period, probably after 1685, he formed a partnership with John Wotton. After Wotton's death in 1704, his executors and Robert Fowles sold the partnership to John Mead, distinguished in banking history as the man who introduced the practice of

[26]P.R.O., E.351/2122–4.
[27]*Hoare's Bank: A Record 1673–1932* (London, 1932), 4–6, 16–17, 20; E. T. Powell, *The Evolution of the Money Market (1385–1915)* (London, 1915), 112.

issuing pass-books to his clients. Mead and Company continued its operations until 1722.[28]

A large cache of papers has survived relating to the Fowles and Wotton banking enterprise during the 1680s and 1690s. As cashiers they issued receipts for deposits and allowed their clients to write checks upon their accounts.[29] One of their statements of account survives, issued to Mr Charles Atherton on December 14, 1699, listing interest and principal paid on his loan.[30] Fowles and Wotton accepted legal writings of their clients for safekeeping.[31] At the same time they continued the craft of goldsmiths, for a document mentions fourteen parcels of uncut Indian diamonds which they sold, placing the money on deposit for their clients.[32] As investors Fowles and Wotton negotiated mortgages extensively. Among their papers is the waste book of their lawyer listing his legal charges for conveyancing from 1690 to 1700.[33] In two different legal cases, *Bridgman* v. *Fowles* and *Fowles* v. *Bretland*, the types of indentures they employed with their securities were mentioned as being mortgages in fee, with the money transferred through penal bonds and the land conveyed through deeds of lease and release.[34]

By the 1690s Fowles and Wotton received money in London and rents in the country. The receivers for the taxes and aids in Lincolnshire in 1694 appointed Fowles and Wotton as their London agents, to accept all monies paid from the county in bills of exchange. After cashing the bills Fowles and Wotton were to deposit the money in Exchequer for tallies, to be transferred to the tax-farmers.[35] In 1699 the tax-farmer Thomas Austin made a similar contract with these bankers. All monies received from Wales and Cheshire were to be cashed and paid into Exchequer.[36] In 1693–4 they received the rents remitted to London from Lady Rebecca Falkland.[37] Several years later they had evidently employed a rent-collector, as a document dated June 17, 1697 mentions their being hard pressed for money and sending two of their agents to the country to press the tenants.[38] The

[28] Hilton Price, *Handbook of London Bankers*, 100.

[29] See the large number of W. Montagu's assorted checks, notes and receipts, 1685–9, in P.R.O., C.104/107.

[30] *Ibid.*, C.104/124, Part 1.

[31] See the undated letter of Peter Le Neve, 'Mr. Wotton, pray do me the favour to lock up this copy with the rest of the writings of my cousin Neve's estate . . . ,' *ibid.*, C.104/112, Part 2. See also *ibid.*, C.104/125, Bundle No. 6.

[32] *Ibid.*, C.104/108.   [33] *Ibid.*, C.104/124, Part 2.

[34] *Ibid.*, C.104/124, Part 2; C.104/125, Parts 1 and 2.

[35] *Ibid.*, C.104/125, Part 1.   [36] *Ibid.*, C.104/123.

[37] 'The account of John Davis for the rents of the farm and parsonage of Butleigh . . . ,' *ibid.*

[38] *Ibid.*, C.104/123, Part 1.

goldsmiths Cooke and Cary lacked the same facility, and they instructed Fowles and Wotton to receive all the rents due to them in the country.[39]

Before the 1690s Child's Bank had attracted a gentry clientele similar to Hoare's and Fowles and Wotton's, though its origins go back much further. The bank ascribes a continuous connection with a goldsmith's shop founded in Elizabethan times by a family named Wheeler. In the third generation William Wheeler changed the location of the shop to Fleet Street at Temple Bar where he displayed the sign of a marigold. His grandson, the last of the Wheelers to run the firm, died in 1663, leaving a widow who then remarried Robert Blanchard. Through this marriage the foundation of the Wheelers survived. Blanchard continued to run the business at the Marygold, assisted by Francis Child who in 1671 married the late William Wheeler's daughter, Elizabeth. The firm was known as Blanchard and Child until 1681, when Blanchard died leaving his own interest in the bank, as well as the Wheelers', to Francis Child.[40]

In spite of its antiquity there is no evidence that the Wheelers practiced banking alongside their goldsmith's trade. With no tradition as a royal moneylender, the bank was not faced with the problem of reorienting its finances after the Stop of the Exchequer. The transition to goldsmith-banking began earlier, when Blanchard began to increase his business by accepting deposit accounts. Plague and fire halted the growth of the firm for a while during the 1660s, but soon the banking part of the business eclipsed its other functions. According to an analysis of the Grand Ledgers of the bank, made by a former archivist, the new accounts opened in 1679 amounted to 206 deposit accounts, 27 goldsmithing accounts and 20 mixed accounts of both banking and the goldsmith's craft.[41]

Blanchard's bank in 1663 was a small shop with none of the apparatus of rent-collection, conveyancing or legal expertise characteristic of the firm of Clayton and Morris. His deposits came more and more from country gentlemen wanting mortgage securities, yet his bank had no network of agents linking his potential deposits in the country with his headquarters in the City. Hoare's Bank and Messrs Fowles and Wotton only acquired rent-collectors by the 1690s. Before then Blanchard devised another solution to give his bank a reach into the country economy. The ledger he kept from 1663 to 1679 devotes almost one-third of its pages to

[39] *Ibid.*
[40] *D.N.B.*, Vol. IV, 240.
[41] S. W. Shelton, 'The Goldsmith Banker,' in *Studies in the History of Accounting*, ed. A. C. Littleton and B. S. Yamey (London, 1956), 248.

one Christopher Cratford's affairs with the bank.[42] Cratford was a lawyer who hired the services of Clayton and Morris to receive the country rents due to Blanchard's bank. After 1672 these scriveners played a similar parental role to other goldsmith-banking firms, with Cratford acting as a middleman. Through this connection goldsmith-banking matured through its relationship with the more advanced structure of the scriveners' bank.

Before he moved into banking circles Christopher Cratford acquired a practical training in the problems bankers faced with their gentlemen clients. To his goldsmith-banking patrons Cratford filled a role similar to the position that Stephen Monteage, Thomas Manley and Anthony Keck held with Clayton and Morris. From 1659 to 1664 Cratford kept the court of the manor of Lamer, Herts., for Dame Jane Garrard.[43] By 1662 he was in the service of the Earl of Worcester, later to become the first Duke of Beaufort, whom he served as steward of his London household. With this position Cratford became the intermediary between the Somersets and their legal adviser, Chief Justice Sir Orlando Bridgeman. This connection with the great authority on mortgages and conveyances sharpened Cratford's knowledge of mortgage law. A series of letters from this period from Cratford to the Somersets reveals how extensive his knowledge had become. A friend of Bridgeman's had loaned the Countess of Worcester £5,500 through a scrivener, a Mr Hanson, and the lender sought Bridgeman's advice as to the legality of the loan and security. On June 21, 1662 Bridgeman instructed Cratford to write Lady Worcester that her interest was overdue and to instruct her to write a letter telling him when she planned to make good her payment.[44] On August 12, 1662 Cratford relayed Bridgeman's advice about a particular of lands the lady had composed for sale. Bridgeman was clearly in touch with the land market, for he cautioned her that her terms were too generous. Reduce the number of years' purchase from fifteen years to thirteen, he advised, and add other minor parcels of land to the contract.[45] By comparison, the bank of Clayton and Morris must have had a comprehensive appeal to other families like the Somersets, since it offered all these services under one roof

[42] Ibid., 251.
[43] Hertfordshire Record Office, Garrard MSS 225, 226, 228. I am indebted to Mr Andrew Federer for this reference and to his directing my attention to the subsequent references to Cratford in the Wiltshire Record Office.
[44] Wiltshire Record Office, MS 1300/234.
[45] Ibid., 237.

– a storage for valuables and expert legal advice about land sale, as well as the transference of land through mortgage covenants.

Bridgeman saw no conflict of interest between his influence on behalf of his clients and his role as Chief Justice. In 1662 he prepared the covenants and sealed the contracts in Lady Worcester's mortgage.[46] In the matter of a private Act relating to the earl's affairs, the Lord Chief Justice used his authority to borrow from the Clerk of the House of Lords the original bill, which he then mislaid.[47] Gradually, however, Cratford began to offer his own legal advice to the Beauforts, filling in details where Bridgeman only remitted instructions. On November 6, 1662, he commented on the problem of entail and reversion in a manor which the earl was offering for sale.[48] The tone of the letters changed in the closing months of 1662 from 'Lord Bridgeman instructs me to tell you' to 'I was with my Lord Bridgeman who tells me.'[49] Rather than passing along the particulars which the Somersets had drafted for Bridgeman's advice, Cratford rewrote these articles in a form he knew the Chief Justice would approve.[50] Then, in January 1663, Cratford gave the earl his own opinions about his lordship's plans to sell land, with the comment that if the earl approved his suggestions, he would then seek Bridgeman's advice.[51] When the correspondence ends in April 1664, Cratford had gained the confidence of the earl without interrupting his connections with the Lord Chief Justice.

With his expertise in 'court keeping,' his knowledge of the financial problems of a noble family living both in London and the country, as well as his tutelage in conveyancing practice under Bridgeman, Cratford had skills alien to goldsmith-bankers acquiring a clientele of country gentlemen. As he moved into banking circles in the City, he kept his independence, acting as intermediary for several bankers rather than the employee for any one foundation. He became a link between bankers and their clients, and this connection depended upon another point of contact, the bank of Clayton and Morris. The first recorded accounts of Cratford with Clayton and Morris began in 1669 and continue through the ledgers which survive until 1685. The significance of these accounts is unmistakable. As the lawyer for goldsmith-bankers, Cratford contracted the receiving services of Clayton and Morris. He instructed his bankers' clients either to pay their monies directly to the scriveners' agents in the country, or, when these deposits were not simple cash payments, to remit bills and notes to

---

[46] *Ibid.*, 238.   [47] *Ibid.*, 248.   [48] *Ibid.*, 242.
[49] *Ibid.*, 242, 244.   [50] *Ibid.*, 245.   [51] *Ibid.*, 247.

the scriveners' bank in London for collection.[52] The banker John Coggs of the King's Head, Strand, left his rent book with the scriveners, who then recorded each payment as they received it.[53] Inland bills received in London were collected and recorded in the same manner, as well as payments remitted to Exchequer by the sheriffs, and also debts and receipts delegated by warrant and thus subject to the legal pressures Cratford might exert. Unless he intervened beforehand to direct that certain sums be invested in mortgages, each deposit with the scriveners was then remitted to each respective banking house. Child's Bank kept a separate account of these negotiations.

The scriveners offered credit in the time between these payments were collected and paid out to each goldsmith. In 1677 they issued a note for £6,000 to John Mawson of the Golden Hind in Fleet Street to be drawn on the account of Blanchard and Child. On June 8, 1677 Cratford instructed Peter Clayton to pay off the note to Mawson.[54] The money under Cratford's control increased greatly after the Stop of the Exchequer in 1672, representing an impressive picture of how country capital was increasingly swelling the reserves of private bankers in the City. From October 1669 to October 1672 the scriveners received £23,933 into Cratford's account. In the subsequent three-year period, October 1672 to October 1675, £74,968 was credited to his account. There follows a break in the ledgers and an omission of several folios which contained a continuous record for the next period. But when the accounts resume in October 1677 and continue until November 1679 – a period of just more than two years – £68,454 had been assigned to Cratford's credit with the scriveners.[55] These accounts suggest that private banking houses arising to prominence in the years after 1672 rarely had anything more than primitive collection facilities for drawing their clients' accounts to London. Into

---

[52]Cratford was an intermediary through Clayton and Morris with goldsmith-bankers. Receipts and debits in his accounts with the scriveners were placed and taken by clients and servants of the scriveners and goldsmiths. For instance, Sir Charles Duncombe's servant Bartlett appeared at the scriveners' shop on his master's business, and his name is credited and debited in their accounts. In most entries only the servant or client's name appears, with no designation to a goldsmith's account. This suggests that another set of records was kept, now missing, like John Coggs's rent book, where the ledger entries were reassigned to their proper goldsmith's account. Names of goldsmith-bankers recurring in these accounts are Blanchard and Child, Thomas Carwood and John Hind, Benjamin Hinton, John and George Snell, and Charles Duncombe.

[53]G.L., MS 6428, iii, fol. 28 (March 25, 1677).

[54]Christopher Cratford to Peter Clayton and Thomas Leman, June 9, 1677, Box 4, L.S.E.

[55]This total was drawn from Cratford's accounts with the scriveners, G.L., MS 6428, I, fols. 49v–50r; 266v–267r; II, 35v–37r; 244v–246r; 354v–356r; III, 38v–39r; 177v–178r; G.M.R., MS 84/1/4, fols. 50–2, 184, 249.

this vacuum came Christopher Cratford, and possibly there were others like him who devised methods of attracting capital outside London into the hands of private bankers.

In the example of Child's Bank this dependence upon Cratford lessened during the 1680s. From Michaelmas 1682 until Michaelmas 1686 Clayton received for Francis Child and his partner John Rogers the sum of £96,325 into an account separate from Cratford's.[56] After Blanchard's death the business of his successor increased to the degree that the bank began to issue regular statements of account to its clients. By 1690, when Clayton's abilities to receive goldsmiths' deposits slackened, Child's Bank's deposits, recorded in its own ledgers, reached £160,000. By 1694 the bank's deposits had contracted to £109,000, though by 1704 the figure rose again, to £177,000.[57] Other methods enabled the bank to absorb in its deposits, by procedures unapparent from the ledgers surviving from the period.

If private banking houses acquired their own means of deposit collection, their dependence upon lawyers did not diminish. With the decline of the Scriveners' Company lawyers were unrivaled as conveyancers, and consequently they assumed a greater role in the affairs of private banking. The scribal traditions of the money-scriveners taught them a familiarity with contracts; the same legal foundations were foreign to the craft of goldsmiths. Goldsmith-bankers had no more knowledge of law pertaining to securities than ordinary citizens, wrote the author of *The Mystery of the New Fashioned Goldsmiths* in 1676, and he considered their ignorance to be a barrier to the skillful investment of their deposits.[58] Without proper legal advice bankers were likely to run into trouble. As an example, Joseph and Nathaniel Hornby of the Star, Lombard Street, in May 1686 arranged a faulty mortgage contract unrestricted to further sub-conveyancing. They failed to register one of the indentures of the loan, and, failing to imitate the policy of the bank of Clayton and Morris, kept no copies of the original contract under their control. The Hornbys' own names were included in the contract for which they then became liable; they were sued over complications arising from the negotiations.[59]

As conveyancing became the domain of the legal profession, knowledge of land law gave lawyers access to their clients' financial affairs. Lawyers

---

[56] G.M.R., MS 84/1/4, fols. 43v–45r, 161, 235.
[57] Shelton, 'Goldsmith Banker,' 253.
[58] *Ibid.*, 7.
[59] *The Case of the Creditors of Joseph and Nathaniel Hornby* . . . [n.d.].

frequently acted as brokers in mortgage negotiations, putting lenders and borrowers in touch. Occasionally lawyers lent their own money to clients restoring their estates. The attorney Peter Walter, for instance, combined his legal practice with moneylending. In 1686 he became steward to Lord Paget. Gradually the young attorney acquired a practical knowledge of leases, land, contracts and bills of exchange. By careful management of the coal mines on Lord Paget's property, Walter increased the lord's capital, at the same time diverting part of the profits into his own hands. By 1700 he calculated his capital to be £13,357 0s. 0d. His businesslike methods applied to land management were so successful that he soon received commissions from other great landlords, like the Holles and Pelhams, 'court keeping' on their estates and handling other aspects of their finances. With his huge profits he then loaned money to his clients. Walter was an unusual figure in the success he had, though the incipient connection between law and moneylending was implied throughout the legal profession of the early eighteenth century.[60]

Mortgage law was too complex for bankers to master, largely because the law was constantly in a state of change. The printed reports of lawyers formed a guide to these legal developments, but they were not inclusive, and the reports were often superseded by subsequent decisions at the time of their publication. Unless the security was protected with the best legal opinion, the lender's title was risky and his credit in the loan suffered. To keep abreast of contemporary legal opinion on mortgage law bankers must either have sent their own agents to attend the sessions of Chancery, as Clayton and Morris hired Anthony Keck to be their 'ears' in such matters, or they must have contracted the services of specialists in mortgage law to devise each conveyance to conform to current practice.

With the constant changes in mortgage law the best opinion lay at the bench of Chancery. No clear distinction there was drawn between the self-interests of lawyers once they became judges. During the early eighteenth century judges had become scandalously involved in the affairs of private

[60]H. Erskine-Hill, '"Dextrous Attorney": Peter Walter, Esq. of Stallbridge (1664?–1746),' in idem, ed., *The Social Milieu of Alexander Pope: Lives, Examples and the Poetic Response* (New Haven, 1975), 103–31; M. Birks, *Gentlemen of the Law* (London, 1960), 182–3; R. Robson, *The Attorney in Eighteenth-Century England*, Cambridge Studies in English Legal History (Cambridge, 1959), 143–4; F. M. L. Thompson, 'Land-ownership and Economic Growth in England in the Eighteenth Century,' in *Agrarian Change and Economic Development*, ed. E. J. Jones and S. J. Woolf (London, 1969), 54; B. L. Anderson, 'The Attorney and the Early Capital Market in Lancashire,' in *Liverpool and Merseyside: Essays in the Economic and Social History of the Port and the Hinterland*, ed. J. R. Harris (New York, 1969).

clients, as is shown in the papers of the Holford family. Sir Richard Holford of Lincoln's Inn, called to the bench in 1689, became a Master in Chancery in 1694. He continued his activities as a practicing lawyer, placing large sums of money out at interest and engaging in private litigation in pursuit of his interests. His eldest son, Robert Holford, became a Master in Chancery in 1712, and in line with what was now a family tradition, Robert Holford's sons, Peter and Robert, both followed the path of their forebears, taking the same positions in the court. At the time Robert Holford became Master, he received an account of his late predecessor Sir Robert Legard's investments of monies, bonds, securities and deeds left with him by suitors in Chancery. Both Sir Richard and Robert Holford engaged in the same speculative practices with their suitors' assets, investing many of these deposits in mortgages of their own lands, like banks which take in deposits to make reinvestments in mortgages. These practices were so widespread all along the bench that in 1725 a committee of the Privy Council made an investigation, ordered all Masters with dubious accounts to make these deficits and forbade further malpractice with suitors' interests.[61]

Lawyers and judges with capital to lend diverted clients from bankers unable to protect their securities with the same legal assurance. How bankers worked with their lawyers is unclear. Was it the practice for bankers to have lawyers in their retinue, as employees, as did the bank of Clayton and Morris in the seventeenth century? Or was it more frequently the case in the early eighteenth century that bankers sought the advice of lawyers in their own chambers, paying fees for each commission? Were lawyers like Christopher Cratford common in the eighteenth century, men who specialized in bankers' affairs, yet retained their own independent status? These questions concerning the actual relationship of bankers to their lawyers are as yet unanswered, though it seems safe to conclude at this stage that goldsmith-banking oriented to mortgage lending became gradually dependent upon the legal profession, giving it a character it lacked during its Restoration years.

Another type of expertise – land assessment – lay also beyond the ordinary skills of bankers. A modest idea of the problems of banking and land surveying comes from the Verney papers at Claydon House. This concerns the bank of Snow and Paltock of the Golden Anchor in the Strand, the

[61]G.L., MS 15, 583–95, 602; *The Accompts of the Several Masters of the High Court of Chancery of the Securities, Effects and Cash, Belonging to the Suitors of that Court, Deposited in Their Respective Hands* (London, 1725).

business established by Jeremiah Snow. During the 1720s the bank began to buy lands adjacent to the Verneys, to sell at a profit through mortgages arranged by the bank. On one piece of property in East Claydon they leased back an estate, with the stipulation that the lessee had the land surveyed and remitted to them any credit arising if an alternative valuation proved a discrepancy in the value per acre of land. The Golden Anchor had no surveyor of its own, and no suggestion was made that the bank's lawyers should perform simple mensuration for the valuation. Upon the bank's own suggestions, scientific circumscription of the property would decide the value of the land. By succumbing to the word of a judgment exterior to its own powers, the bank recognized its dependence upon other professional advice, on which, like legal counsel, it was now reliant.[62]

However the relationship of bankers to their lawyers and surveyors was organized during the early eighteenth century, mortgage lending necessarily changed the relationship of bankers with their clients. As bankers coordinated the work of lawyers and surveyors, their roles as brokers to their loans changed, as they now held before their clients keys to the credit of the negotiation. Previously the borrower's risk of ruin under the conditioned penal bond had placed bankers in an awkward position in the negotiation. Denied access to the records describing personal credit, brokers were removed from the credit process. They might place lender and debtor in touch with each other and write the covenants, but the nature of the penal bond contract was so intensely personal and threatening that there was no satisfactory way bankers could assume the risks of the negotiation. Penalty disappeared when long-term mortgages replaced conditioned penal bonds. At the same time, other liabilities were inherent in real security concerning its long-term capital value as well as the clarity of its legal title. These were technical problems which often the parties to the contract were unable to ascertain themselves. During the 1690s no less an authority than John Locke received inquiries concerning the value of mortgages, a sign of how complex mortgage lending had become.[63]

The services associated with the banking mortgage tended to overshadow the other aspects of its investment because the procedures of credit, conveyancing and management were so complex. The detail in the Clayton papers presented in the preceding chapters shows how mortgage finance gave their bank a specialization oriented to landowners. Discount-

---

[62]I am indebted to Dr John Broad for this information.
[63]*The Correspondence of John Locke*, ed. E. S. deBeer, Vol. VI (Oxford, 1981), 148–9; Vol. VII (1982), 12, 14, 16–17, 72–4, 161, 195, 311, 331–6.

ing foreign bills and exchanging foreign money into English coins imply an elaborate network of communications from the bank into the international trading community. If the banker issues letters of credit abroad, he must somehow establish contacts he can trust. An entirely different structure into another social milieu is implied in a bank offering exchange services of any magnitude, as opposed to a bank characterized by its mortgage operations, with its arms spread in entirely different directions to other social groups. Mortgage finance dominated a banker's function, even in its cash-keeping aspects, since the rents and other income received were earmarked to repay loans. To this extent the deposit and lending functions of banking were complementary.

A small group of goldsmiths after 1685 began to supersede the position Clayton and Morris had formerly held, with a clientele in the country. At the same time, some of the goldsmith-bankers drawing their deposits from the country and negotiating mortgage loans for their clients seem also to have speculated in foreign exchange. Sir Francis Child kept a separate account book apart from his Grand Ledgers in which he recorded his exchange transactions.[64] Nevertheless, exchange did not characterize private banking in this period, any more than pawnbroking or goldsmithing. In his inspection of banking records D. M. Joslin found that all the private banking establishments by 1720 had severed most of their contacts with the mercantile community, as landowners became their clients. By the middle of the eighteenth century there were two distinct types of private banks in London. One group of bankers in the City answered the needs of the merchants, and these establishments were of fairly recent origin. The other group of private bankers, mostly located in the West End, had landowners primarily as their clients.[65] It was the latter group which performed the older-style banking, and its historical genealogy went back over one hundred and fifty years to the first money-scriveners.

Clayton's operations were perceived at the time by other bankers as unique functions, compatible with their own work. First, there is Sir Francis Child's comment in 1671 about Clayton's role in mortgage credit, tacitly recognizing that a highly specialized process of valuation was at work, which others might duplicate in some manner if they were to compete. Secondly, Christopher Cratford's use of the scriveners' collection

[64]Shelton, 'Goldsmith Banker,' 250.

[65]D. M. Joslin, 'London Private Bankers, 1720–1785,' *Economic History Review*, second series, VII (1954); D. M. Joslin, 'London Bankers in Wartime 1739–84,' in *Studies in the Industrial Revolution Presented to T. S. Ashton*, ed. L. S. Pressnell (London, 1960), 157, 159, 176. See also Sir J. Steuart, *An Inquiry into the Principles of Political Economy*, Scottish Economic Classics (Chicago, 1966), 483, n. 2.

mechanism acknowledged a greater banking institution than the goldsmith-bankers had with their own organizations. Both points assume that among the purple of the banking community there was some accurate perception of exactly what services the scriveners rendered their clients which their own organizations did not. No less a person than Sir Robert Vyner knew that Anthony Keck enjoyed a critical and confidential relationship with the scriveners' bank. If he and other bankers did not know the exact work Clayton's agents performed, there can be little doubt that when the publications of Manley, Monteage and Keck appeared, these works would be taken by other bankers to comprise statements about various stages in the process of valuation, conveyancing and land management. No other bank of the period produced such published records of its techniques. These works are testimony to the unique contribution of Clayton and Morris in banking history, the integration of the mortgage in fee as a viable instrument of banking credit. The cash-keeping side of the scriveners' banking business, shared with the goldsmith-banks, was unworthy of comment in the same way that mortgage investment attracted attention for its singularity, unless one considers Monteage's *Rent-Gatherers Accompts* to be more a guide to an aspect of receipt than a treatise on land management. At all these points the work of Clayton and the money-scriveners preceding him came to the attention of banking goldsmiths.

Deposit banking in the course of the seventeenth century was oriented around the two loose traditions of money-scriveners and goldsmith-bankers. There was continuity, broadly speaking, in the depositing nexus of these early banks. Pressure to expand their roles as loan-brokers promoted significant change in the private banking structure. The scriveners emerged from a notarial and legal foundation, while the goldsmiths appeared first in the banking world as specialists in foreign exchange. In spite of their different origins, both groups came to hold capital from a common source. Neither the differences nor the similarities among the body of money-scriveners and the commonalty of goldsmith-bankers were strong enough to promote banking traditions of any permanence. It seems that most significance lay not in the body of scriveners or the generality of goldsmiths adhering strictly to either their craft or the banking possibilities surrounding it, but rather in those few unique individuals who took the initiative to introduce new banking techniques in advance of the common practice. If Clayton's bank was an isolated example of the period, unrepresentative of other banks, so also were the minority of goldsmith-banks different from their fellow bankers.

APPENDIX 1

GROWTH OF CLIENTS' DEPOSITS

———————— • ————————

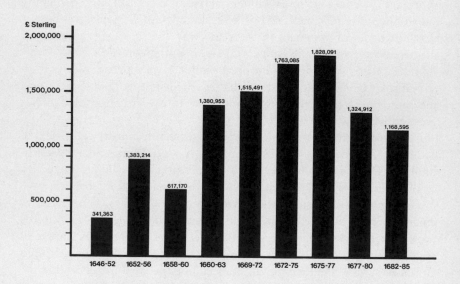

GROWTH OF THE BANK

————— . • —————

These figures indicating the relationship of moneylending and the growth of the scriveners' bank were compiled from entries in their ledgers. Only consecutive ledger entries can be compared for this purpose; where there is a gap in the evidence, e.g., between 1663 and 1669, no relationship is apparent. The figures were taken from the scriveners' 'proper' accounts of their own cash credits and debits. '(A) Loans granted' refers only to those loans made in their own names and not to contracts negotiated on behalf of their depositors.

Before 1669 there was little or no correlation between the time loans were made and paid off within the various accounting periods. Loans made in one accounting period might be paid off and entered in the consecutive accounting periods. Nevertheless, the discrepancies are so great between loans repaid in one period and the cash credited during the previous term as to confirm the suspicion that the scriveners were lending in their own names capital which was not their own. Presumably part of their own capital was invested in their own names, but it is clear from the table that this was not their only source, and that loans registered in their own names were drawn from another base. From 1652 to 1663 the loans repaid into the accounts of Abbott and the young scriveners Clayton and Morris were larger than the loans they actually granted in their names and even greater than their cash credits.

When Clayton and Morris began their own operations in 1658, they made a clear distinction in the ledgers between the accounts they kept for Abbott's executors and their own 'proper' accounts. The old bank and the new foundation thus appeared in the books as two separate foundations

Table I

	1646–52	1652–6	1658–60	1660–3	1669–72	1672–5	1675–7	1677–80
From the bank's Profit and Loss Accounts { (A) Loans granted	£5,267	£27,726	£21,460	£64,192	£72,779	£320,748	£242,733	£332,302
(B) Loans repaid	£4,481	£19,271	£13,505	£35,108	£50,831	£60,254	£5,013	£4,000
(C) Cash	£12,671	£38,795	£23,026	£78,822	£157,949	£780,500	£267,246	£708,723
(D) Clients' deposits	£341,364	£1,137,646	£617,170	£1,380,953	£1,515,491	£1,704,038	£1,828,081	£1,324,912

with a common source of depositors. From Abbott's death until 1660 the
bank's deposits sank to £617,170 at the same time that the two scriveners,
with virtually no assets of their own, placed £21,450 on loan, of which
£13,505 was repaid before 1660. Abbott's executors made no loans to
Clayton and Morris to begin their new enterprise. The only likely source
of capital they had to manipulate was the bank's deposits of the late Robert
Abbott's clients. His two scriveners were gambling on the possibility that
they could capture the same clientele, which they did; from 1660 to 1663
they more than doubled their capital on deposit.

After 1669 the relationship of these figures changed. As the foundation
of Clayton and Morris became an established bank with an increasing
specialty in mortgage finance, they saw a sharp decline, especially after
1675, in the relationship between loans granted and loans repaid either
before or during the subsequent accounting periods. The tendency was for
loans to be repaid over a much longer period than was the case previously,
when short-term loans were common policy. If the mortgage contracts
were not honored within the time set in the contracts, debtors were usually
allowed the option of extending their loans and paying the relevant fees. As
the figures indicate for 1675 to 1677 (A) and 1677 to 1680 (A), the loans
granted came from a much wider base than the principals repaid within the
same category.

After 1672 the scriveners' accounts show that the loans repaid in one
accounting period were less than the cash credited in the preceding. At the
same time, during the agricultural recession of the 1670s, the scriveners
made their greatest investments in mortgages. This presumed an ever-
increasing source of capital. Yet from 1672 to 1675 they loaned in their
own names £320,748, while their cash credits were £780,500, and the
same relationship of greater cash to lesser loans continued until the consecutive accounting period ended in 1680.

Were they lending more from their ever increasing profits, as reflected in
their assets (excepting the period 1675 to 1677), or were they relying on
their clients' deposits as a source of their own lending capital? There is no
clear answer to this problem. The years 1675 to 1677 appeared in their
ledgers as a setback of a sort, when their capital assets declined from
£780,500 in the previous accounting period to £267,246. If they were not
'cooking the books' in the aftermath of the Exchequer Crisis, this probably
meant no more than that the greatest part of the mortgages they granted in
the previous period (£320,748) were not repaid in the next accounting
period. Their loans amounted to 90.1% of their assets. This is an artificial
figure; there is no reason to believe that these investments were actually

made from their assets. Nevertheless, the high ratio of loans to assets, as reflected in the ledgers, betrays some confidence that the setback was not a real loss. And, during the same period, their clients' reserves increased to the greatest amount, £1,828,081. If the scriveners did not draw upon their deposits during this period, to meet the reductions in their own lending capital, they were following a new policy contrary to the tradition of the enterprise.

APPENDIX 3

GOLDSMITH-BANKERS, 1670–1700

————————— • —————————

The first enumeration of goldsmith-bankers was published in *The Little London Directory* of 1677, containing forty-four banks keeping 'running cashes.' Later, F. G. Hilton Price arranged the fruits of his research to list goldsmith-bankers for the random years 1670, 1687 and 1700, followed by subsequent lists of bankers. Six banks accounted for in Hilton Price's lists for 1670 and 1687 do not appear in *The Little London Directory* (Hornby, Pinckney, Snow and Walton, Tassell, Warner and Walstead). If other banking houses appeared and then disappeared between these intervals, the actual numbers of goldsmith-banks operating during the later seventeenth century was greater than these lists enumerate.

However, within the lists themselves and Hilton Price's notes there are unwarranted assumptions confusing the numbers of distinct banking houses. There is no reason to suppose, for instance, that when one bank appeared at the address of a defunct establishment, even displaying the sign of the former business, the new bank was linked to the old. Thus, when John Ballard succeeded the great Edward Backwell at the Unicorn in Lombard Street, he exhibited an emblem similar to his predecessor's. The evidence for Backwell, however, does not suggest that his firm bore any subsequent relationship to Ballard's bank. Comparable evidence, in another example, involving the origins of Gosling's Bank, seemed to place the origins of this firm in the time of Cromwell. According to this genealogy Gosling's derives from the foundation of Henry Pinckney who established the Three Squirrels in Fleet Street during the Commonwealth. After his death, *c.* 1678, his brother William Pinckney, of the Golden Dragon, Fleet Street, moved his business to the Three Squirrels. The bank

233

of the Pinckneys then passed to the Chambers brothers. Abraham Chambers acquired the Three Squirrels in 1683, and by 1687 he was located also on the same street at the Golden Falcon. By 1687 the Three Squirrels was in the occupation of James Chambers, brother of Abraham Chambers. This is insufficient evidence to conclude that there was an institutional connection between the Pinckneys and the Chambers whereby one business had a continuous life. It may be that the Chambers acquired no more than the lease and the name from William Pinckney or his heirs. Likewise, no one has determined that there is a direct connection between Sir Francis Gosling's Three Squirrels in Fleet Street and the seventeenth-century firm of the same name.

In at least three instances there appear to be fewer distinct banking houses than these lists suggest. Samuel Hankey's bank, The Ring, in Fenchurch Street, was established by 1687 but defunct by 1700, according to Hilton Price. Henry Hankey was at the Ring and Ball in Fenchurch Street by that time, raising the possibility that this was a single, family concern surviving two generations with a slightly different name, rather than two distinct banks with separate lives. In another example, the bank of Snow and Walton appears at the Golden Anchor, Strand, in 1670 and 1687 and by 1700 under Thomas Snow's name, though the same business does not appear in the interim list of 1677. Thomas Pardo had a bank The Golden Anchor in Lombard Street at that time, the only date Snow's bank of the same name is missing. Doubts arise also as to whether the bank of Heneage Price, the Golden Lion without Temple Bar (1687, 1700) and Michael Shrimpshaw's bank in the previous period, The Golden Lion, Fleet Street (1677) were two separate institutions.

At least ninety-three separate goldsmith-banks can be accounted for between 1670 and 1700. The incomplete list for 1677 includes, presumably, those banking houses adhering to the description of banking made in 1676 by the author of *The Mystery of the New Fashioned Goldsmiths*. There is less certainty that a decade later, in 1687, and then in 1700, houses appearing in the lists for the first time followed the same pattern. From 1670 to 1687 at least eleven houses survived the period, though by 1700 only four of the foundations of 1670 had survived: Blanchard and Child, the Hoares, the Hornbys (failed by 1701) and John Warner. In the lists of 1677, 1687 and 1700 at least thirty-three new banks appeared. Three of these banks – Brassey and Caswell, Freame and Gould, and William Wright – have disputed dates of origin and may have arisen somewhat later, in the eighteenth century. Of the banks remaining, only two foundations lasted beyond 1736: Hankey's and Middleton, Campbell and Company, the ancestor of Coutts and Company.

At least five of the seventeenth-century goldsmith-banks had any permanence, connected institutionally through the generations:

1. James Hoare at the Golden Bottle, Cheapside [Hoare's Bank]
2. Charles and Valentine Duncombe and Thomas Martin at the Grasshopper, Lombard Street [Martin's Bank]
3. Blanchard, Child and Company at the Marygold, Fleet Street [Child's Bank]
4. Henry and Samuel Hankey at the Ring and Ball, Fenchurch Street [Hankey's Bank, until 1865]
5. Middleton, Campbell and Company at the Three Crowns, Strand [Coutts and Company]

Goldsmiths Keeping 'Running Cashes,' 1670–1700

Name	Address	1670	1677	1687	1700
1. John Addis [Adys] & Co.	Sun, Lombard St				
2. Ald. Edward Backwell	Unicorn, Lombard St	x			
3. Atwell & Courtnay	Exchange Alley, Lombard St			x	x
4. John Ballard	Unicorn, Lombard St		x	x	
5. Robert Blanchard & Francis Child	Marygold, Fleet St	x	x		
Child & Rogers	Marygold, Fleet St			x	
Francis Child & Co.	Marygold, Fleet St				x
6. John Bolitho & John Wilson	Golden Lion, Lombard St		x		
7. Job Bolton	Bolt and Tun, Lombard St		x		
8. Brassey & Caswell	Acorn, Lombard St				x
9. Abraham Chambers	Golden Falcon, Fleet St			x	x
James Chambers	Three Squirrels, Fleet St			x	x
10. Mr Churchill	—, Strand		x		
11. John Coggs	King's Head, Strand		x	x	
Cogg & Dann	King's Head, Strand				x

Name	Location				
12. John Collier	Unknown	x			
13. John Colville	Unknown	x			
14. Thomas Cooke & Nicholas Cary	Griffin, Exchange Alley		x		
15. Cooke & Venables	Lombard St				x
16. Mr Cuthbert	Cheapside		x		
17. Charles Duncombe & Richard Kent	Grasshopper, Lombard St		x		
Charles & Valentine Duncombe				x	
Richard Smythe	Grasshopper, Lombard St				x
18. Bernard Eales	Lombard St			x	
19. John East	Sun, Strand	x	x	x	x
20. John Ewing & Benjamin Norrington	Angel & Crown, Lombard St		x	x	
21. Thomas Fowles	Black Lion, Fleet St	x	x	x	x
Fowles & Wotton	Black Lion, Fleet St				x
22. Freame & Gould	Three Anchors, Lombard St				x
23. Ralph Gerrard	Three Lions, Lombard St				x
24. Samuel Hankey	Ring, Fenchurch St			x	

237

Goldsmiths Keeping 'Running Cashes,' 1670–1700 (cont.)

Name	Address	1670	1677	1687	1700
25. Henry Hankey	Ring and Ball, Fenchurch St				x
26. John Harling	Heart and Crown, Lombard St	x			
27. James Herriot	Naked Boy, Fleet St		x	x	x
28. John Hind & Thomas Carwood	'over against the Exchange' in Cornhill	x	x		
29. Benjamin Hinton & Co.	Flower de Luce, Lombard St	x	x		
30. James Hoare	Golden Bottle, Cheapside	x	x	x	x
Sir Richard Hoare	Golden Bottle, Fleet St				
31. John Holmes		x			
32. Joseph & Nathaniel Hornby	Star, Lombard St	x	x	Nathaniel x	x
33. Roger & John Hudson	Royal Exchange, Fleet St				x
34. Jenkins & King	Lombard St				x
35. James Johnson [John Johnson]	Three Flower de Luce, Cheapside		x	x	x
36. Mr Kenton	King's Arms, Fleet St		x		
37. Mr Ketch	Black Horse, Strand		x		

No.	Name	Sign / Address				
38.	Thomas Kiborne [Kilborne] & Capill [Capell]	King's Head, Lombard St			x	
39.	Joseph Knight	Flower de Luce, Great Russell St Covent Garden		x		
40.	Henry Lamb	Grapes, Lombard St	x	x	x	
41.	James Lapley	Three Cocks, Cheapside		x	x	
42.	Richard Lassels	Unicorn, Strand	x	x		
43.	George Lewis	Angel and Crown, Strand	x			
44.	John Lindsay	Angel, Lombard St				x
45.	John Mawson & Co.	Golden Hind, Fleet St	x		x	
46.	John Mead	Goat, Strand	x			
47.	George Merttins	Peacock, Cornhill	x			
48.	Isaac Meynell	Lombard St				x
49.	Middleton & Campbell	Three Crowns, Strand	x			
50.	Edward Mompessen	Birchin Lane	x			
51.	Richard Morson & Co.	Anchor and Three Crowns, Lombard St	x			
52.	Henry Nelthorpe	Rose, Lombard St			x	
53.	Thomas Pardo	Golden Anchor, Lombard St	x		x	

Goldsmiths Keeping 'Running Cashes,' 1670–1700 (cont.)

Name	Address	1670	1677	1687	1700
54. Captain Pearce	Three Golden Cocks, Cheapside				x
55. Richard Peirson	Acorn, Fleet St				x
56. Peter Perceful [Percival] & Stephen Evans [Evance]	Black Boy, Lombard St		x	x	x
57. William Pinckney	Golden Dragon, Fleet St	x	?	x	
58. Philip Pinckney	Sun, without Temple Bar				x
59. Jonathan Portman	Lombard St	x			
60. Heneage Price	Golden Lion, without Temple Bar		x	x	x
61. Thomas Price	Goat, Lombard St		x		
62. Stephen Ram	Angel, Lombard St			x	
63. Thomas Rowe	George, Lombard St	x	& Thomas Green x		
64. John Rowland	Lombard St			x	
65. Robert Ryves		x			
66. Shales & Smithin	Unicorn, Lombard St			x	
67. Michael Shrimpshaw [Scrimpshire; Skrimshire]	Golden Lion, Fleet St		x		

No.	Sign / Address				
68. Richard Snagg	Flying Horse, Lombard St	x	x		
69. George Snell	Fox, Lombard St				x
John Snell	Fox, Lombard St			x	
70. Jeremiah Snow	Lombard St				x
71. Thomas Snow	Golden Anchor, Strand	x			
Snow and Walton	Golden Anchor, Strand		x	?	x
72. Richard Stayley	Covent Garden			x	
73. Humphrey Stocks [Stokes]	Black Horse, Lombard St			x	x
Robert Stokes	Black Horse, Lombard St	x			
74. Andrew Stone	Grasshopper, Lombard St	x			
75. John Sweetaple	Black Moor's Head, Lombard St		x	x	x
76. John Tassell	Bunch of Grapes, Lombard St		x	?	x
77. John Temple & John Seale	Three Tuns, Lombard St			x	
78. John Thursby	Lombard St		x	x	
79. Benjamin Tudman	Crown, Lombard St	x			
80. Bernard Turner	Golden Fleece, Lombard St				x
81. Bernard Turner & Samuel Tookie	Fleece, Lombard St			x	

Goldsmiths Keeping 'Running Cashes,' 1670–1700 (cont.)

Name	Address	1670	1677	1687	1700
82. Sir George Viner	Lombard St	x			
Sir Robert Vyner	Lombard St	x			
83. Peter Wade	Mearmaid, Lombard St		x	x	
84. Maj. John Wallis	Angel, Lombard St		x	x	
Wallis & Studley	Angel, Lombard St				x
85. Robert Ward & John Towneley	Ram, Lombard St		x		
86. John Warner	'without Temple Bar', Strand	x	?	x	x
87. Robert Welstead	Hare, Lombard St	x	?	x	x*
88. Peter White and Churchill [Thomas Churchey]	Plough, Lombard St		x	x	
89. Joseph Wilson	Plough, Lombard St			x	x
90. Thomas White	Blew Anchor, Lombard St		x	x	
91. Thomas Williams	Crown, Lombard St	x	x	x	
92. Gilbert Whitehall	Unknown	x			
93. William Wright	Golden Cup, Covent Garden				x

* According to Horsefield, Welstead was bankrupt by 1695 and Joseph Hornby failed in 1701: ' "The Stop" of the Exchequer Revisited,' *Economic History Review*, second series, XXXV (1982), 525.

APPENDIX 4

CLAYTON MSS
IN PUBLIC COLLECTIONS

———————— • ————————

The Clayton papers are the most dispersed of all Stuart private banking records, and at the same time the most complete archive.[1] At some time before Sir Robert Clayton's mansion in the Old Jewry was destroyed (*c.* 1865), the Clayton family transferred the banking papers of the seventeenth-century firm to their estate at Marden Park, where they preserved the records of the estate. Before the First World War the family sold Marden Park to the Greenwells, and, with at least one exception,[2] left the bulk of their remaining family papers with the new owners.

The Greenwells began to disperse the Clayton papers in their ownership in several stages. Before the first sale, in 1929, Sir Peter Greenwell separated and retained the estate muniments from the seventeenth-century business records. When the Greenwells sold Marden Park after the Second World War, the estate muniments were deposited in the Surrey Record Office.[3] Sir Peter presented to the Surrey Archaeological Society another collection of seventeenth-century business records, which had apparently been uncovered during the war, when Marden had been an army hospital.

[1] I published another description and list of the Clayton papers, with a comparison with other banking archives, in *Bulletin of the Institute of Historical Research*, LII (1979), 91–9.

[2] The Claytons sold their estate in Buckinghamshire in 1953. The papers which they had taken with them from Marden Park were deposited in the Buckinghamshire Record Office, which transferred those papers concerning the Clayton's former estates in Surrey to the Surrey Record Office (Appendix, XXVIA).

[3] In two separate deposits in 1950–1 (Appendix, XXVIB). In 1951 the Surrey Record Office received another deposit from the Claytons' solicitors (Appendix, XXVIC).

These papers are now on permanent loan in the Guildford Muniment Room.[4]

By far the largest and most diverse group of the Clayton papers are those which were sold at Sotheby's on March 26, 1929 to three principal purchasers.[5] The Public Record Office of Ireland acquired about 700 items concerning Clayton's affairs in County Wexford and his administration of the second Duke of Buckingham's Irish estates.[6] Hodgson's purchased 5,389 'deeds,' which in fact were a variety of estate documents, including title deeds. Divided by lots into counties when Hodgson's resold these documents, many of these papers are now in county record offices.[7] A private dealer, G. Michelmore, acquired a number of the Clayton manuscripts, including a collection of about 3,500 seventeenth-century letters.[8] While many of the Clayton manuscripts now in archives can be traced back to the original sale and to several resales through dealers, undoubtedly there are many papers still in private hands.

[4] Appendix, VIIA–E.
[5] *Catalogue of Valuable Printed Books ... and Manuscripts ... to be Sold ... 25 March 1929, and Three Following Days (1929)*, 71–3. This describes eighteen lots of papers from the Clayton collection to be sold on the second day of the sale, March 26. They were owned by George Sherwood, a private dealer in manuscripts, who had acquired them from the Greenwells. He later sold a collection of Clayton papers apart from those he had acquired from the Greenwells in 1929 (D. C. Coleman, 'London Scriveners and the Estate Market in the Later Seventeenth Century,' *Economic History Review*, second series, IV (No. 2, 1951), 226 n. 1, 230 n. 3).
[6] Appendix, XXVA. See also *57th Rept. of the Deputy Keeper of the Public Records in Ireland* (Dublin, 1936), 49–52.
[7] *Hodgson's Catalogue: Books and Manuscripts Sold 15–16 May 1929, no. 21 of 1928–29* (London 1929), 39.
[8] It was from Michelmore in the Royal Opera Arcade that the Guildhall Library purchased in 1929 four account ledgers of Clayton and Morris (Appendix, VIIIE). Michelmore sold one part of the Clayton correspondence to the University of Birmingham, which later transferred these papers to the London School of Economics (Appendix, XVIIA). In 1958 Michelmore sold the other part of correspondence to the University of Illinois at Urbana-Champaign (Appendix, IXA).

Repository	Reference	Description
Clayton MSS in public collections		
I. Bodleian Library, Oxford	MS Eng. Misc. b.96 fo. 24	A. Clayton family pedigree, *c*. 1835
	MS Don. c.68 fos. 1–25	B. Business papers, including letters addressed to Clayton by Laurence Hyde, first Earl of Rochester
	MS Eng. Lett. c.12, c.14, c.16	C. Business papers, including letters to C. and M. from Sir John Bramston, 1662–72, Sir Charles and Robert Wolseley, 1671–6, Henry Hastings, first Baron Loughborough, 1663–6, Philip Barrow, 1654–76, Thomas Stanley, 1651–74
	MS Eng. Lett. c.309	Letters of Robert Clayton to his uncle C., on the Grand Tour
	MS Eng. Lett. c.192, c.309	D. Miscellaneous Clayton letters and papers
	MS Eng. Lett. c.201	E. Business papers, including letters to Clayton and Morris from Sir Thomas Foot, 1658–79, Earl Rivers, 1671–5, Sir John Heath, 1672–6, and the scriveners' agents, 1670–4
II. Buckinghamshire Record Office	MS D/CE (unfoliated)	A. Ireland. Thirty letters between Clayton and Morris, 1662–77
		B. Northamptonshire and Leicestershire, twenty-five letters concerning estate matters among Thomas, Peter and William Clayton, 1664–79
		C. Miscellaneous correspondence concerning family, estates and other business matters, 1664–98
	Clayton MS A.1–4	D. Business, personal and public affairs of Clayton and Morris
		E. Papers of Sir George Jeffreys, first Baron Jeffreys of Wem
		F. Clayton estate accounts and vouchers, etc., 1715–1847

Repository	Reference	Description
III. Columbia University, Butler Library	Montgomery Collection Spec. MS Coll. Buckingham	A. Accounts of Clayton, Morris, John Wildman, Martin Clifford and Thomas Spratt, trustees for the estate of George Villiers, second Duke of Buckingham, 1675–7
		B. Documents concerning Clayton's trusteeship with George Villiers, second Duke of Buckingham
	ibid., 1646–700	C. Clayton's miscellaneous business accounts
IV. Essex Record Office	D/DWh	A. Clayton Deeds
	D/DAc	B. Particulars, legal papers of numerous Essex estates
V. Folger Shakespeare Library, Washington	X.d. 492 (1–70)	A. Household bills, *c.* 1659–75; inventory of John Southwell's shop, 1669; miscellaneous business papers
	X.d. 492 (71–88)	B. Miscellaneous business papers concerning the account of George Villiers, second Duke of Buckingham, with Clayton and Morris, *c.* 1660–87
VI. Greater London Record Office	A/CSC/699–701, 705–13, 718, 719	A. Clayton's transactions concerning property in Capel Court, London, 1663–8
	Q/EV/129	B. Agreement relating to felling of trees in Garrowden Park, Leics. (Duke of Buckingham's trust), 1678
VII. Guildford Muniment Room	84/1/1	A. Abbott's business ledger, 1653–6
	84/1/2–4	B. Clayton and Morris's business ledgers, 1658–60, 1660–3, 1682–6
	84/2/1	C. Peter Clayton's miscellaneous business accounts, 1669–85
	3/1–4	D. Surrey deeds
	3/1/11(1) & (2), 3/1/39, 3/2/3, 3/2/5, 3/3/4, 3/3/42, 3/3/46, 84/1/1(2)	E. Surrey deeds
	3/1/32, 3/3/39, 3/4/15	F. Miscellaneous

Repository	Reference	Description
VIII. Guildhall Library, London	400–1, 404–5	A. Abbott family papers, 1648–83
	1993, 2135	B. Business affairs of George Villiers, second Duke of Buckingham, with Clayton and Morris
	2931	C. Abbott's account book, 1646–52
	2931a	D. Abbott's business papers, 1639–58
	6428	E. Clayton and Morris's account books, 1669–72, 1672–5, 1675–7, 1677–80
	1871, 5286, 20484–8, 20581	F. A collection of schedules, rentals and other particulars, relating to estates in London and Middlesex, in the possession or under the administration of Clayton, 1648–1721
	8871	G. Deeds relating to property in or near Lothbury, 1659
	5386	H. A collection of draft leases, title abstracts and other legal papers in the possession or under the administration of Clayton, c. 1640–c. 1690
	10049	I. Letters and papers relating to Clayton's business affairs with John Palgrave
	8394	J. A collection of assignments, petitions to the Court of Exchequer, accounts and other documents connected with post fines, relating to various capital and estate transactions by Clayton, 1683–1723
	8493A	K. Original minutes of the committee appointed to investigate a 'petition of several merchants and traders in and about the city of London consisting of several exact and undue proceedings of the commissioners and other officers of the customes' (April 5–May 3, 1689)

Repository	Reference	Description
	15604–621, 20484	L. Miscellaneous business papers concerning rebuilding, mortgages and rentals in and near London, 1648–1721, etc., poor relief, Corporation of the Poor
	1993, 2135	M. Business affairs of George Villiers, second Duke of Buckingham, with Clayton and Morris
	1572, 8493a	N. Miscellaneous papers concerning Clayton's mayoralty and career in parliament, 1681, 1689
	3542, 3615	O. Letters patent by James II to Clayton of the manor of Kennington, Surrey, April 21, 1686; other Kennington papers
IX. Illinois University at Urbana-Champaign	Clayton Collection	A. Receipts, bills, bonds, promissory notes, petitions, wills, affidavits, indentures. Correspondents to Abbott, Clayton and Morris, A, Ba–Bod, Bod–By, Ca–Cr, D–F, Ga–Gr, Ha–Ho, I–Mo, Py–Wa (c. 3,000 items)
X. John Rylands University Library of Manchester	Eng. MS 899	A. Twenty letters from Anthony Isaacson of Newcastle to Clayton and Sir Jeremy Whitchcott, concerning the sea coal trade to London, 1675–7
	Rylands Ch. 3642	B. Ireland. Account of bills of exchange and money returned out of England to John Morris, c. 1663
	Rylands Chs. 2520	C. Rentals and timber estimates of Clayton's estates in Lincolnshire, c. 1660–98
	Rylands Chs. 3641, 3645–56	D. John Southwell, ironmonger of London and cousin of Clayton. Miscellaneous business and family affairs
	Eng. MSS 906, 943, 959, 986	E. Business correspondence of Clayton and Morris, 1656–1707
	Rylands Chs. 3682, 3698, 3776	F. Receipts and miscellaneous business papers, 1659–97
	Rylands Chs. 3642, 3757, 3840	G. Legal affairs

	Repository	Reference	Description
XI.	Kent Record Office	Neame Collection, U214	A. One hundred and twenty particulars and legal papers; *c*. ninety title deeds relating to property in Kent parishes, 1586–1707
		Clayton MSS E7/1–63, E8/1–18, E19/1–20	B. Particulars and other estate papers pertaining to Kent
XII.	Leeds Central Library	Symington MSS Acc. 1202/102	A. Detailed typescript catalogue of Buckingham, Colepepper, Fairfax Papers, in alphabetical order of correspondents, based on 189 entries (*c*. 500 items, 1625–75)
XIII.	Leeds University Library	Brotherton Collection, Yorkshire Deeds (Clayton Papers)	A. Thirty-five volumes of particulars and correspondence and forty-eight boxes of deeds, bonds and indentures concerning Clayton's and Morris's transactions in Yorkshire, many pertaining to the Fairfax and Buckingham estates (unlisted and uncatalogued)
XIV.	Leicestershire Record Office	35′29	A. Deeds, particulars, wills and other legal papers concerning Abbott, Clayton and Morris's estates in Leicestershire
XV.	Lincoln City Library	5226 fos. 7, 12	A. Correspondence from Sir Charles Dymoke to Clayton and Morris
XVI.	Lincolnshire Archives Committee	Hill 301A–B	A. Correspondence of Dymoke Walpole to Morris, 1660, 1672–8 (sixteen items); correspondence from Clayton and Morris to their agents, 1672–4
		B.R.A. 1297/1, P.S.J. 3/2/1, Smith 1/5/11	B. Lincolnshire deeds, 1654–82
XVII.	London School of Economics, British Library of Political and Economic Science	Clayton Papers	A. Receipts, bills, bonds, promissory notes, petitions, wills, affidavits, indentures. Correspondents to Abbott, Clayton and Morris, Bod–By, Ca–Cob, Cos–Cut, Gu–Gy, Ho–Hy, Mo–Mz, N–O, Pa–Pe, We–Wh, Wi–Z (748 items preserved as a separate collection, unlisted and uncatalogued)

Repository	Reference	Description
XVIII. London University Library	MS 553	A. Twelve documents concerning the Clayton family, 1659–97, including papers on the education of Peter Clayton
XIX. Marsh's Library, Dublin	Z3.1.1	A. Case of N. Peters and his wife, relating to a quarry near Dolphin's Barne and trespass thereon by the workhouse authorities. Reposal to R. Clayton to the governors of the workhouse for teaching trades to the children (extracts, eighteenth century)
XX. National Library of Ireland	MSS 30, 325, 810, 3294, 8535, 10786	A. Ireland. Correspondence, chancery and exchequer answers and bills, deeds, conveyancers, letters of attorney, leases, many concerning Clayton's ironworks in Enniscorthy, County Wexford (*c.* 700 items)
XXI. Northamptonshire Record Office	Clayton MSS 1–185	A. Indentures, deeds, particulars of land, mostly in Northamptonshire and Rutland but occasional documents to lands elsewhere
XXII. Norfolk Record Office	3210–3437	A. Norfolk deeds, particulars, bonds, wills, legal papers and other materials relative to Clayton and Morris's transactions in Norfolk B. Howard of Castle Rising (eleven items)
XXIII. Nottingham City	M.1622, 1625–8	A. Deeds of the manors of Warsop and Salterford
XXIV. Oxfordshire County Record Office	Misc. Lancs. II/2, VI/14, Clayton I/22, 31	A. Deeds, leases of Abbott, Clayton and Morris
XXV. Public Record Office of Ireland	IA-40-40 & 41	A. Ireland. Proposals for reform of the Irish, customs, second Duke of Buckingham's land in Ireland, leases, indentures, many concerning Clayton's ironworks at Enniscorthy
XXVI. Surrey Record Office	60/1/1–60/10/3	A. Documents concerning the Claytons' estates in Surrey; Bletchingley parliamentary elections (various), 1660–1702; records of the farmers of the post fines, 1674–87, 1690–1

Repository	Reference	Description
	60/1/10	B. Muniments of Bletchingley and and other estates of the Clayton family in Surrey, particulars of properties to be sold or mortgaged to Morris and Clayton in Surrey, London, Kent and Lincolnshire, 1659–80 (61/5/1–66)
	389/1/3–16	C. Deeds concerning the manor and burgage tenements in Bletchingley
XXVII. Wiltshire Record Office	84/47, 212A/37/4 & 5, 212B, Ram. 6	A. Deeds, indentures of Wiltshire manors, 1658–77
XXVIII. Yale University, Beinecke Library	84/47, 212A/374 & 5, 212B Osborn Collection, MS 202/23	A. Accounts of Clayton and Morris, trustees for the estate of George Villiers, second Duke of Buckingham, 1671–3; miscellaneous business accounts with Buckingham, c. 1660–85
XXIX. British Library	Add. MS 45902	A. Clayton papers re House of Lords: 1. Notes of fees to be paid when George Villiers, first Duke of Buckingham, took his seat 2. List of petitions, etc. due to be heard, November 21–5, 1685 and held following the prorogation of parliament
XXX. Glamorgan Record Office	CL/Deeds.I	A. Papers concerning financial transactions of the Earls of Pembroke, 1635–97. Deeds and other papers concerning various estates in Wales
	CL/Deeds.II	B. Deeds from the Clayton papers relating to Sir Robert Thomas of Llanvihangle and to land in Penmark, 1626–88
XXXI. South Glamorgan Central Library, Cardiff	3.586	A. Correspondence to Morris, Clayton and Peter Clayton, 1670–92, from Sir John Chichester and other clients
XXXII. Shakespeare Birthplace Trust	DR 76/2	A. Particulars of Warwickshire manors
XXXIII. National Library of Wales	8472E	A. Miscellanea from Clayton MSS
	11016E–11021E	B. Clayton letters re Welsh affairs
XXXIV. William Salt Library		A. Letters of Lord Aston to Clayton, with miscellaneous papers regarding property at Standon, Herts (sixteen items)*

* *Collections for a History of Staffordshire Edited by the Staffordshire Record Society* (Stafford, 1941–2) 127–37

INDEX